IN SEARCH OF HEAVEN ON EARTH

RACHEL STORM

IN SEARCH OF
HEAVEN ON EARTH

BLOOMSBURY

Pictures reproduced with kind permission of:
Mary Evans Picture Library (15); the Hulton Picture Company (1, 6, 11, 14, 16, 17); Popperfoto (18, 19); Radha R. Sloss (3, 4); Topham Picture Source (8, 10).

First published 1991 by Bloomsbury Publishing Ltd, 2 Soho Square, London W1V 5DE

A CIP record for this book is available from the British Library

ISBN 0 7475 0550 0

Designed by Geoff Green
Typeset by Hewer Text Composition Services, Edinburgh
Printed and bound in Great Britain by Clays Ltd, St Ives plc

CONTENTS

INTRODUCTION

To get a feel for the New Age, simply go into any New Age bookshop. The air will be lightly scented with incense and aromatherapy oils, the talk will be hushed, even reverent, and a taped cassette of waves lapping on a beach, or perhaps some Tibetan chanting, will be gently playing in the background.

A noticeboard will be swamped with information on forthcoming events, from rebirthing courses to sacred dance classes, tarot readings, meditation sessions and holidays to the pyramids. There may well be a couple of stands displaying crystal or Celtic jewellery, and another of New Age magazines. The books themselves will cover every imaginable esoteric, religious and occult tradition – as well as many freshly concocted spiritual paths – while some shelves will groan under the weight of volumes promising miracle cures of the 'heal yourself' variety.

And that's about as far as the unconverted get: a brief visit to a shop and a vague recollection of having heard the term 'New Age' somewhere before. But the New Age is much more than just a passing fad. In one guise or another, it has been around for centuries. And today, with the inroads it is making into mainstream life, its future looks secure.

So what exactly is the New Age? For many critics, a shop is a particularly appropriate place from which to approach the movement – they see it as little more than a commercial venture. Nonetheless, the demand for New Age consumer goods is there and continues to grow – New Age shops are simply supplying their customers with the tools they need in order to transform themselves into fit citizens of heaven or earth: the approach of the year 2000 is rekindling visions of an earthly paradise, and the New Age promises its adherents a place therein.

But the approach of the millennium is not the only reason for an upsurge of interest in the New Age. The twentieth century has witnessed a widescale distrust in external teachings and traditional seats of authority. Thousands of people have turned their backs on the religion they were born into and instead have determined to find their own forms of spirituality and their own paths to enlightenment. It is here, then, that *In Search of Heaven on Earth* starts – with a look at the twentieth century roots of the New Age.

For New Agers, the arrival of heaven on earth is virtually all down to the individual. They must transform themselves – and self-transformation will lead to world transformation. Citizens of the New Age assume total self-responsibility, achieve their true potential – and become divine. Fully empowered, they create their own reality – an earthly paradise. Chapters Three to Seven look at ways throughout history in which individuals have attempted to escape the confines of self and find heaven in the here and now – whether through sex, drugs, self-awareness seminars or material gain.

Some prefer to call the New Age the Aquarian Age – the astrological age of the water carrier characterized by peace, harmony and under-standing. Most astrologers date the Aquarian Age from the 1960s, the 'Death of God' decade when the age of Christ or Piscean Age, gave way to an all-encompassing spirituality, embracing all manner of religions. Certainly, the 1960s saw an influx of Eastern gurus and spiritual paths to the West, bringing with them alien, exotic and often intensely appealing routes to enlightenment. These paths will be covered in Chapters Seven and Eight.

Of course, the Christian tradition is not without its own promise of a New Age – Christ's second coming and 1000-year reign on earth. The more concrete these Christian predictions become, however, the further those making the predictions tend to stray from the main-stream, often leading their flocks into the twilight world of sects.

Christian fundamentalism is gaining an increasing following as we approach the year 2000. But the Bible's teaching of man's dominance over nature is increasingly seen as being at odds with a new 'wholistic' understanding of our place on the planet. Growing environmental awareness has already lead many to reject conventional or funda-mentalist Christianity in favour of paganism or nature spirituality, both of which the New Age embraces. Like Christians who believe in Armageddon, 'greens' also have their apocalypse: the environmental crisis. Chapter Nine looks at the Christian tradition of heaven on earth while Chapter Ten looks at green spirituality.

Where politics is concerned, the socialist, anarchist or communist dream has long been held up as a type of heaven on earth. These ideologies, promising automatic emancipation for all through changes in the way society is organized, contrast with the majority of religions, which promise salvation only for those who become devotees. Political paths to utopia are explored in Chapters Eleven and Twelve while the book's final chapter takes a close look at today's New Age – at its teachings, ideals and pitfalls.

Perhaps the New Age heaven on earth is nothing more than a utopian dream. Many argue, however, that the earthly paradise is taking shape all around us, that everywhere frogs are being transformed into princes and scales are falling from eyes. While increasing numbers of people would support such a viewpoint, others would say if you buy that, you'll buy anything.

ONE | MYSTERY AND MASTERY

The iron gates swing noiselessly shut, closing out the screech and jangle of downtown Madras. High above, fronds of coconut trees blot out the searing heat. For the dust-grimed traveller, this is utopia. This is, it turns out, the headquarters of the Theosophical Society, the grand-dame of New Age movements.

On either side the sanded track dark figures glide silently about their work, skirting the temples to Hindu, Islamic, Zoroastrian and Christian gods. Dense shrubland gives way to an avenue of plane trees. At the base of each a small plaque bears the name of a country – England, Uganda, Senegal, France. One place lies empty – the jagged stump and name-tag, South Africa, identify its fate. A movement committed to 'universal brotherhood' has no time for apartheid.

Past the trees a greystone arch carved with symbols of the world's religions leads to the sacred banyan tree, its multiplying shoots and branches forming a fantastic, impenetrable cathedral. On holy days, Indians flock there to pace around its girth, while beneath its branches the rise to power of the Indian National Congress, founded in 1885, was nurtured.

The roots of the Theosophical Society were laid towards the end of the nineteenth century, on the tail of the furore over the theory of evolution. Knowledge and beliefs had collapsed into a welter of uncertainties: as one of the unhappily enlightened many remarked on hearing of Darwin's ideas, 'Leave me my ancestors in Paradise and I will allow you yours in the Zoological Gardens.'[1] Many seekers after truth were ready for some new, and preferably concrete, vision of utopia.

One such vision was provided by a fat, flamboyant Russian aristo-crat, Mme Helena Petrovna Blavatsky. Born Helena Hahn in 1831, the wild-eyed young woman deserted her ageing Vice Governor husband to travel the world, earning her keep as a medium's assistant and bareback rider in a circus. Eventually HPB, as she became known, fetched up in New York – a city humming with the new craze for spiritualists. It was a heaven-sent opportunity for her to make her mark.

With the support of an American lawyer and honorary colonel, Henry Steel Olcott, HPB began to conduct run-of-the mill seances, materialising teacups and rings to the accompaniment of table-rappings and the tinkling of astral bells. Time passed merrily by when, at a meeting of an esoteric study group in September 1875, Col Olcott passed HPB a note. 'Would it not be a good thing to form a society for this kind of study?' he enquired. HPB was struck by the idea, and the Theosophical Society came into being.

The Society exists 'to promote a knowledge of Theosophy, which is the cornerstone of all the major religions. However, it has no dogma or official body of beliefs'. While 'dogma' is out for Theosophists, 'doctrine' is most certainly in.

'Is [Theosophy] no more than a vague philanthropic philosophy which any student is entitled to colour according to his fancy?' asks Ianthe Hoskins, general secretary of the Society's British headquarters in central London. 'Not at all,' she continues, 'the title of Mme Blavatsky's major work is itself a recognition that there exists a DOCTRINE, a teaching, "the accumulated Wisdom of the Ages", handed down from one generation to the next by enlightened seers of whom every civilization and culture bears ample record.'[2]

The 'major work' referred to is *The Secret Doctrine* which, along with her other magnum opus *Isis Unveiled*, Mme Blavatsky declared was dictated to her by 'ascended masters', in particular the Tibetan-based spirit-beings or Masters of Wisdom, Mahatmas Koot Hoomi and Morya. During the 1890s a study of the two books documented two thousand plagiarized passages in *Isis Unveiled* and claimed that *The Secret Doctrine* was largely compiled from standard works of reference.[3]

More was to come. London's Society for Psychical Research sent one of its members to look into Mme Blavatsky's claims. The verdict: HPB was 'neither . . . the mouthpiece of hidden seers, nor . . . a mere vulgar adventuress; we think that she has achieved a title to permanent remembrance as one of the most accomplished, ingenious, and interesting impostors in history'.[4]

What was most brought into question was the authenticity of the Mahatma Letters – replies, allegedy from the Mahatmas, to queries from the Theosophists. In 1988, the Theosophical Society conducted an independent investigation into their origin. The study concluded that HPB had at any rate not penned the letters herself, although little light was shed on the writer's true identity.

Though Mme Blavatsky may have been an impostor, her movement foreshadows many of the beliefs, hopes and stumbling blocks of innumerable present-day New Age groups. One striking similarity is the Society's tendency to disparage knowledge and the mechanical workings of the mind in preference for an enlightened and transforming wisdom.

Former Indian film star Radha Burnier, the current president of the society, writes, 'Knowledge can leave one stagnating, sterile, or even be productive of various forms of folly. But wisdom is synonymous with transformation.'[5] To press home the point, the façade of the icecream-pink, aptly-named Great Hall at the society's international headquarters supports a long line of sculptured elephant heads – the ancient symbol of wisdom. In pursuit of enlightenment, Theosophists study anything from the Jewish Kabbalah, an esoteric mystical doctrine, to Christian and Sufi mystics, the tarot, *Upanishads*, meditation and spiritual ecology. But Mme Blavatsky's works remain their chief source of wisdom.

Hand in hand with the Theosophists' notion of transformation goes their theory of reincarnation – thereby placing the theory of evolution within a spiritual context. Whereas many found the idea of evolution profoundly humiliating – the Bible, after all, claimed mankind was 'a little lower than the angels' – the Theosophists took the idea on board. But whereas the Darwinian theory 'postulates an unbroken sequence of linear development from simpler to more complex or "higher" forms of life', Theosophists see evolution as 'the impulse of conscious life to take on forms which fulfil its inner needs'.[6] Through spiritual evolution, they say, man is perfectible. We are on 'a pilgrimage of consciousness toward a wider and wider universality'.[7]

According to Ianthe Hoskins, 'We are the birthplace of the New Age movement, the sprouting ground. We have prepared the way. The other movements have grown out of us like a banyan tree throws out its shoots from the trunk.' As Theosophist Dr Yves Marcel puts it, 'The time has come to make Theosophy the guiding principle for a new age.'[8]

The Theosophical Society teaches that humanity is divided into seven Root Races, each one representing, on one level, a paradigm of consciousness. We are currently in the fifth Root Race, the Aryan, when man's consciousness will unite itself with the spiritual soul. The seventh Race entails such bliss that it lies way beyond the limits of imagination.

While succeeding each other chronologically, the Root Races overlap and intermingle, experiencing internal decline and renewal. Throughout the Races, each individual possesses a divine spark, a fragment of the true self which will eventually enjoy perfect bliss. But the important point to remember is that 'nothing prevents our making earth a paradise now if we decide to make it so'.[9]

The fourth Race – that in which man achieves enormous progress – is called the Atlantean, after the lost continent of Atlantis. The story of the submerged continent of Atlantis begins with Plato, who described it as an advanced, golden age civilization in his works *Critias* and *Timaeus*, written around 355BC. Apparently, the god Poseidon 'equipped the central island with godlike lavishness; he made two springs flow, one of hot and one of cold water, and caused the earth to grow abundant produce of every kind'.[10] Rich and powerful, with glorious multicoloured buildings, a gold, silver and ivory temple, horse racing and rivers and lakes, the 'sacred island' flourished for generations for, 'so long as the divine element in their nature survived, [the rulers] . . . obeyed the laws and loved the divine to which they were akin [and] . . . saw soberly and clearly that all these things flourish only on a soil of common goodwill and individual character'.[11] Then, however, their divine nature became mingled with and weakened by mortal stock. The dream of a sacred civilization ruled over by divine beings who care both for the community and the individual persists among today's New Agers.

Interest in Atlantis was revived in the 1880s when a flurry of books exploring the culture of the vanished continent appeared. The desire to discover the exact siting of the long-lost utopia has obsessed millions – and thousands of books have appeared on the subject. According to Plato and the Theosophists it is under the Atlantic Ocean, but the American prophet and seer Edgar Cayce (1877–1945), who founded The Association for Research and Enlightenment, declared that it lay off the West Indian archipelago. Apparently, Cayce correctly predicted the deaths of two American presidents; so some think there may be a case for believing him. A hundred years on, in the early 1980s, a Soviet research vessel hunting for Atlantis made two expeditions to a site off Portugal, returning with reports of a submerged circus arena, staircases and arches. The site they investigated focused on the submerged Mount Amper, and the divers photographed what appeared to be man-made buildings on its summit as well as tidal marks on its slopes, which would indicate that the mountain was once above sea level. The findings were reported in the mainstream press with scepticism, and soon reports emerged saying that the Soviets were using their Atlantis investigations as a cover for spying on Western military installations.

Early Theosophists believed heaven on earth was well within their grasp. In its heyday, the Society was committed to establishing a new world order to prepare the way for a one-world government and religion. The plan is not so very different from the dreams of many of today's New Agers who, like the Theosophists, believe world transformation will be brought about through personal transformation.

To lead mankind forward to the next stage of evolution, the Theosophists called on the services of a young Indian, Jiddu Krishnamurti, marked out by the ascended masters as the 'Lord Maitreya'. Many believed Krishnamurti achieved divine status in the late 1920s. Increasingly unhappy with the role thrust upon him, however, Krishnamurti left the Theosophists in 1930 after four years as a messiah to pursue a solitary, self-effacing life as a teacher, taking numerous members of the society with him and declaring that truth was a 'pathless land' and could not be approached by any path, any religion or any sect. Nevertheless, the Theosophical Society remained the stamping ground for innumerable mystics of the day. At its height, it had millions of members throughout the world. It now has branches in some sixty countries and a total membership of more than 33,000.

Nehru, the first Prime Minister of independent India, was one of the Society's most notable alumni, and Mahatma Gandhi was also associated with the group. Theosophists are recognized as having helped the cause of Indian independence, not only through fighting for it politically but also because their admiration for India's ancient wisdom encouraged Indians themselves to look on their heritage with fresh eyes. Indeed, Gandhi first read the *Bhagavad Gita* after being given it by two Theosophists when he was studying law in London.

Other former Theosophists include the poet W. B. Yeats (1865–1939), the composer Alexander Scriabin (1872–1915) and artists Wassily Kandinsky (1866–1944) and Piet Mondrian (1872–1944). The belief that binds Theosophists together, irrespective of time and place, is that heaven on earth is attainable – and imminent. As Kandinsky put it, 'A great era has begun: the "Spiritual Awakening" . . . We are standing at the threshold of one of the greatest epochs that mankind has ever experienced, the epoch of great spirituality.'[12]

Pre-empting the musical *Hair*, a hit in the 1960s, some viewed the late nineteenth century as the dawning of the Age of Aquarius. 'The sun passes from Pisces into Aquarius in a few years,' wrote Theosophist George Russell to Yeats. 'Pisces is phallic in its influence. The waterman is spiritual so the inward turning souls will catch the first rays of the new Aeon.'[13]

Yeats had little doubt that 'Our civilization was about to reverse itself, or some new civilization about to be born from all that our age had rejected . . . because we had worshipped a single god it would worship many or receive from Joachim de Fiora's Holy Spirit a multitudinous influx'.[14]

Joachim of Fiore was a thirteenth century Calabrian mystic who believed that history was divided into three ages – the first the age of the Father, the second the age of the Son and the third the age of the Spirit when men would live in a blissful earthly paradise and possess full knowledge of God. This third and final age, said Joachim, was now dawning. New Agers are saying the same today.

According to Professor Norman Cohn, writing in 1957 of the influence of Joachim of Fiore, 'The phrase the Third Reich . . . adopted as a name for that "new order" which was supposed to last a thousand years, would have had but little emotional significance if the phantasy of a third and most glorious dispensation had not, over the centuries, entered into the common stock of European social mythology.'[15]

Ironically, in his prophetic poem 'The Second Coming', written years after his youthful optimism, Yeats asked 'And what rough beast, its hour come round at last, Slouches towards Bethlehem to be born?' Heaven on earth hadn't delivered. Instead of an imminent utopia, he sensed a new order in which 'the ceremony of innocence is drowned' – the rise of fascism.

For Yeats, along with many others, the big draw of the Theosophical Society was the opportunity it gave him to take part in occult ceremonies – though HPB did warn members of the dangers. Members would work with ritual symbols to effect changes within the self and, by way of preparation, study ancient texts and follow ascetic, highly regimental lifestyles. Scriabin learnt the hard way: his dabblings in the supernatural terrified him to the extent that he scarcely dared play a piano sonata he had composed while under occult influences. Though most Theosophists tended to veer away from black magic, Mme Blavatsky's review *Lucifer* carried the first public statement of the Hermetic Order of the Golden Dawn, a secret occult society founded in 1888. The Order was said to originate from an ancient German occult group, but its roots remain uncertain. It may have been the offshoot of a German magical society heavily influenced by HPB; there again, its history may have been a hoax.

Yeats joined the Order two years after its foundation. 'We who are seeking to sustain this greater Order must never forget that whatever we build in the imagination will accomplish itself in the circumstance of our lives,' he wrote. In the 1950s the Rev Norman Vincent Peale preached much the same line in his *The Power of Positive Thinking* – for him, the emphasis was on creating material success.

Like Theosophists, members of the Golden Dawn believed that personal transformation was closely linked to world transformation: hand in hand with the dawning of a new age went the evolution of the superhuman. To join the Order, initiates had to 'solemnly promise and swear that with the Divine permission I will from this day forward apply myself unto the GREAT WORK which is so to purify and exalt my spiritual nature that with the Divine Aid I may at length attain to be more than human, and thus gradually raise and unite myself to my Magus and Divine Genius, and that in this event I will not abuse the great power entrusted to me'.[16] Once admitted to the Order's ranks, they had to 'maintain a benevolent and fraternal relationship towards each other and a strict silence towards all the outer world . . .' They were told that 'the chief will not tolerate disregard of these most essential conditions. Unity of will is the occult condition precedent to a realization of our aspirations, unserving Fidelity on your part both to the ideals of the Higher Life and to the Chiefs of the Order will constitute the most practical evidence you can give of your desire to assist your brethren. To know, to do and to be silent is the triad of Occult Obligation'.[16a]

In the last years of the nineteenth century the Order began to disintegrate – hastened, it seems, by Aleister Crowley's initiation into its ranks on the prompting of MacGregor Mathers, one of the group's founders. Crowley, a self-confessed Satan worshipper – who even went so far as to file his teeth into sharp points to achieve a serpent's kiss – was happy to be known as the Beast 666, the Anti-Christ from Revelations. Some say that Mathers was eventually killed by his protégé in a psychic dual. At any rate, Mathers died in 1918 while Crowley went on to play a leading role in satanic circles.

All three founding fathers of the Golden Dawn – Mathers, William Woodman and William Wynn Westcott – were associated with the Freemasons, a secret society or society of secrets to which the Theosophists are closely linked. Inside the Universal Shrine at the Theosophical Society's international headquarters, pride of place is given to the masonic symbols of the square and compasses.

'Freemasonry is not a religion,' say Theosophists, 'but it is probably the oldest brotherhood in existence today.'[17] Both societies claim to uphold and strive for 'the Brotherhood of Man', although for many modern-day masons this tends to amount to a Brotherhood of the Elect Few. According to Tolstoy's Freemasons in *War and Peace*, their aim is, like that of the Theosophists, 'diligent self-purification' in order to 'enlighten their minds' and so regenerate mankind.

Theosophist Annie Besant was herself initiated into a branch of Freemasonry known as the Co-Masonic Order which allows women members and was set up to 'show the hidden meanings behind the ancient ritual'. In 1902 she introduced it to England, and afterwards to India. A journalist and mistress of George Bernard Shaw, Annie Besant was drawn into Theosophy after reviewing *The Secret Doctrine* and eventually became president of the Theosophical Society in 1907 after Mme Blavatsky's death in 1891.

According to Mme Blavatsky, the ancient masonic ritual was passed on through the Rosicrucians – mystical adepts who claimed to be custodians of an arcane wisdom that transcended Christianity. Rosicrucianism seems to date from the early seventeenth century when three tracts appeared in Germany proclaiming the existence of a secret brotherhood of mystical initiates. The tracts are now considered to have been a hoax, but they promised exactly what the Theosophists, and today's New Agers, are seeking – a transformation of the world and of human knowledge which would usher in a new epoch of spiritual freedom. During this new epoch, man would unlock the secrets of nature and govern his own destiny in accordance with harmonious, all-pervading cosmic laws.

One of the Golden Dawn's founders, William Woodman, was Supreme Magus of the Rosicrucian Society of Anglia and for a time Rosicrucianism was revitalized, then dying down until 1915 when the Ancient Mystical Order Rosae Crucis (AMORC) was founded. AMORC apparently teaches its members to 'knock the "t" out of "can't"'. Based in San José, California, it has branches throughout the Western world and claims some 250,000 members. Some have their doubts about AMORC's intentions, claiming members spend their time conducting 'prosperity affirmations' – mind-over-matter money-making ventures. Recently, AMORC has been going through leadership struggles, and accusations have been made about the organization's stewardship of millions of dollars.

The masons also claim to have links with the twelfth century Knights Templar. Their common ground is Solomon's Temple, an occult symbol for the perfection of the individual. King Baldwin II (r. 1118–31) of Jerusalem is believed to have given the Knights Templar part of his royal palace, next to the site of the Temple, as a reward for their chivalrous deeds in the Holy Land; today, masons symbolically re-enact Temple myths in their secret rituals. The Seal of Solomon, the six-pointed star, is a symbol of both the masons and the Theosophists.

It has been claimed that the Knights Templar were guardians of the Holy Grail. At any rate, many Theosophists are preoccupied by the Grail legend and in 1908 Theosophist Herbert Whyte – Knight Lancelot as he became known – founded a children's group, the International Order of the Round Table, with the help of Annie Besant. In the 1930s the Round Table became an independent movement, although it still teaches Theosophical ideas, including reincarnation. It now has branches in twenty-two countries, including New Zealand, Australia, Germany, France, Italy and Sweden.

In a letter to members of the Order, Ethel Whyte, wife of the Round Table's founder, voiced her belief in the dawning of a new age in which the members of the Round Table would have a major part to play. 'Each one of us, dear Companions, can be in his or her small way a herald of the GREAT PEACE BRINGER, by making ourselves tiny centres of peace, and we can only become such centres as we learn to cooperate with the GOOD, the TRUE and the BEAUTIFUL everywhere.'[18] One of the Round Table's 'voluntary disciplines' is to spend 'not less than five minutes each morning . . . picturing the perfect man'. According to a leading patron of the Order, the reasoning behind the routine is that 'every civilization, really great, has kept before it an ideal vision of perfect manhood to bequeath to its youth'.[19] While the Theosophists' ideals of chivalry have decidedly sexist overtones, Annie Besant was a staunch campaigner for women's rights.

Today's senior Knight of the World, Philippa Hartley, describes the Order as 'the brotherhood of kindness'. Through nourishing the 'intuitive understanding' and 'extreme spirituality' of the young children in her care, she believes they will come to have a 'transforming effect on the world'.

Seated around a Round Table, members of the Order conduct elaborate ritualistic ceremonies celebrating 'the eternal ideals and spirituality of mankind which little children intuitively understand'. One chair is always left empty to represent the presence of the king. The children, who may join the order from the age of five, are not told who inhabits the chair but must attribute to its absent occupant their highest spiritual ideal.

For the more significant ceremonies, the children wear white robes and tabards, coloured according to their spiritual progress. Beginning as Pages, they progress through the stages of Companion and Squire before finally reaching the office of Knight, at which point they are awarded a scarlet tabard. In a ceremony reminiscent of masonic ritual, the seated children hear a knock at the door and are told to 'go see who knocks'.

'Why have you come?' asks one of their number.

'We have come to learn more about the king and how to serve him,' comes the reply.

'Who is the king?'

'The perfect man.'

'How will we find him?'

'We shall find him as we serve him.'

The ritual of the Order of the Round Table finishes with a candlelit ceremony, to 'allow the light to come in'. It is, say members, 'a very beautiful, very spiritual occasion'. Today, interest in the Grail legends is enjoying an upsurge and numerous 'Grail Groups' have sprung up, their members publishing books, holding lectures and worshipping the Grail as the light of truth. Many experts claim that the English town of Glastonbury in Somerset is Avalon, the distant island where

Arthur's funeral boat landed, or the resting-place of the Holy Grail. In 1190, monks of Glastonbury abbey claimed they had found the remains of Arthur and Queen Guinevere lying in a hollow log coffin alongside a lead cross inscribed with the words 'Here lies buried the renowned King Arthur in the Isle of Avalon'. Whatever the truth behind the various theories, Glastonbury has become a 'spiritual capital', a magnetic attraction for New Agers.

The notion of an ideal being, whether focused in King Arthur or the giant race of Atlanteans, found its philosophical expression in Friedrich Nietzsche's Superman who would usher in a new age of liberty. 'I teach you the superman,' he announced. 'Man is something that should be overcome.'[20] Almost exactly a hundred years later, New Age authority Marilyn Ferguson wrote '. . . we are not victims, not pawns, not limited by conditions or conditioning. Heirs to evolutionary riches, we are capable of imagination, invention, and experiences we have only glimpsed. Human nature is neither good nor bad but open to continuous transformation and transcendence. It has only to discover itself'.[21]

Nowadays Nietzsche is regularly accused of being a forerunner of Nazism. The Theosophists, too, have been accused of inciting racial hatred. In turn-of-the-century Germany, numerous Volkischen or people's groups sprang up, proclaiming their Germanic purity and sometimes reinstating nationalistic myths and the pagan gods. Some of them dedicated themselves to the eradication of Jewish influences in the Fatherland, and others infused their teachings with the glamour of the occult by borrowing heavily from Theosophy.

The Order of the New Templars, founded in Austria in 1907, conducted Grail ceremonies and restricted membership to those with blond hair, blue or grey eyes, pale skins and slim hands and feet. The Templars' founder, Adolf Lanz, a former Cistercian monk, believed Aryans were caught in a cosmic struggle against the forces of darkness. In a 1908 issue of his magazine, *Ostara*, he drew on the Theosophists' ideas of race and set out a blueprint for the restoration of Aryan world domination. Annie Besant was named as one of his sources.[22]

Hitler is said to have been a keen subscriber to *Ostara*, and Lanz claimed that Hitler was one of his pupils. The American prophet Edgar Cayce (1877–1945) put forward an intriguing theory when he hinted that Hitler and Stalin were both reincarnations of the Atlanteans, the Theosophists' fourth Root Race. He believed Atlantis was destroyed when its inhabitants began to worship power.

Lanz, who preferred to be known as Lanz von Liebenfel, also developed a movement called Ariosophy, a term he coined in 1915. Like the Order of the New Templars, Ariosophy borrowed many occult teachings from Theosophy. In the late 1920s, Lanz wrote that 'No longer will parliaments determine the fate of the people. In their place will rule wise priest kings, genial patricians with an understanding of ariosophical mysticism and leaders of chivalrous and spiritual secret orders'.[23] In his book *The Occult Roots of Nazism*, Nicholas Goodrick-Clarke recounts how two Ariosophists were closely involved with Nazi leader Himmler in the 1930s.

The Theosophists' doctrine of races and talk of Aryans is more than likely to have proved irresistible fodder for the Nazis' publicity campaign. But some believe the Theosophists have more to account for. Certainly Alice Bailey, who was closely involved with the Theosophists for several years before breaking away to found the Arcane School in 1923, described Jews as 'an international minority of great aggressiveness, exceedingly vocal' and claimed that 'there is no other problem like it in the world today'. Jews, she said, were guilty of 'the sin of separateness'.[24] Bailey's many books lay down the principles by which humanity will be able to enter a New Age and are avidly read by today's New Agers.

According to today's Theosophists, '[though the word] "Aryan" calls up ugly associations with the racist ideology of German National Socialism . . . it seems not unlikely that Nazi and proto-Nazi ideologues pilfered and distorted Theosophical terms and teachings . . . characteristically twisting and debasing it to support their arguments for racial superiority . . .'[25] Moreover, they say, Theosophists were persecuted by the Nazis – along with the Freemasons and Jews.

In an attempt to counter attacks that they are anti-semitic, Theosophists claim that 'Jewish people are an intrinsic part of the Fifth or "Aryan" Root Race, making their own special contribution to the development of that Race'.[26] And in *Isis Unveiled*, Mme Blavatsky commended the Jews, saying, 'How faithfully and nobly they have stood by their ancestral faith under the most diabolical persecutions.'

Repeatedly, though, the urge for unity, a new world order and the 'brotherhood of man' has been transformed into nationalism. In an isolated castle in Ireland the poet Yeats aimed to establish a nationalist group which would use masonic methods to achieve

Irish independence. Then, quite naturally, he believed, the earthly paradise would transpire.

Today, many Theosophists have taken refuge in an otherworldly mystic gentility while awaiting 'a coming new Race [which] will be centred far from Europe, seeing the history of humanity as a whole which has many diverse parts'. Visitors to the Madras headquarters have variously described it as 'the garden of doddering delights', 'an isolated paradise' and 'an idyllic respite from the world'. A utopia, of kinds, it may well be.

An ageing American-born woman, former assistant to a maharajah, holds nightly soirées in her colonial bungalow overlooking the Bay of Bengal. There, Theosophists from around the world gather to listen to classical records on her old-fashioned gramophone and discuss the Kabbalah, or tarot, or *Bhagavad Gita*. The days are passed studying mysticism, listening to sitar music and meditating. The outside world rarely impinges. Some, at least, seem to have found their heaven on earth.

TWO | AWAKENINGS

In 1907 satanist Aleister Crowley was 'enormously encouraged' by an article evaluating his influence and work. Written by Florence Farr, a friend of Yeats and member of the Golden Dawn, the review appeared in the pages of an influential journal, *The New Age*.

A weekly magazine, *The New Age* was taken over that year by A.R. Orage with backing from George Bernard Shaw. Subtitled *An Independent Review of Politics, Literature and Art*, *The New Age* covered politics, moral issues, philosophy and psychoanalysis. On spiritual matters, it was informed by Shaw's belief that 'There is only one religion, though there are a hundred versions of it'.[1]

Among the magazine's contributors was the philosopher-scientist H.G. Wells who, in 1905, had spread his vision of a one world community through *A Modern Utopia*. The book concludes: 'There will be many Utopias. Each generation will have its new version of Utopia, a little more certain and complete and real . . . Until at last from dreams Utopias will have come to be working drawings, and the whole world will be shaping the final World State, the fair and great and fruitful World State, that will only not be a Utopia because it will be this world.'[2]

Before becoming editor of *The New Age*, Orage had written two books on Nietzsche and, while teaching at a school in Leeds, had fallen across Theosophical theories. Soon, his new-found vision of cultural reform inspired him to set up the Leeds Arts Club as a platform for his ideas. Among the club's speakers were W.B. Yeats and social reformer and poet Edward Carpenter.

For fifteen years, Orage threw himself into *The New Age*, working all hours for little reward other than that of spreading the vision of an ideal world and of fostering countless new talents – including that of New Zealander Katherine Mansfield: '. . . you taught me to write, you taught me to think, you showed me what there was to be done and what not to do' she said of her mentor.[3] Doubtless, Mansfield's unconventional behaviour went down well with *The New Age* circle who had moved a long way from the somewhat fusty intellectualism of Theosophy. In the year Katherine Mansfield began writing for *The New Age*, the journal published an article by Edward Carpenter. The piece, typical of the changing times, called for 'the coarse, the concrete, the vulgar and the physiological side in human life and passion'.[4]

It was Mansfield's inclination for experiencing the new and exotic which drew her to the Ballet Russe. In 1909 Vaslav Nijinsky – who died insane in 1950 crying out 'I am God, I am God' – performed with the company in Paris under the command of Sergei Diaghilev. Soon, England was swept with a craze for all things Russian. The 'drama' of Russian dance satisfied a craving for wholeness which science and religion seemed unable to fulfil.

More than a decade later Katherine Mansfield wrote, 'One must live more fully and one must have more POWER of loving and feeling. One must be true to one's vision of life – in every single particular – and I am not. The only thing to do is to try again from tonight to be stronger and better to be WHOLE.'[5]

As it turned out, it was to be Russians who set her on the path towards achieving her goal – in particular the charismatic mystic, or eccentric philosopher, Gurdjieff, whose teachings permeate today's New Age movement. Gurdjieff was born George Gorgiades in Alexandropol, a Russian village in territory that had long been disputed with the Turks. The date was sometime in the 1870s. His mother was an Armenian and his father a Greek carpenter and, according to Gurdjieff, a bard. It was, says Gurdjieff, his father's singing which first aroused his interest for esoteric knowledge passed down orally through the ages.

Educated at Kars municipal school and by private tutors, Gurdjieff claims to have witnessed various psychic phenomena as a child, such as strange table tappings, which prompted him to become 'extremely interested in supernatural phenomena'.[6] After finishing his formal education, he became obsessed by the desire to discover more about the Sarmoung Brotherhood, an esoteric school 'according to tradition

. . . founded in Babylon as far back as 2500BC'.⁷ Taking his dog with him, he set out on his travels, journeying throughout Central Asia and the Middle East in search of the secrets of the ages.

He fell in with the Community of Truth Seekers, a group who believed in a single world religion. Sometime in the distant past, said the Seekers, this one-world universal religion had faded out of existence, but it could still be identified in fragments of rituals, monuments and beliefs that lay scattered throughout ancient civilizations.

If Gurdjieff is to be believed – and much of his life story, including his date of birth, is in doubt since he had a self-confessed habit of deceiving people – he met with mystics, princes and sages on his travels, including the Monopsyche Brotherhood, the Essenes, Dervishes and Buddhists. He also rested several months at the monastery of the Sarmoung Brotherhood – though it is uncertain whether he met up with any monks.

Fifteen years or so passed in this way, interspersed with time spent as a carpet salesman, a corset-mender and, so it has frequently been alleged, a Tzarist spy. By his own confession, Gurdjieff would make money by any means whatsoever – which often included cheating people. He also began to develop his powers of hypnotism.

At the end of his odyssey, sometime between 1910 and 1913, Gurdjieff returned to Russia, convinced he had hit upon the Truth. Apparently, the doors of a certain school had opened for him – a school where he came to understand how to bring together all the principles of esoteric teaching. This school was called the Universal Brotherhood – the phrase used by Mme Blavatsky and the Freemasons to describe their respective organizations.

According to Gurdjieff's account, the next decade was spent attempting to establish some sort of vehicle for his teachings. He had reckoned without the intervention of the Russian Revolution and, while gathering a considerable following, he squandered on dead-end ventures the fortune of several million roubles he had acquired on his travels.

One of the bright spots during this period was his meeting with Peter Ouspensky, a Russian mathematician and philosopher preoccupied by the evolution of man's consciousness. The two found much in common and Ouspensky began to lecture on Gurdjieff's ideas. Ouspensky had already long been interested in Theosophy, and had stayed at the Society's Adyar headquarters for six weeks in 1913.

A year earlier, his book *Tertium Organum* had been published. The book, which deals with the development of mankind's consciousness, immediately attracted attention – including, when it was finally translated into English, that of Lady Rothermere, wife of the owner of the *Daily Mail* and *Daily Mirror*.

Before long Ouspensky was whisked to London, on the request of Lady Rothermere, where he was an instant hit with many truth seekers of the day – Orage and the poet T.S. Eliot would frequently attend meditation sessions with him. It was to one of Ouspensky's lectures, introducing the ideas of Gurdjieff, that Orage took Katherine Mansfield in 1922. The secret knowledge that Gurdjieff had acquired and that had captured the imagination of thousands was, put simply, that man is a machine.

'All the people you see, all the people you know, all the people *you may get to know*, are machines . . . working solely under the power of influences,' Gurdjieff told Ouspensky. '. . . But there is a possibility of ceasing to be a machine . . . When a machine knows itself it is then no longer a machine, at least, not such a machine as it was before. It already begins to be *responsible* for its actions.'[8] Gurdjieff taught that the habitual mechanicalness of man is caused by his alienation from his true self, and from the world around him. In order to become whole, man and the world must coalesce into a harmonious body. The thinking, very much that of today's environmentalists and New Age disciples, was spelt out in the early 1970s by John Bennett, one of the master's foremost disciples. Only by realizing the importance of Gurdjieff's insistence on mutal dependence with the surrounding world – 'reciprocal maintenance', as he called it – would the ills of the times be cured. 'I have confidence,' said Bennett to a group of Gurdjieffians, 'that this action will succeed and that many of you here today will see the birth of the New World.'[9]

According to Gurdjieff, Bennett explained, 'everything that exists in the universe depends on other things for its maintenance and must in its turn maintain the existence of others . . . this applies to us men also.'[10] Many modern-day physicists say much the same, emphasizing the interconnectedness, or 'wholism', of all matter. Interestingly, Ouspensky often expressed his altered states of consciousness in mathematical language – his flashes of insight, of seeing unity within diversity, lay beyond the realms of everyday language: numbers became ideas, or symbols for a higher reality.

This 'wholism' was precisely what Katherine Mansfield, and many like her, were seeking. 'The world to me is a dream and the people in it are sleepers,' she wrote in October 1922, echoing Gurdjieff's belief that 'man is asleep'. 'I have known just instances of waking but that is all. I want to find a world in which these instances are united. Shall I succeed? I do not know. I scarcely care. What is important is to try and learn to live – really live – and in relation to everything – not isolated (this isolation is death to me).'[11]

Many of Gurdjieff's disciples were to learn how to achieve unity the hard way – through slave labour. For some time, Gurdjieff had been looking for a site for an institute where his ideas could be put into practice. In February 1922 he arrived in London where, in the leafy lanes of Hampstead, Lady Rothermere and her circle hoped to trap their prize. With his handlebar moustache, shaved head and gimlet eyes, Gurdjieff was an intriguing figure. The Home Office, however, was unimpressed by Lady Rothermere's idea – possibly because tales of Gurdjieff's rumoured former life as a Tzarist spy had crept out.

According to the master's own account of his departure, 'France seemed . . . to be the most suitable base for the diffusion of my ideas. England, owing to its insular situation, would not have allowed any development in this respect; an Institute founded there would have taken on the narrow character of a local institution.'[12]

And so it was, with backing from Lady Rothermere, that Gurdjieff finally set up the Institute for the Harmonious Development of Mankind in October 1922 at Le Prieuré, a former monastery set in a large though languishing estate at Avon near Fontainebleau south of Paris. According to Bennett, Gurdjieff created at Le Prieuré conditions that enabled the residents to experience their full potential for self-transformation.

At the end of September 1922 Orage resigned his editorship of *The New Age* and prepared to move to Le Prieuré. On his arrival he was ordered to stop smoking, and start digging. It was not a task Orage enjoyed but, determined to persevere, he put all his effort into it. It took some four or five months for him to achieve 'breakthrough': 'When I was in the very depths of despair,' he said, 'feeling that I could go on no longer, I vowed to make extra effort, and just then something changed in me. Soon, I began to enjoy the hard labour . . .'[13]

According to Gurdjieff, Orage had broken through to a new level of consciousness, the reason being that he had ceased to understand things simply with his intellect and had begun to experience them directly. Gurdjieff taught that human beings, quite literally, spend their lives asleep, living out a routine existence, preoccupied by trivialities. Occasionally, in moments of peak intensity, they become self-aware and will catch a glimpse of their true potential at which point they begin to exist. The title of one of Gurdjieff's books sums it up – *Life is Real Only Then, When 'I Am'*. Many present-day 'transformation trainings', which aim to introduce participants to a new concept of reality, teach precisely this philosophy – one even calls itself 'I AM'.

Before long, the intelligentsia of the United States, Britain and continental Europe were flocking through the ornate gates of Le Prieuré to be humiliated, slave driven, and lodged in small, ice-cold rooms. One disciple, Louis Pauwels, writes how 'after two years of "work" . . . I found myself in hospital, as weak as a kitten, one eye nearly gone, on the verge of suicide'.[14] But life at Le Prieuré was devoted to more than hard labour. Dancing also came high on the list of activities, the idea being that once the energy had been drawn away from what Gurdjieff called the 'noise machine', or interfering mind, and directed into the muscles, a higher state of consciousness could be achieved.

On the birthday before his death in January 1990, Bhagwan Shree Rajneesh's disciples performed a Gurdjieffian dance for him in the Buddhahall at his Indian ashram. It was an extraordinary display of self-discipline. For Bhagwan's followers, Gurdjieff is in line with Mahavira, the omniscient teacher of Jainism, born in India in the sixth century BC. Jainism teaches reverence for all life, denies a creator god and offers a path to spiritual liberation. One of today's Gurdjieff-inspired systems, Arica, makes use of 'psycho-calisthenics' – physical exercises intended to break down habitual patterns in the body.

Once his disciples were familiar with dancing, Gurdjieff had countless tricks up his sleeve to shock them out of their habitual patterns of behaviour and into heightened states of consciousness. Sometimes he would set them impossible tasks, then cancel his instructions at the last minute; at other times he might tell them to repeatedly dig and refill a hole.

Innumerable success stories emerged from Le Prieuré. Whether it was due to Gurdjieff's system, or whether it was simply that the free thinkers of the day found a form of salvation in submitting themselves to the caprices of a master is open to question. It could be that they glimpsed immortality through, as Eliot put it in 'The Waste Land', 'The awful daring of a moment's surrender' – and in doing so were merely returning to all that Nietzsche and those of his ilk disparaged as slavish humility.

Katherine Mansfield moved to Le Prieuré in October 1922. Although she was already extremely ill she was put to work peeling vegetables and weaving baskets. 'At 34 I am beginning my education,'[15] she wrote a month later. On the instruction of Gurdjieff, in whom she had absolute confidence, she spent much of her time on a wooden platform in a cow shed, following an old peasant remedy for tuberculosis, combatting the extreme cold by wearing her fur coat night and day. Writing from Le Prieuré, she explained '. . . in the deepest sense I've always been disunited . . . It is a living death. So I have decided to make a clean sweep of all that was "superficial" in my past life and start again to see if I can get into that real living simple truthful FULL life I dream of . . .'[16] Her death at Le Prieuré, ten weeks after her arrival, fuelled rumours of the bizarre practices that went on there.

Gurdjieff had a huge appetite for life – he drank and ate to excess – he had a reputation for being a superb cook – and he went through women as if face to face with Armageddon. Orage possibly felt that his master lived out the basic urges – 'the coarse, the concrete, the vulgar and the physiological' – that Edward Carpenter had extolled in the pages of *The New Age*. Like Carpenter, Gurdjieff believed that sex in itself had a mystical value, claiming that 'It is a very big thing when the sex centre works with its own energy'. For Gurdjieff, women were 'only the means to an end'.[17]

By 1923 funds were running low at Le Prieuré and Gurdjieff decided it was time for his disciples to introduce his work to the United States. Orage was sent ahead to prepare the way. The crowning event of the tour was a dance display staged in New York in January 1924. According to one of the audience, William Seabrook, 'What excited and interested me was the amazing, brilliant, automatonlike, inhuman, almost incredible docility and robot-like obedience of the disciples. They were like a group of perfectly trained zombies . . . if they hadn't learned supreme coordination they'd have broken their arms and legs, and maybe their necks . . . But what I felt the demonstrations showed, even more than their control over themselves, was the terrific domination of Gurdjieff, the Master. At his command, they'd race, spread out, at breakneck speed from left to right across the stage, and at another low command from him, freeze in full flight . . . Once I saw Gurdjieff push a dancer who had been "frozen" by his command . . . The dancer tumbled and rolled over several times, then rolled upright and was back again, apparently without volitionally *assuming* it – in the original frozen position.'[18]

One member of the troupe, Olgivanna Hinzenberg, passed a Sunday afternoon at the matinée performance of a Russian ballet performance. Sitting next to her was the architect Frank Lloyd Wright. The two fell in love and in 1932 set up the Taliesin Fellowship, based on Le Prieuré, and which still exists on a farm in southern Wisconsin. It is, some say, dominated by a hierarchy of Gurdjieffians. Certainly, in the early days, much of the disciples' time was spent hard at work turning Taliesin into a country estate commensurate with Wright's lofty ideals. Interestingly, Wright called one of his house designs the 'Usonian' style – a name taken, he said, from Samuel Butler's utopian never-never land novel *Erewhon*, though no one has been able to find it mentioned there.

Another of Wright's favourite writers was Major Clifford Douglas, a British economist whose work Orage also greatly admired – he had serialized Douglas's first book in *The New Age*. Douglas put forward an economic theory known as social credit, which when put into practice would, he claimed, usher in a utopian era of plenty, freedom, leisure and human dignity. In 1930, after seven years spent spreading Gurdjieff's teachings throughout America, Orage set up *The New English Weekly*, devoted to Douglas's ideas.

Social credit was based on a belief that people simply don't have enough money. Under the new system, retailers would be given credit which would enable them to sell their goods at prices people could afford. Major Douglas's ideas continue to be put forward by affiliates of today's New Age. Rather than using money as a means of wielding power, writes Eric de Maré in a 1990 issue of *Resurgence* magazine, it should exist as a convenient method of exchange. The human race is suffering from 'unreal monetary problems' whereas it should be enjoying 'simple living of a highly creative quality in a state of personal liberty'. Such a lifestyle 'is likely rapidly to reduce world populations as life becomes more fulfilling for the individual man and woman'. The solutions de Maré puts forward are, he admits, 'not the author's own; they are those of the engineer and costing expert, Major C.H. Douglas . . .'[19]

At around the same time that Orage was circulating the Major's ideas, Andrew MacLaren, born in 1883 and educated at the Glasgow School of Art, was espousing a theory of land taxation reform – that people should be taxed on their land holdings rather than their incomes. MacLaren's theories began to interest members of *The New Age* circle: 'If I were Prime Minister, I would make Mr Andrew MacLaren minister of Land'[20] said George Bernard Shaw, the magazine's backer. In 1922 – the year Orage left for Le Prieuré – MacLaren became Member of Parliament for Burslem.

In the 1930s MacLaren started a group known as the School of Economic Science, devoted to the study of his theory of land value taxation. Before long, the School was taken over by MacLaren's son, whose name – Leonardo da Vinci MacLaren – indicates his parents' high hopes for him. A trained barrister, Leon still lives in London. In his early working years, he wholeheartedly adopted his father's economic theories and himself went into politics. But under his leadership, officially established in 1947, the School of Economic Science was to change dramatically. Gradually, Leon had come to believe that the key to social betterment lay not in social transformation through politics but in personal transformation. It was a reversal of the road Orage had beaten.

The gurus who had influenced MacLaren's change of heart were none other than the two philosopher mystics Gurdjieff and Ouspensky. Following a car crash in France in the summer of 1924, Gurdjieff had felt unable to invest the same enthusiasm in his work at Le Prieuré. Convinced his consciousness had regressed to an earlier stage of evolution, he felt the strenuous role of transformation catalyst was temporarily beyond him. Moreover, the American tour had not realized its full money-making potential and the Le Prieuré coffers were far from healthy.

Although Le Prieuré struggled on until 1933, when it was finally sold, the place had lost its vital energy. Gurdjieff turned instead to writing. The resulting book, *All and Everything: Beelzebub's Tales To His Grandson* deserves recognition as one of the most obscure books to have been penned. 'It was in the year 223 after the creation of the World . . . Through the Universe flew the ship Karnak of the "trans-space communication",'[21] he wrote. The bizarre science-fiction world Gurdjieff created finds a later echo in the work of the American L. Ron Hubbard, founder of the Church of Scientology. As part of his science of mental health, Hubbard describes how Xemu, an evil tyrant who lived 75 million years ago, froze people in alcohol and glycol and dropped nuclear bombs on them.

Though frequently travelling to America, Gurdjieff made his home in Paris where he scratched a living through psychic healings. Bennett visited him there in October 1949 and recalls Gurdjieff announcing, 'Either I will make the old world "tchic" or it will make me "tchic" . . . When *Beelzebub* is published a new force will come into the world.'[22] Within a week, Gurdjieff was dead.

Meanwhile, Ouspensky had set up house in London where his lectures continued to attract numerous followers. Unlike Gurdjieff, who emphasized the experiential approach, Ouspensky believed transformation could be achieved through rigorous intellectual enquiry. As a result he was a far less controversial character than Gurdjieff, but nonetheless attracted a devoted following. That following received perhaps their most habit-breaking experience when, shortly before his death, Ouspensky radically altered his views, declared 'There is no System' and told his disciples they must look elsewhere for the truth. It was, according to a woman present when he made the announcement, a shattering experience.

In 1988 a Gurdjieff-Ouspensky offshoot, the Alexandria Foundation, ended in a similar manner. In a letter to his followers, leader Gary Chicoine wrote, 'I have no spiritual instruction or advice to give to anyone. I have literally burned and destroyed all my books, pamphlets and writings . . . I disown them . . . My renunciation of spiritual leadership is total, absolute . . . You may as well give up on me, for I have truly given up on you.'[23]

The teaching of the two Russians persists, however, through numerous organizations. One, the London-based Gurdjieff–Ouspensky School, provides 'a system of inner development to awaken consciousness and change the being of ordinary normal women and men . . . This system comes from higher mind and has been taught by word of mouth through generations of teachers and students from ancient times to our own. This school is on the direct line of oral transmission first introduced to the West through G.I. Gurdjieff'. At the school, members are told they will learn 'to change both your knowledge, that is, what you know, and your being, that is, what you are'.[24]

Ouspensky died in London in 1947 – the same year Leon MacLaren took over the reins of the School of Economic Science. Perhaps MacLaren recognized the need for some new system for all those whose light had suddenly been extinguished. Before developing his own system, however, he had to come to grips with the work of the two Russians. To do so, he attended meetings of the Society for the Study of Normal Psychology, known as the Study Society – one of the numerous small groups devoted to unravelling the mysteries of Gurdjieff's and Ouspensky's teachings. Members of the Study Society were drawn largely from the intelligentsia of the day and were organized by Dr Francis Roles, a Harley Street paediatrician. MacLaren eventually began to lead classes at the Society, and to introduce its teachings to the School of Economic Science.

In 1961 Dr Roles along with other senior members of the Study Society journeyed east where, in the teachings of the Indian Shankaracharya of the North, they believed they had hit upon the source of Gurdjieff's teaching. MacLaren was quick to follow the Society's eastward path and soon afterwards he himself visited the Shankaracharya. On his return, he gave up his job as a barrister and began to work full-time for the School of Economic Science.

The Shankaracharyas follow the teachings of a Brahmin called Shankara (c. 788–820AD) whose school of Vedanta (so called because it is based on the interpretation of the ancient Vedic writings) is known as non-dualistic or advaita Vedanta. Shankara taught that reality lies in the one eternal Absolute and that the world as we know it is illusion, created by the interpretation we choose to impose on it. The aim of man is to realize, through inner experience, his union with the Absolute. According to the SES this could be achieved through developing 'self' consciousness. The attraction for disciples of the Gurdjieff and Ouspensky system is clear.

Self consciousness, for the School of Economic Science, is closely allied to self control. Students are expected to govern their lives by a strict system of rules – inspired, perhaps, by Gurdjieff's belief that rules are the alarm clock that wake the sleeping man. They also work tirelessly at menial, often unnecessary manual jobs in the hope of breaking through to a new level of consciousness. In his *Journey to the East*, Hermann Hesse noted that 'a long time devoted to small details exalts us and increases our strength'.[25] Like Gurdjieff, Hesse was dedicated to the aim of building up a harmonious 'self', and became immensely popular with the counter culture of the 1960s.

In addition to the Vedantic and Gurdjieffian input, the School of Economic Science has taken on board the vision of utopia portrayed in Plato's *The Republic*. There, society is based on a highly disciplined class system – comparable to the Hindu caste system – at the top of which come members of a power-wielding elite known as Philosopher Rulers. Through their lengthy, rarified philosophical education, these 'saviours of society' acquire 'the characteristics of order and divinity as far as men may'. Philosophy is not, however, possible 'among the common people' and the Rulers 'will have to employ a great deal of fiction and deceit for the benefit of their subjects'.[26]

Though Plato has been condemned as a totalitarian, he has also been hailed as a forerunner of nineteenth- and twentieth-century left wing 'utopian planners'. Whatever their political colour, members of the School of Economic Science study Plato's work, believing it puts forward 'the clearest and truest ideas for a smooth-running society'.[27]

According to Plato, education is the most efficient tool with which to transform society. As well as holding classes for adults in subjects such as 'the Platonic Academy in Florence in the fifteenth century under Marsilio Ficino', the School of Economic Science runs a private school for children in central London. In the early 1980s it hit the British headlines for its unorthodox teaching practices. Criticism centred on pupils being trained in Hindu philosophy, Sanskrit and meditation, together with the school's practice of disciplining pupils with the cane and cold showers. In Plato's *Republic*, the ideal education will not concentrate on 'purely intellectual pursuits' but will be that in which 'the mind as a whole must be turned away from the world of change until its eye can bear to look straight at reality, and at the brightest of all realities which is what we call the good'.

Some say that members of the SES are expected to agree to arranged marriages. Certainly, in Plato's *Republic*, it is believed that 'we must, if we are to be consistent, and if we're to have a real pedigree herd, mate the best of our men with the best of our women as often as possible, and the inferior men with the inferior women as seldom as possible, and bring up only the offspring of the best'.[28] Some women have allegedly used the SES as a dating agency, thereby in a sense willingly participating in 'positive eugenics', since members of the School are seen as superior to outsiders.

The School even conducted an experiment in creating the perfect woman in the 1960s and '70s, taking a young girl away from her SES parents and training her up in its teachings and traditions. In Plato's *Republic*, the family is abolished, children are looked after in state nurseries, and later educated by the state.

Like the ancient Greeks, members of the SES hanker after a golden age – a long-ago time when everyone lived in peace and harmony. Since then, they believe, humanity has degenerated. While for some, the School provides an opportunity to recapture a taste of Edenic bliss, others recount tales of drudgery and mental suffering.

Each year, the movement holds an art exhibition in the grounds of one of its properties, Waterperry House, a gracious Oxfordshire mansion. Exhibitors include top names from the art world and SES philosophy informs the whole occasion – even down to the meticulous tidiness of the event.

Artistic endeavour is encouraged because, like Gurdjieff's dances, it requires self-control, discipline and dedication. Not surprisingly, the more precise arts such as calligraphy and lithography are favoured. 'The creative process is a variety of meditation, concentrating and stilling the mind,' explains an SES member. 'We are looking at ways of lifting art and people into another dimension, of freeing the spirit.'[29]

Art in Action is organized with painstaking precision by the School's 2000 British members. Among them are doctors, lawyers, teachers and businesspeople. The women wear long skirts and both they and the men appear to be in a state of beatific happiness. Former members say this is because negative emotions are held to indicate a lack of self discipline. Classical music – usually the School's recommended composers Mozart and Vivaldi – plays gently in the background and many of the works display a noticeably Eastern influence.

Some exhibitors believe there is something just a little too perfect about the event. 'Maybe it's odd because it's what life should be about,' says one. 'Maybe you need a group like that to find your utopia.'

THREE | DO WHAT YOU WILL

S omewhere on the banks of the Loire, so the story goes, lies a beautiful abbey with 9332 apartments, gracious staircases of porphyry, marble and serpentine, and fine, old-fashioned arcades. The abbey is home to both men and women – provided they are handsome, well-built and sweet-natured. Because 'ordinarily monks and nuns made three vows, that is of chastity, poverty and obedience, it was decreed that there anyone could be regularly married, could become rich, and could live at liberty'.[1] This utopian monastery has, in fact, only one rule: *Fay ce que voudras* (Do what you will).

The Abbey of Thélème is the fictional invention of François Rabelais (c 1494–1553), a humanist keen to put forward his vision of personal liberty as the world moved slowly into a New Age of individualism. In the twentieth century, Rabelais has been hailed as a prophet for the Aquarian Age. Certainly, his creed, 'Do what you will', has reverberated down through the centuries, as an inspiration to countless individuals and communities intent on making earthly life just that little bit more heavenly – if not a true heaven on earth.

On the whole, 'Do what you will' has served as a justification for free sexual expression. Sex could be the means not merely for personal but for social transformation: the key to a world of sexually liberated individuals living in a free love society. With the rediscovery of classical Greek and Roman authors, many Renaissance humanists turned their backs on the theological bias of former scholarship. One Greek text which was translated dozens of times during the Renaissance described life on the Isles of the Blessed, a magical heaven on earth where marriage is unknown and promiscuity rules the day.

The Renaissance also gave birth to Thomas More's best-seller, *Utopia*, published in 1516. The sexual habits of More's community are more in line with those of Christian teaching. There, pre-marital sex is punished by celibacy for life, adultery by slavery and repeated adultery by death. Thankfully, More made it quite clear that in his case, utopia meant nowhere. All the same, he had good authority for taking a stern attitude towards sexual behaviour. 'It is good for a man not to touch a woman,' said St Paul. 'Nevertheless, to avoid fornication, let every man have his own wife . . . for it is better to marry than to burn.'[2] In the eyes of many through the ages, Christianity went hand in hand with sexual suffocation. God knew Adam had sinned when he saw he had covered his nakedness, and so sex and sin became inextricably linked.

According to Mother Ann Lee, British founder of the Christian Shaker sect in the mid eighteenth century, God had revealed to her that the original sin in the Garden of Eden was sexual intercourse. At their peak, in the early nineteenth century, the Shakers had some 6000 members living in twenty-three self-supporting communities in America. Today, only the merest handful remain: extinction will inevitably overtake a sin-free society if sex itself is considered sinful. Despite the depressing conclusion that sin is necessary for humanity's continued existence, Mother's belief holds sway in numerous religious circles. Christians have repeatedly 'envisaged the transformed human animal as . . . shrivelled and inert in sexuality'.[3]

On their wedding night, members of the Unification Church, or Moonies, are expected to perform a sexual ritual intended to symbolize the redemption of Adam and Eve, whose first attempt at living in heaven on earth in the Garden of Eden went horribly wrong. But with the second coming, in the shape of Unification Church founder Rev Sun Myung Moon, the original state of purity will be restored. 'Let us humbly listen to the voice of our original mind and search for the announcement of the Messiah,' states the *Divine Principle*, the book which lays down the movement's theological doctrine. 'Let us calm our mind and pay attention to the hope-giving news that announced the New Age.'[4]

Self-abnegation can go to extreme lengths. The early church father Origen (?185–?254), following the Bible's advice, made himself a eunuch. The practice has not died out. In 1990 it was reported that priests of a secret Roman Catholic sect in Spain were said to have castrated themselves or inserted rings in their genitals, and that local hospitals were often called upon to carry out emergency surgery.[5] The priests might be accused of masochism. Certainly, they vie with the Marquis de Sade (1740–1814) – the original sadist – for sexual ingenuity.

The 'Divine Marquis', as he was known, adopted Rabelais as a guru, naming one of his characters the 'Marquise de Thélème' after Rabelais' Abbey. He even attempted to set up a real-life Thélème of his own at his Provençal home of La Coste, but the enactment of his fantasies often proved impossible – he spent much of his life in jail.

Just as Rabelais was hailed as prefiguring a New Age, so de Sade has been hailed as the prophet of the world we live in today. Anticipating the sexual revolution of this century, he dealt with the question of the relationship between sexuality and human freedom, believing that it was through following the 'natural' urge for pleasure that true transcendence was attained: '. . . abandon all your senses to pleasure, let it be the one object, the one god of your existence . . . nothing must be as holy as pleasure.'[6] His distaste for what he saw as the weakness of Christianity has been held to anticipate Nietzsche. Moreover, anticipating Sigmund Freud (1856–1939), he claimed that: 'The act of enjoyment [sexual pleasure] is a passion which . . . subordinates all others to it, but which simultaneously unites them.'[7]

For de Sade there was to be no nonsense about souls uniting during sex – empathy merely acted as a distraction from the individual's ecstasy: '. . . the idea of seeing another enjoy as he enjoys reduces him to a kind of equality with that other which impairs the unspeakable charm despotism causes him to feel. 'Tis false as well to say there is pleasure in affording pleasure to others; that is to serve them. On the contrary by causing them hurt . . . 'tis then he dominates, is a tyrant.'[8] A unification of sorts could, however, be obtained through sadistic sex. By recognizing the complete control of the torturer, the victim confirmed the torturer's existence. For de Sade, then, sex was a means of coping with the existential crisis.

De Sade saw sex not as a means to self-abandonment, or loss of self, but as a route to self-actualization – a way to discover the authentic self – and the more divorced from emotion, the better. As for virtue, '. . . might it not be the appearance of virtue which really becomes necessary to social man?' he asked. 'Let's not doubt that the appearance alone is quite sufficient to him.'[9] De Sade, on the other hand, was interested in the 'real'. In all contexts, including the sexual, the pursuit of the real as opposed to the illusory surfaced in the 1960s, reawakening interest in de Sade – and in 1990, the 250th anniversary of de Sade's birth, the 'Sade industry' took off – 'de Sade' champagne and chocolates were on sale, while stage plays and a feature film of his life ran to packed houses.

Like Rabelais, de Sade delighted in infringing taboos, but his anti-monastery in *Justine* (1791) is a long way from the fictional monastery invented by Rabelais. De Sade's monks celebrate the Black Mass, using nuns as the sexual 'altar' to be defiled, and members of religious orders almost invariably enter his works only to take part in orgies. What de Sade's ritual brings to mind is one of the many gatherings conducted by Aleister Crowley.

In 1904 a spirit being called Aiwass appeared to Crowley and dictated *The Book of the Law* to him. The work embodies the Law of Thelema: 'Do what thou wilt shall be the whole of the Law . . . There is no law beyond Do what thou wilt. Love is the law, love under will.'[10] It seems that Rabelais was the inspiration for Aiwass's creed. Crowley was convinced that Aiwass heralded the coming of a New Aeon, the age of Horus, the Crowned and Conquering Child, which succeeded the age of Christ – the 'Dying God'. Although he performed magic to banish Christ, the New Aeon would finally come about when the Law of Thelema, which 'solves all social problems',[11] was instated throughout society. According to Crowley, 'The Law of Thelema avows and justifies selfishness; it confirms the inmost conviction of each one of us that he is the centre of the cosmos. . . . In the New Aeon, each man will be a king, and his relation to the state will be determined solely by considerations of what is most to his advantage.'[12]

In the middle of his career, Crowley moved to Cefalu in Sicily, founded a community in a villa he renamed the Abbey of Thelema, and attempted to put the law 'of freedom and delight' into practice. Life in his 'magical model of society' was one long round of sex magick rituals and meditations. According to one sex magick practitioner, the power of a spell will be heightened tremendously if it is performed at the point of orgasm. While some believe group sex increases the power yet further, and others see sex magick as a chance for an orgy, it is, apparently, 'most effective when performed between a couple in a steady relationship'. The calm of the community was disturbed merely by the jealousies of Crowley's numerous sexual partners. In time, however, said Crowley, these jealousies disappeared: '. . . by sticking to the Law, by training ourselves to treat our sexual life as a strictly personal matter, we abolished jealousy, intrigue and all the other evils usually connected with it.'[13]

The Book of the Law states that 'Each individual has an absolute right to satisfy his sexual instinct as is physiologically proper for him. The one injunction is to treat all such acts as sacraments. One should not eat as the brutes, but in order to enable one to do one's will. The same applies to sex.'[14] Under the influence of Freud's teachings, Crowley developed the idea that sex magick was a form of psychotherapy – the best means of liberating the 'true will of the inmost self'.

Crowley also covered the walls of the villa with imaginative and sexually explicit paintings, or religious icons: in his eyes the sexual organs were the image of God. Crowley was not alone in such beliefs: followers of the Hindu god Shiva believe their deity is symbolized by phallus-shaped pillars known as lingams. A year after arriving in Cefalu, in 1921, Crowley himself, according to his account, became transformed into a deity. Although he kept quiet about his new status, in his writings he declared 'As a God goes, I go'.

The fate of those unable to cope with the freedom offered by Crowley's law, who found 'the responsibility of being truly them-selves . . . too much for them' was to become slaves. When Crowley's law was instated throughout society, the same would apply: 'The bulk of humanity, having no true will, will find themselves powerless. It will be for us to rule them wisely.'[15] The Sicilian community eventually folded amidst scandalous rumours in the press, including the supposed sacrifice of babies – all of which Crowley dismissed as rubbish. One of the few publications to give Crowley a good press was *The New Age* (see p. 18).

It is not surprising that *The New Age* was open to Crowley's ideas. Edward Carpenter of *The New Age* circle shows how closely some of their ideas tallied with Crowley's when he claimed: 'Love indicates immortality. No sooner does the human being perceive this divine nucleus within himself than he knows his eternal destiny. Plunged in matter and the gross body he has learned the lesson of identity and separateness. All that the devil can teach him, he has faithfully absorbed. Now he has to expand that identity for ever unique into ever vaster spheres of activity – to become finally a complete and finished aspect of the One.'[16]

The power to be derived from tapping into sexual energy is one of the oldest tricks in the book – one particularly favoured by disciples of the Greek god Dionysus. Through their abandonment to frenzied pagan rites, ordinary mortals could stop being themselves and catch a glimpse of eternity; they could become 'possessed' and get in touch with the god within them. Dionysus was the name Crowley hit upon for one of his children. More than forty years later, in 1969 – the year Crowley's *Confessions* were published – a group of New York actors staged a show, *Dionysius '69*. As part of the act, members of the audience were invited up on stage to perform sexually with whichever member of the cast appealed to them.

Using the intensity of sex as a means to enlightenment and power is a method which has been taken up by various occult groups, including the Ordo Templi Orientis. Founded in Germany in 1902 the 'OTO' was revived in England nine years later by Aleister Crowley and still has many branches today. The Temple Ov Psychick Youth, founded in the early 1980s by pop musician Genesis P. Orridge, is just one of several groups heavily influenced by Crowley. Members make a point of practising sex magick and claim that 'Thee Temple of Psychick Youth's perception ov life and its sexuality is limitless'.[17]

While in the popular mind Crowley is notorious for having regularly conducted black masses, these rituals were, says one of his biographers, technically speaking Gnostic masses which, because of their sexual component, should be considered grey rather than black. Gnostics exist on the heretical margin of Christianity, seeking a direct knowledge of, rather than a faith in, the divine. Once this knowledge has been achieved, the devotee is beyond the strictures of society, beyond all notions of good and evil, beyond the bounds of moral judgement and, quite simply, incapable of sinning. This individual freedom can be achieved only by turning away from the world and becoming an outcast, either through extreme asceticism or extreme libertinism.

Over the centuries, Gnostic sects have, with unflagging regularity, been condemned for their sexual permissiveness and treated to the kind of distrust and disparagement later reserved for hippies. To some extent, rumours were whipped up by the mainstream churches which felt threatened by the obvious appeal of their liberal beliefs. Some Gnostics were, however, given to indulging in ritual orgies simply to prove their sin-free status – no one with an iota of sin remaining in them would think to so risk their place in heaven.

In the second century, Gnostics were apparently intent on efforts 'to rouse the soul from its sleepwalking condition and to make it aware of the high destiny to which it is called',[18] thus demonstrating more than a passing similarity to followers of the Russian mystic Gurdjieff, who aimed that his followers should break through to a condition of wakefulness. Certainly, as with Gurdjieffians, the emphasis for most Gnostics was on inner psychological experience.

From the twelfth to the sixteenth centuries, numerous Christian sects flourished in Europe, members of which – like the Gnostics – considered themselves beyond the realm of sin. For many, free love was an outward sign of their spiritual advancement. As Professor Norman Cohn recounts in his *The Pursuit of the Millennium*, the Abbot of St Victor near Paris alleged that the Amaurians, who claimed to be the first 'spirituals', 'committed rapes and adulteries and other acts which give pleasure to the body. And to the women with whom they sinned and to the simple people whom they deceived, they promised that sins would not be punished'.[19]

The Brethren of the Free Spirit, who surfaced sporadically from the thirteenth century to the close of the Middle Ages under a succession of inspirational preachers, were perhaps the most notorious spiritual libertines – although not always egalitarian. One adept announced that, just as cattle were created for the use of human beings, so women were created to be used by the Brethren. Though the analogy with Gurdjieff can only be drawn out so far, he, in a similar fashion, declared that 'women are only a means to an end'. Gurdjieff believed that sex was one of the few functions which had not become automized – or destroyed – by over-intellectualism. Apparently, his own sexuality was such that, according to one of his female disciples, he was virtually able to bring her to orgasm while she ate dinner at a neighbouring table.

The Brethren, like Joachim of Fiore, believed in three ages of existence – the first was the age of the Father, the second the age of the Son, and the third the age of the Spirit – a new age or earthly paradise. In each of the three ages of existence, incarnations of the divine being would appear – Abraham, Christ and the Brotherhood respectively. 'With God I have created myself and I have created all things, and it is my hand that supports heaven and earth and all creatures . . . Without me nothing exists,' said one libertine.[20] Another, Sister Catherine, wrote 'Rejoice with me I have become God'.[21] Others went yet further: 'When God created all things I created all things with him . . . I am more than God,' said one.[22] Today, 'Everyone is God! Everyone!' says actress and New Ager Shirley MacLaine, a belief accompanied by the idea that each individual, as God, creates reality.

Like Gurdjieff, the Brethren attracted a following of spiritual groupies who, with divine ecstasy, experienced their sexual union with the Brethren – or God. Sometimes nudity and sex were ritually integrated into the act of worship, to symbolize the perfect, guilt-free existence in the Garden of Eden prior to the Fall. In strict contrast to the Moonies, the Brethren even had their own favoured way of sexual communion – the 'delight of Paradise' – which was supposed to be that practised by Adam and Eve in the Garden of Eden. And of course the more time one spent in Paradise, the more spiritual one became. While not involved in direct sexual activity, the Brethren and their followers would 'love bomb' one another, publicly hugging and kissing whenever they met.

Using surprisingly similar language to today's New Agers, the Brethren claimed that 'the perfect man is the motionless Cause'.[23] Werner Erhard, self-styled guru of the 'Me generation', encourages trainees at his enlightenment seminars to be always 'at cause' rather than 'at effect'.

While the Brethren taught that, strictly speaking, everyone was capable of being deified, in practice it was a status held only by the élite. The Brethren did, nevertheless, sow the seeds of a variety of socialism, inspired by their millennial vision. According to Norman Cohn, 'In the later Middle Ages it was the adepts of the Free Spirit who conserved as part of their creed for total emancipation, the only thoroughly revolutionary social doctrine that existed.'[24] On a practical level, the Brethren's deified state did away with any notion of ownership and they would beg, borrow and steal whenever they felt the need – justifying themselves by saying that among the free in spirit, all things belonged to everyone.

Utopian socialists have often dreamt of an early paradise where bodies, as well as goods, are freely shared. At the end of the eighteenth century 'founder of French socialism' Comte Henri de Saint Simon sought the 'rehabilitation of the flesh' and dreamt of a world peopled by 'men and women giving themselves to several without ceasing to be united as a couple'.[25] In this socialist utopia the inheritance of wealth would be abolished and working men set free from their bonds.

One of Saint Simon's most ardent followers, Barthélemy Prosper Enfantin, attempted to put the reformer's ideas into practice – while adding a mystical element of his own. In the late 1840s, Enfantin christened himself 'le Père', believing that his union with 'la Mère' would bring about a new world. (Likewise, the Rev Sun Myung

Moon's marriage to Hak Ja Han in 1960 would enable him to establish the ideal family, the ideal nation and the ideal world.) Enfantin's la Mère was not, however, forthcoming. Novelist and Saint Simonian George Sand, several of whose works were informed by anti-marriage polemic, was approached, but declined the offer. Enfantin eventually retreated to the outskirts of Paris where he turned his family home into a commune – for men only. Moreover, all the members of the community had to take vows of chastity.

Several of Enfantin's female disciples took umbrage at being excluded from paradise. One, Léonore Labillière, was so disgusted with the turn events had taken that she eventually established her own 'free love' community, La Maison des Poètes in the mid-nineteenth century. Based high in the Pyrenees, the community aimed to revive the spirit of courtly love. Men were there merely to woo their chosen woman with ballads and poetry – to suffer, pine and plead their cause in as winsome a way as the troubadours of old. Inevitably, the community soon fell apart.

While researching her experiment, Léonore Labillière visited the Oneida Community, founded in the 1840s and originally called the Perfectionists, in New York state. The community's leader, former theology student John Humphrey Noyes, believed that the second coming had taken place in 70AD, doing away with the ten commandments but upholding the New Testament commandment of love. Like the Brethren, he believed that he himself had passed beyond the boundaries of sin, and with respect to the workings of his community, he taught that: 'In the kingdom of heaven, the institution of marriage which assigns the exclusive possession of one woman to one man, does not exist . . . In the kingdom of heaven, the intimate union of life and interests, which in the world is limited to pairs, extends through the whole body of believers; ie *complex* marriage takes the place of simple. The new commandment is that we love one another, and that, not by pairs, as in the world, but *en masse*. We are required to love one another *fervently*, or, as the original might be rendered *burningly*.'[26]

From their foundation in 1848, the Oneidans proved to be industrious workers. Their self-discipline may have been developed by the Community's practice of 'karezza'. Apparently invented by Noyes, this was the art of engaging in protracted sexual intercourse without reaching the point of orgasm. In the 1960s, a utopian community known as Kerista also practised a type of polyfidelity. Founded by

Brother Jud and Even Eve, members worshipped Sister Kerista –
supposedly Jesus's sister – and were organized into groups of twelve
men and twelve women known as Best Friend Identity Clusters.
Sexual relations outside the BFIC were forbidden. Like most free
love experiments, the community has since foundered.

Back in the nineteenth century, another experiment in free love
communal living was conducted by Thomas Lake Harris who eventually settled at Fountain Grove, California with his Brotherhood of the
New Life. Laurence Oliphant, a British former Member of Parliament
and diplomat, was attracted to Harris when he visited London in
1868. After donating $100,000 to the movement, and withstanding
the rigours of a two-year probation, he was finally allowed to join the
community. Two years later, Harris sent Oliphant back to England
where he worked as a war correspondent for *The Times*, sending his
earnings to the distant utopia. While in London, Oliphant married
– having first received Harris's permission and having successfully
persuaded his wife, Alice, to hand all her jewellery over to the
Brotherhood.

In time, the dream began to turn sour and former disciples began
to describe what went on in the Brotherhood. For example, 'One man
states that the men and women washed each other in a complete nude
state. Another says he was commanded by Th.L.H. to have sexual
intercourse with five separate women in one day . . . We have the
statements of some dozen men who all tell the same tale of sexual
abuses.'[27] Others complained of their spartan lifestyle, contrasting
it with the luxury in which Harris lived, and claimed they were
reduced to slavery. Then, Harris, who had preached fervently against
marriage, got married and moved out of the community, selling his
final interest in it in 1900.

Laurence Oliphant, by now back in the United States, had been
one of those who added his penn'orth to the rumours surrounding
Harris. Disillusioned with his master, and convinced that he himself
had hit upon the route to enlightenment, he demanded the return
of the money he had handed over on joining the community. Harris
referred to Oliphant as Lucifer and attempted to have him declared
insane, whereupon Oliphant and his wife left for Haifa in Palestine,
where they set up their own group, Sympneumata.

The aim of Sympneumata was to practise and pass on an enlightenment technique aimed, like that of the Oneida Community's karezza,
at uniting the spiritual and physical sides of man through prolonged

sexual excitement. Unlike karezza, however, it seems that spiritual breakthrough did not require sexual intercourse. Instead, the missionary couple taught that all one had to do was to sexually excite a partner by lying next to them.

Both Sympneumata and the Oneidans' practice of karezza were probably influenced by Tantrism, a ritual practice common to both Hinduism and Buddhism. Tantrism teaches that, within the act of sex itself, the two experiences of bodily and spiritual ecstasy become merged into a transcendent unity. As with some Gnostics, sex was seen to fire off a divine spark, giving rise to knowledge of the divine.

It was Aleister Crowley who, according to his biographer John Symonds, cemented the bridge between Tantrism and the Western esoteric traditions. Certainly, his belief in the power of sex is similar to that of the Tantrics. Moreover, like Crowley's law of 'Do what you will', Tantrism holds that what is natural cannot be wrong – and like the Divine Marquis, some Tantric initiates believe that spiritual englightenment can be achieved by ritualistically infringing certain taboos.

Tantrism of a kind informs other traditions, too. According to a modern-day witch, or Wiccan: 'The Great Rite, or ritual sexual intercourse, is like Tantric Yoga. It releases power and is an extremely sacred ceremony.'[28] For a French group of witches, Wicca-Française, 'a collective orgasm will permit a powerful projection in space-time'.[29] For others, 'Sex has the power to transform reality.'[30]

The Wiccan Rede, or law, is none other than: 'An' it harm none, do what you will.' While some say the law's origin is buried in the mists of time, others say that Gerald Gardner, who revived modern-day witchcraft with his book *Witchcraft Today*, published in 1954, borrowed the Rede from Aleister Crowley. Certainly, the two met shortly before Crowley's death.

Tantrics often deliberately cultivate obscene language in order to increase the intensity of the sexual experience. The 1960s, which heralded a revival of interest in Tantrism, was also the decade that gave rise to the 'free speech', sometimes described as the 'foul language', campaign.

In 1967, Malcolm Muggeridge proclaimed, 'The curtain, indeed, is falling if it has not already fallen on all the Utopian hopes which have prevailed so strongly for a century or more. I personally rejoice that it should be so because I know that then, looking desperately into the mystery of things, we shall once again understand that fulfilment must be sought through the spirit, not the body or the mind, and will be realized, if at all, elsewhere than in this world of time and space.'[31]

Not quite. Across the Atlantic David Berg, 'the original hippie', was rallying the mood of the times into the Family of Love, usually known as the Children of God. Up and down the beaches of California, hippie groups had discovered you could get high on Jesus – and now Berg was throwing in an added revelation – 'God is Sex!'[32]

Few movements have quite so openly – or controversially – proclaimed the mystical, revolutionary and redemptive nature of sex as the Children of God. In a letter to his followers, which might just as well have been pinned to the noticeboard at California's Berkeley College, Berg proclaims:

YE CANNOT BELONG TO BOTH THE SYSTEM AND THE REVOLUTION, the forces of reaction and the forces of change! It's impossible; as Jesus said, you'll either hate the one, and love the other, or hold to the one and despise the other. You'll either stay in the System or drop out.[33]

And the way to drop out?

ENJOY YOURSELF AND SEX AND WHAT GOD HAS GIVEN YOU TO ENJOY, WITHOUT FEAR OR CONDEMNATION! . . . Let yourself go in the bosom of God and let God do it to you in an orgasm of the Spirit till you're free! . . . Power to the people! – Sex power! – God's power! – Can be your power! Amen? – Be a sex revolutionist for Jesus! – Wow! – There we go again! Hallelujah! – Are you comin'?[34]

The appeal to anti-establishment youth was powerful. Soon, all those outside the movement were dismissed as 'systemites' – and the women within the movement were recruiting new members through sex – a practice known as 'flirty fishing'. The term came from St Matthew's gospel: '"Brother," Jesus said, "Follow me and I will make you fishers of men," and the disciples straightaway left their nets and followed him'. 'The husbands practically have to be pimps for their own wives!' wrote David Berg. 'God bless them! They've got to help manage them and protect them and guide them.

They need the fishermen to help them fish. Oodles of men do it for money in the World! Why not for God?'[35]

Before long he was reporting, 'Our dear FF'ers are still going strong. God bless'm, having now witnessed to over a quarter-of-a-million souls, loved over 25,000 of them and won nearly 19,000 to the Lord, along with about 35,000 new friends.'[36] Disciples can also gain spiritual freedom by participating in porn films. And the viewers, presented with 'the beauty of God's creation', benefit too.

Berg has also caused a good deal of controversy for his attitude towards child sex. In a Children of God publication, *Heaven's Children*, he writes: 'Of course, as there are no longer any such things as Man's legalistic laws against incest in the loving Kingdom of *God*, everyone loves *everyone* and is completely free in His all-encompassing Love! So I make wonderful, sweet, precious love to my now beautiful teenaged Techi! She seems thrilled and delighted with having this wonderful love-dream with Grandpa . . .'[36a]

In 1983 Berg predicted that Western civilization was on the point of being destroyed by a nuclear holocaust, heralding the period of chaos before Christ's second coming. The Children moved east, from their communes scattered throughout Europe. Nothing happened, and many returned home to await the end of the world, now set for 1993.

Among today's communes, that of the Bhagwan Shree Rajneesh – the 'sex guru' or 'god of vagina' – has been one of the most notorious, possibly because his synthesis of Western Psychology and Eastern religion tends to attract the better educated and heeled.

Rajneesh introduced many Westerners to Tantrism and is some-times referred to as a 'Tantric Master'; his books include *The Tantra Vision* and *Tantra: The Supreme Understanding*. In the latter he writes, 'For Tantra you have to use the energy of sex. Do not fight with it: transform it. Do not think in terms of enmity: be friendly to it. It is your energy, it is not evil, it is not bad. Every energy is just natural. It can be used for you, it can be used against you.'[37] Therapies offered by followers of Rajneesh – 'sannyasins' as they are known – have included 'Neo Tantric', 'Orgasmic Undoing', and 'Pleasuring', along with innumerable non-sexually-oriented classes.

As well as having been influenced by the Tantrics, Rajneesh – or Osho as he was called in his latter days – drew inspiration from writers D.H. Lawrence and Havelock Ellis, as well as Nietzsche, Gurdjieff and Ouspensky.

In *From Sex to Superconsciousness* (1979) Rajneesh teaches that 'the lust inside each of us may become a ladder with which to reach to the temple of love, that the sex inside each of us may become a vehicle to reach superconsciousness' and that the 'longer intercourse lasts, the more possibility there is of making sex a door to samadhi' – the culmination of meditation in which the adept frees his mind of all disturbing and extraneous thoughts and images. He even went so far as to predict that a universal understanding of Tantrism would usher in a new age. 'The day we fully develop a scripture of sex, we will produce a new race of humans,' he claimed.[38]

For Frenchman Claude Vorilhon, sex has the power to forestall Armageddon. Vorilhon tells how in December 1973, when he was just twenty-seven years old, he was visited by the Elohim, or 'those who came from the sky'. The Elohim supposedly renamed Claude 'Rael' – 'The messenger of those who come from the sky' – and introduced him to the secrets of the universe.

25,000 years ago, so their story goes, mankind was created in a test-tube by an inferior breed of chemist. These chemists, or genetic engineers, originally lived on a distant planet but were exiled after offending the government. Eventually they appeared on planet earth which they turned into a cosmic laboratory, creating the birds and bees, plants and cities – and man. Unfortunately, the chemists bungled the operation by failing to give their men and women souls. Not only were the chemists forgetful; some were stupid, too. It was these chemists – the lowest of the low – who created the Australian Aborigines. When not concocting creation, the aliens would entertain visiting friends and family, who checked in at their embassy, the Temple of Solomon.

Rael claims that he is the last prophet to appear before a nuclear war engulfs planet earth. To forestall such an Armageddon, he suggests his followers, known as Raelians, practise 'sensual meditation', which enables humans 'to deprogramme the Judaeo-Christian inhibitions of guilt whilst at the same time not falling into the ethereal mysticisms of the oriental teachings'. At the same time, 'the sensual meditation allows the human to discover his/her body and especially to learn how to use it to enjoy sounds, colours, smells, tastes, caresses and particularly a sexuality felt with all one's senses so as to experience the cosmic orgasm, infinite, absolute which illuminates the mind by linking the one who reaches it with the universes s/he is composed of and composes'.[39]

Members of the Raelian movement, who number some 20,000, are expected to practise sensual meditation each day. In the manner of an extra-terrestrial dating agency, the movement produces tapes to which followers are urged to listen with a partner of complementary sex, so that devotees can come together in spiritual and physical harmony. Each summer, at international camps held in France, followers are encouraged to express their true feelings by wandering around naked and indulging in 'an element of permissiveness'.[40]

Dr Wilhelm Reich's science fiction-style conception of the universe foreshadows that of the Raelians. Reich, a medical doctor and clinical assistant of Freud from 1922 to 1928, discovered orgone – a type of energy which, he said, comes from the sun and is concentrated in the sexual organs during orgasm. Apparently, orgone energy can be trapped in a carefully constructed orgone accumulator – a wood and metal box something like the orgasmatron in Woody Allen's film *Sleeper*.

Just how life-enhancing the blue-coloured substance is can be deduced from the sense of well-being following orgasm, Reich claimed. Moreover, when concentrated, the very same energy can apparently be used to treat illnesses from hay fever to ulcers – one modern-day witch, explaining her coven's tendency to conduct ceremonies 'sky clad', or naked, said that the 'Ki, or orgone certainly flows more easily when you're naked'.[41] Eventually, Reich developed his theory into a complex theological system. Christ was in direct communication with the cosmic orgone forces, he claimed, while hostile alien troops, intent on capturing the precious energy, were zooming earthwards in their flying saucers to steal it away. Before long, orgone became the sci-fi elixir of both a personal and world transformation.

Although Reich gathered many orgone disciples, he met with continual opposition from the establishment. Eventually, the US Federal Administration attempted to take him to court for making unproven claims about his orgone box. When he failed to appear at the trial, he was jailed and died in prison of a heart attack. Though Reich's ideas seem bizarre, he has been recognized as rescuing Freudian ideas from being used merely to 'normalize' individuals – returning them to a repressive society rather than enabling them to find heaven – and is seen to have used sex as a means to transform society.

Norman O. Brown, author of *Love's Body* (1966), also developed Freud's ideas, believing that by analysing mankind as a whole, rather than simply the individual, humanity could experience an earthly resurrection of the body, thereby entering into a heavenly state of being. Humanity, says Brown, is incapable of accepting death, seen as the ultimate separation, and is therefore incapable of accepting true life. What he calls for is a merging of the inner self and the outside world, a Dionysian body-consciousness, a supreme awareness of our sexuality which – as in all mystic moments – will remove us from the realm of time into a paradise. For Nietzsche, the Dionysians lived according to 'the evangel of cosmic harmony, each one feels himself not only united, reconciled, blended with his neighbour, but as one with him . . . he feels himself a god, he himself now walks about enchanted and elated even as the gods whom he saw walking about in his dreams'.[42]

Some of today's New Agers attempt to fulfil Norman O. Brown's theories by living out full-body sexuality, believing it will enable them to live in flesh and blood reality for ever and ever – provided they keep their cells moving with regular bodily and sexual contact. But whereas Brown believed that sexuality should be removed from the purely genital arena, the Eternal Flame, as some who hold this belief are called, recommend classes in 'How to release death from your sexual organs' and 'How to experience your living, moving cells through soft entry ejaculation'.[43]

Another New Age leader, Robert Ferris, or Shunyata – the 'Laughing Yogi', as he is called – also believes sex can open the door to a divine state of bliss. Of 'Cherokee, Armenian, Egyptian and German ancestry', Shunyata believes that 'we traded our Supreme Divine state eons ago for the Human adventure of self discovery'. Humanism, then, of which Rabelais with his Abbey of Thélème was the great inspiration, is seen as the cause of man's expulsion from heaven on earth.

Through 'Soul Centering' and 'Sacred Sexuality' however, says Shunyata, 'Our fragmented Consciousness is now preparing to realize and celebrate its Totality.'[44] In his 1990 book *Temple of Paradise* he describes how 'the vision of the Golden Age lives on in the soul of each and every one of us'. The route back lies via 'Ejaculatory control', 'Different levels of orgasm' – and even 'Erotic chastity'. Shunyata runs a small retreat centre in Bali, conducts ceremonies worldwide and has counted among his followers Timothy Leary, the high priest of LSD. 'Sex is sacred,' announced Leary in the 1960s. 'People of like sexual temperament must form their own spiritual cults.'[45] Drugs, like sex, often go hand in hand down the road to Paradise Now.

FOUR | CHEMICAL ENLIGHTENMENT

Long ago, deep in the mists of time, the authority of the ancient Vedic deities began to wane. The demons saw their chance and a power struggle ensued, the gods' strength growing ever weaker and weaker. The balance of the whole cosmos was in jeopardy. Eventually, the great god Vishnu came to the aid of the deities. 'Forget about your quarrel with the demons,' he said, 'and seek their assistance in churning from the ocean a precious drink.' So the gods and demons together placed a vast mountain in the middle of the seas and, using the snake Vasuki as a cord, began to turn the mountain and so churn the ocean. Eventually, the milky sea brought forth new deities: Varuni, goddess of wine, Lakshmi, goddess of good fortune – and Soma, the 'precious drink' manifested as a god, which restored the strength of the older deities.

The ancient myths show Soma in a variety of forms. Sometimes he is a bull, sometimes a bird, an embryo or a giant. But above all, Soma is the link between mankind and heaven. Soma was almost certainly a hallucinogenic plant – probably a mushroom – which provided a passport to an earthly paradise. Not only did its juice heighten spirituality, but it was also credited with miraculous healing powers and with bestowing immortality on all who drank it – as did the Greeks' ambrosia. Known in other mythologies as Haoma or Amrita, Soma formed an essential part of ancient Hindu rituals and the god is celebrated in more than a tenth of the *Rig Veda*'s psalms.[1]

Down the ages, soma's divine powers have been attributed to numerous other hallucinogenic and intoxicating drugs. Not only are the drugs seen as a path to enlightenment, to instant heaven on earth, they are also often worshipped as gods and can become the focus of a religion. Conversely, hallucinogens and intoxicants are often condemned by other religions as the force of evil – as, for instance, the 'demon drink'.

In his 1932 novel *Brave New World*, Aldous Huxley depicts a futurist society whose inhabitants are solaced with the drug 'soma'. Just a mere cubic centimetre of the substance 'cures ten gloomy sentiments', enabling them to 'take a holiday from reality' whenever they like.[2] The drug is also the focus of a religious ceremony to their founder, Ford, in which they drink to their annihilation and end up in an 'orgy porgy' session.[3] Happiness lies on tap, for soma is 'euphoric, narcotic, pleasantly hallucinant . . . All the advantages of Christianity and alcohol; none of their defects'.[4]

While soma enables everyone to realize their society's ideals of 'Community, Identity, Stability',[5] Huxley's *Brave New World* wavers on a fine line between a utopia and dystopia. Soma – and indeed universal happiness – is used as a control mechanism, a means of keeping the populace content. Everyone can do what they want because nobody wants to 'run afoul of group standards'.

The god Soma was, however, also held to be the prince of poets – the source of inspiration and divine power of creativity. Drugs have often been used to access a new world or instant paradise, but their actual creative use is uncertain. S.T. Coleridge's 'Kubla Khan' (1816) might have been written under the influence of drugs, but according to the controller of Huxley's *Brave New World*, soma keeps the citizens perpetually happy and 'You've got to choose between happiness and what people used to call high art': the presence of soma makes high art an impossibility.[6]

When Huxley was introduced to the hallucinogenic drug mescaline in 1953 by English psychiatrist Humphry Osmond he was instantly won over. Four years later, Osmond coined the term 'psychodelic' to describe the hallucinogenic drug experience. The word was later amended to psychedelic – apparently, the former was thought to have too negative connotations.

In *The Doors of Perception*, published a year after his first mescaline experience, Huxley is convinced that consciousness-expanding drugs can be used as a short-cut to mystical experience. The book's title is taken from a line in William Blake's 'Marriage of Heaven and Hell': 'If the doors of perception were cleansed, everything would appear to man as it is, infinite.' According to Huxley, mankind is labouring under the burden of the brain – a 'reducing valve' which stems the flow of experience. Drugs can release the valve, allowing humanity to become whole again – one with the infinite and the divine. By 1962, the year his utopian novel *Island* was published, Huxley's conversion to hallucinogenics was complete.

Often, the desire to transcend mortality appears to stem as much from a fearful fascination with death as from a search for paradise. With drugs, 'bad trips' and intermittent paranoia seem to heighten the anxiety. In *Island*, Huxley describes the death of Lakshmi on psychedelics – and Huxley himself took LSD on his deathbed. Within a few years of the book's publication, a number of 'transcendental communities' modelled on *Island* had sprung up in the United States. They were the inspiration of Timothy Leary, the aforementioned high priest of LSD.

The mind-changing properties of LSD (lysergic acid diethylamide) were accidentally discovered in 1943 when a Swiss chemist experimenting with a fungus found in rye plants began hallucinating. Medieval peasants had already discovered the strange effects of lysergic acid as a result of eating cheap rye bread. The effect, which include impaired vision, was known as St Anthony's fire.

Although eating rye bread had unexpected mind-altering effects, witches' 'magic ointment' was used intentionally. Believed in medieval times to help witches fly through the night on broomsticks, the substance has been recreated in modern times. A doctor at a German university tested out a recipe on himself and a colleague. The ingredients included deadly nightshade, thornapple, henbane, wild celery and parsley and caused the experimenters to fall into a trancelike sleep for twenty hours. When they woke up, the men compared notes and found they had experienced almost identical dreams of flying through the air to a mountain top and participating in erotic orgies with monsters and demons.[7]

In 1960, Dr Timothy Leary, a Harvard University lecturer, had his first taste of psychedelia in the form of 'sacred mushrooms' and, like Huxley, was instantly converted. The following year Leary took LSD. But it was the Good Friday Experiment, sometimes known as 'The Miracle of Marsh Chapel', conducted on Good Friday 1962 by Harvard student Walter Pahnke that really rocked the boat. It took place in a chapel at Boston University. Twenty students were gathered together, half were administered the psychedelic drug psilocybin, and the other ten a placebo which produced a temporary feeling of well being. Then, for more than two hours, the students participated in a religious service of prayers, organ music and readings. Afterwards, it was found that the religious experience of the control group was far less intense than that of those who had taken the psychedelic. According to Leary, recounting the impact of the event, 'Nine out of ten divinity students shakingly recounted awesome mystical-religious experiences, and two of them promptly quit the ministry!'[8]

Back at Harvard, Leary's psychedelic research eventually grew too hot for the authorities to handle and both he and Richard Alpert, a fellow academic interested in psychedelic research, were expelled from the university. After founding the International Federation for Internal Freedom, they set up the Castalia Foundation in Millbrook, New York state, named after Hermann Hesse's sacred order in *The Glass Bead Game* (1943). Ralph Metzner, another Harvard academic, was also on the staff. Leary was faced with the 'Messianic task of accelerating evolution (ie psychosocial Revolution) including an alteration of human consciousness leading to the immediate mutation of social and economic forms'.[9] Once all society learnt to drop out, said Leary, then everyone would be free, 'a god in the Garden of Eden'.[10]

Because of the complicated legal situation in the United States, psychedelics were not advertised as part of the Foundation's 'experiential workshop' curriculum. Instead, Gurdjieff's training in self-awareness was on offer, along with dance, diet and a variety of therapies. 'Every effort will be made to create transcendent experiences through non-chemical means' – a brochure promised.[11] Viva, Andy Warhol's acolyte was one of the many who travelled out to Millbrook in the 1960s. 'I knew I was having a nervous breakdown so I got my sister to drive me to Millbrook, New York to see Timothy Leary,' she said in an interview in *New York* magazine. 'Tim Leary had been the first one to turn me on to drugs. He told me to take psilocybin, the hallucinogenic mushroom, and I took it out of curiosity . . . I stayed with him for about a week but he wouldn't let me have anything except a few sniffs of methedrine from my finger so I painted a mural, walked in the woods and made it with some guys.'[12]

In 1966, Leary founded the League for Spiritual Discovery (LSD) – acid, quite literally, became a religion. The first LSD service was dedicated to 'The Death of the Mind'. By turning LSD into a religion, Leary hoped to sidestep the legal clampdown on acid, introduced that year in California. LSD would be transformed into a sacrament to be taken only when in a state of grace. Devotees were encouraged to confess their sins before swallowing the pills. The League's Bible was *The Politics of Ecstasy*, another Leary/Alpert venture. 'The purpose of life,' they wrote, 'is religious discovery. When you turn on, remember: you are not a naughty boy getting high for kicks. You are a spiritual voyager furthering the most ancient, noble quest of man. When you turn on, you shed the fake-prop TV studio and costume and join the holy dance of the visionaries. You leave LBJ and Bob Hope: you join Lao-Tse, Christ, Blake. Never underestimate the sacred meaning of the turn-on.'[13]

Leary's ventures tended to be practised in a spirit of high serious-ness. Nonetheless, together with Alpert, he wrote an article which applauded the imagined effect of putting LSD in water reservoirs. 'If an enemy drops LSD in the water supply and if you are accurately informed and prepared, then . . . you should sit back and enjoy the most exciting educational experience of your life (you might be forever grateful to the saboteur).'[14] That sort of prank seemed to belong more to the world of Ken Kesey – or to fantasy. In 1968 the film *Wild in the Streets* – in which a pop singer becomes president – invited teenagers to put LSD in the water supply. Eventually, Leary was jailed for possession of a small quantity of marijuana. He was, said the authorities, pleasure-seeking and irresponsible, an insidious and detrimental influence on society – particularly for his 'advocacy of the use of psychedelic drugs by students and others of immature judgement and tender years' said an attorney.[15]

'Prison,' wrote Leary while incarcerated, 'is an experimental labora-tory for all the emotional and social problems . . . We must all be liberated on both sides of the bars.'[16] After seven months of his ten-year jail sentence, the 'worldly man faced with the task of a Messiah'[17] escaped to Algiers where he sought protection with the Black Panthers. It was refused on the principle that acid was a barrier to revolution and Panther leader Eldridge Cleaver put Leary under house arrest. Leary remained committed to internal revolution and ended up back in jail.

In a 1989 interview, Leary announced, 'I was a suburbanite in the fifties, I was expanding consciousness in the sixties. It's inevitable to be doing software in the eighties.'[18] After taking a passing interest in the colonization of outer space, Leary now preaches that the new worlds of the future will be discovered through the personal computer screen, through learning to use 'the human nervous system, according to the instructions of the manufacturers'.[19] By fulfilling their genetic potential, human beings can reach cosmic fusion – but most will need high doses of LSD to achieve such heights.

Dr Humphry Osmond, who introduced Huxley to mescaline, a derivative of the cactus plant peyote, was himself introduced to the drug by a Peyote Chief of the Native American Church in the 1940s. During the 1870s, when the American Indians were being deprived of their lives, lands and identities by the white man, peyote became the focus of a Native American cult, known simply as Peyotism. As the fighting on the plains grew less and less, and the power of the white man grew more and more, peyote gave the Indians a unique source of power and wisdom – a replacement, of sorts, for all they had lost – from lands to bison, to their whole way of life.

For 1960s counter-culture, the white murder of Indians was the beginning of 'this great scandal of the closing of the doors of perception of the Naked Human Form Divine'.[20] By forging a mystical bond through peyote, the Indian tribes were able to reaffirm their identity in a way which transcended the white man's efforts to interfere with their way of life. But before long, the white man began to attempt to deprive the Indians of their brand of spirituality. In 1899 the session laws of Oklahoma prohibited the practice and in 1907 many Peyotists were arrested.

It was scarcely surprising that the acid apostles related to the Peyotists. The Peyotists had roots, had a drug god and provided a vision of a back-to-nature utopia all but in reach – provided authority could be overcome in time. For the counter-culture, the white man was authority in any shape – whether parental, state or brain. But like the Indians, they wanted to preserve their identity and create a heaven on earth outside the system. And like the Peyotists, so it seemed, drugs provided them with rituals, identity and a sense of bonding, allowing them to dissolve into one another, forming a tribe with invisible and invincible boundaries.

Gradually, Christianity began to seep into Peyotism, bringing with it a glimmer of white respectability. Sometimes a form of baptism was introduced to the peyote-taking ceremony, and in some groups the spirit of the drug became identified with Christ. Whereas the white man finds Christ in the Bible, Indians should look for Christ through peyote, said a peyote missionary. Eventually the Native North American Church of God legitimized the use of peyote, and by 1960 Peyotism was said to be 'the major religious cult of most

Indians of the United States between the Rocky Mountains and the Mississippi . . . and additionally in parts of southern Canada, the Great Basin and east-central California'.[21]

Peyote also appealed to ethnic, organic ideals. 'I prefer mescaline and peyote to synthetic drugs,' said Viva. 'I can't see anything wrong with taking something that actually grows out of the ground . . . Under drugs I think the answer is love and the constant orgasm. You just keep coming. That puts you in the Kingdom of Heaven. I guess religion is just a whole sexual sublimation.'[22]

Today, many alternative magazines in the United States carry advertisements for peyote and information about Peyotists Groups. 'Peyotea is a Sacramental Ally Containing Wildcrafted Native American Herbs, specially packaged for Ceremonial use,' runs one. 'Each order includes one Peyote Button a peyote pamphlet a listing of Peyotists Groups and PEYOTEA for seven people . . . Wear your Full Color Peyote Button in support of religious freedom!'[23]

In January 1966 the Trips Festival, a vast, psychedelic multi-media event was held at the Longshoremen's Hall in San Francisco. One of the shows was staged by an organization called America Needs Indians, founded by Stewart Brand who had come across the Peyote cults in Arizona and New Mexico. A tepee was set up and slides and films depicting Indian life were projected onto mammoth screens. People began to hold Tribal Stomp dances, to see themselves as working in harmony with the group mind. Another tribe celebrated at the Trips Festival was that of Ken Kesey and his Merry Pranksters, yet more apostles of the great god LSD. Indeed Kesey's Acid Tests – LSD-inspired multi-media 'Happenings' – were forerunners of the event.

Kesey, author of the novel *One Flew Over the Cuckoo's Nest*, was introduced to LSD via the experimental lab of a hospital near Stanford University where he held a creative writing fellowship. The hospital was running experiments in mind-altering drugs – including LSD. At the time Kesey was living on the University's Perry Lane campus. His gospel of LSD soon attracted a host of followers. 'The Lane was too good to be true,' writes Tom Wolfe in *The Electric Kool-Aid Acid Test*. 'It was Walden Pond, only without any Thoreau misanthropes around. Instead, a community of intelligent, very open, out-front people . . . out-front people who cared deeply for one another, and *shared* . . . in incredible ways, even, and were embarked on some kind of . . . *well*, adventure in living.'[24]

Before long, Kesey and the Pranksters moved to a psychedelic paradise in La Honda, California and began to put the acid trip into reality, travelling the country in a day-glo bus. Life was a movie, an experiment in reality. You were either on the bus or off it. 'What they all saw in . . . a flash was the solution to the basic predicament of being *human*, the personal *I*, *Me*, trapped, mortal and helpless, in a vast impersonal *It*, the world around me. Suddenly! – All-in-one! – flowing together, *I* into *It*, and *It* into *Me*, and in that flow I perceive a power, so near and so clear, that the whole world is blind to . . . The – *so-called*! friends – rational world.'[25] The Pranksters were more than any mere community. They were a communal mind, unified into one body, one beingness in the worship of LSD.

Then Kesey devised the Acid Test – a psychedelic version of a Happening. The first public Happening had taken place in 1959 in New York and before long an academic chair in the three-dimensional art-form was created at the University of California. Happenings were seemingly impromptu – but often carefully rehearsed – experiments in creativity with no plot, few, if any, words and often no division between the audience and performers, performance and rehearsal, beginning and end. In a sense, the events enabled participants to transcend individuality into that divine one-ness of the psychedelic experience. But at the same time, they stressed 'the extremes of disrelation' – they were 'in the deepest sense, funny', but nonetheless 'terrifying'.[26]

The Acid Tests were Happenings with LSD, or 'Be-Ins'. 'There was only the present conformation of events, happening,'[27] said Zen and psychedelic philosopher Alan Watts of an LSD experience. For many, LSD was a ticket to a unity beyond 'the extremes of disrelation'. Many of the acid test participants had no idea what they were letting themselves in for. But according to the converts, they were being treated to a supreme form of audience partici-pation, a supreme prank created by LSD-laced drinks – includ-ing Kool-Aid. 'It was a gesture, it was sheer generosity giving all this acid away, it was truly turning on the world, inviting all in to share the Pranksters' ecstasy of the All-one . . . all become divine vessels in unison, and it is all there in Kool-Aid and a paper cup.'[28]

A Be-In, with the luminous, multiplying, seemingly infinite shapes and colours of strobe lighting, was a way of externalizing the drug experience. Today, psychedelic images are used to portray the chaos theory – which to some degree validates the hallucinatory experience by giving a scientific meaning to the meaningless of the universe.

One of the characteristics of hallucinogenics is that '. . . all aspects of the world become meaningful rather than meaningless', according to Alan Watts. 'This is not to say that they acquire meaning in the sense of signs, by virtue of pointing to something else, but that all things appear to be their own point. Their simple existence, or better, their present formation, seems to be perfect, to be an end of fulfilment without any need for justification.'[29]

The emphasis was on experience, words were inadequate. Messages had to come through the senses, not through the mind. Some even believed that before long vibrations might take the place of language. Well before Kesey's 'pranks' in the 1960s, psychologist William James (1842–1910) described the incommunicable nature of a drug-induced experience. After taking a mixture of nitrous oxide and ether he wrote, 'Depth beyond depth of truth seems revealed to the inhaler. This truth fades out, however, or escapes, at the moment of coming to; and if any words remain over in which it seemed to clothe itself, they prove to be the veriest nonsense.' Nevertheless, he continued, 'I know more than one person who is persuaded that in the nitrous oxide trance we have a genuine metaphysical revelation.'[30]

Music was one way of getting through. Originally called the Warlocks, The Grateful Dead were the Acid Tests' house band. Kesey had joined forces with the Dead, allying their mind-blowing music to his mind-expanding path to earthly bliss. Today, the Dead play on. Their core devotees, numbering up to 1000, follow the band's tour route in day-glo painted buses – a psychedelic journey for the 1990s. LSD is still the god – at recent Dead shows it has been reported that the audience was sprayed with water containing LSD, though without the Dead's blessing. Kesey now subscribes to another mega-prank, the Church of the SubGenius, a send-up of other off-beat churches, though by no means so strange as some. A 'cult of screamers and laughers, scoffers, blasphemers and sinners',[31] the Church says the world will end in 1998 – but promises the SubGenii a spaceship ticket to safety. According to Mickey Hart, the Dead's percussionist, 'Psychedelic drugs had an incredible effect. It opened you up to a whole new set of musical values. It altered your time perception, your auditory perception, and allowed you to get together as a group without being competitive.'[32]

In 1990, a spate of deaths linked to Dead concerts and implicating

LSD as a possible cause was threatening to put an end to the utopia. They were certainly not the first warning that drugs could lead to obliteration as well as enlightenment, Janis Joplin being one of the most notable examples. Mickey Hart describes her music as 'springing from a community. It was a certain level of soul-spirit music. It was bordering on religious experience. These people were obviously moving into altered states'.[33]

Ken Kesey was also involved with the Diggers, a collection of 'intentional communes' founded in the early 1960s in San Francisco. They took their name from the seventeenth century Diggers, who were committed to living off shared land, abolishing money and returning to a primitive state of Eden. London tailor Gerrard Winstanley, founder of the early Diggers, determined to 'lay the foundation of making the earth a common treasury for all, both rich and poor'. Once this new society came into being, it would be the kingdom of heaven on earth 'swords and spears' would be beaten into 'pruning hooks and ploughs' and there would be 'abundance of peace and plenty'.[34]

The twentieth-century Diggers looked for heaven in the collective ego which would do away with greed, power and exploitation. Refuting the accusation that acid prevents action, they dealt with the problems that presented themselves on their doorstep. In their shop, the Free Store, they gave away goods discarded by the consumer society, they ran free soup kitchens, started a farming community to provide fresh vegetables, and strove to find accommodation, work and medical contacts for the homeless. Occasionally, they would perform apocryphal stunts – such as when their leader, Emmet Grogan, conducted a public burning of dollar bills, or the time they held a Black Flower Day in protest against a company notorious for pollution, handing grimy daffodils to the organization's top executives.

The Diggers organized themselves through a tribal council. Leaders of the various communes would debate problems sitting in an Indian circle. In the late 1960s, more Digger tribes took off in Britain, and in time, some Diggers formed the Dorinish Island Commune off the coast of Ireland, on land given to them by musician John Lennon.

One tribe united by LSD was that of Charles Manson, who believed messages were conveyed to him through Beatles songs. Manson's followers, The Family, lived in a commune in Death Valley, California. In 1969, Manson led them in nine murders, including that of Sharon

Tate, wife of film director Roman Polanski. 'Wow, what a trip!' one of the Family exclaimed, describing the taste of Sharon Tate's blood to fellow prisoners.[35]

Manson was believed by many of his followers to be the messiah. His prophecies were influenced by Aleister Crowley and Do What You Will was a Family creed. Crowley himself constantly used drugs and made 'extensive and elaborate studies of the effects of indulgence in stimulants and narcotics'[36] which he recorded in 'The Psychology of Hashish', 'Cocaine' and *The Diary of a Drug Fiend*. Some believe that in committing murder, Manson was making a desperate bid to stamp his own identity on a world which, he felt, had denied his reality – that, for him, murder was an existentialist act. After his arrest, Manson was voted Man of the Year by an American underground magazine, and today he continues to be idolized in some circles as an outsider.

'Murder Considered as one of the Fine Arts' was the title of an essay written by Thomas de Quincey (1785–1859), a confirmed opium eater who was almost compulsively obsessed with evil. According to de Quincey, opium was the gateway to an earthly paradise. Writing in his *Confessions of an English Opium-Eater* (1822), and imitating the style of evangelical tracts of the day, he claimed that, '. . . the doctrine of the true church on the subject of opium [is that] . . . the opium eater . . . feels that the diviner part of his nature is paramount; that is, the moral affections are in a state of cloudless serenity; and over all is the great light of the majestic intellect'.[37]

De Quincey believed that in opium he had discovered 'the secret happiness, about which philosophers had disputed for many ages',[38] that the drug had enabled him to enter the 'abyss of divine enjoyment'. But the opium church was not open to just anyone. In fact, wrote de Quincey, 'I acknowledge myself to be the only member – the alpha and the omega.'[39] The masses did, however, use opium – not as an express train to paradise but as a cheap escape from the miseries of everyday life.

For de Quincey, 'Wine robs a man of his self-possession: opium greatly invigorates it.'[40] William James on the other hand, believed that alcohol was capable of stimulating 'the mystical faculties of human nature, usually crushed to earth by the cold facts and dry criticisms of the sober hour'. According to James, 'Drunkenness expands, unites, and says yes. It is in fact the great exciter of the *Yes* function in man. It brings its votary from the chill periphery of things to the radiant core. It makes him for the moment one with truth . . . To the poor and the unlettered it stands in the place of symphony concerts and of literature; and it is part of the deeper mystery and tragedy of life that whiffs and gleams of something we immediately recognize as excellent, should be vouchsafed to many of us only in the fleeting earlier phases of what in its totality is so degrading a poisoning.'[41] Opium was cheaper for most people: a 'ha'pennard o'elevation' would last them a week.[42]

Poet Charles Pierre Baudelaire (1821–67) was attracted to de Quincey's morbid sensibility. Another convert to opium and hashish, Baudelaire excused his vice, explaining that mankind had searched '. . . in the grossest liqueurs, in the most subtle perfumes, under all the climates and in all times, for the means of escaping, were it only for a few hours, from its dunghill dominion, and *"D'emporter le paradis d'un seul coup"*. Alas! Men's vices, horrible as they are supposed to be, contain the proof positive of his taste of the infinite'.[43] The claim is very similar to Huxley's, 'The urge to transcend self-conscious selfhood is . . . a principal appetite of the soul.'[44]

Baudelaire was a frequent visitor, along with Honoré de Balzac (1799–1850) and Théophile Gautier (1811–72), to the marijuana smokers' Club des Haschichins based in a Paris hotel. One of the most curious of murderous tribes, the Assassins, is said to have drawn its name from hashish – hashshashin is Arabic for 'users of hashish'.

The Assassins were an élite corps of killers formed in eleventh-century Persia by Hasan-i Sabbah, leader of a Muslim sect known as the Ismailis. According to legend, the Assassins, high on hashish, were prepared to put their lives at risk without question. It is now considered more likely that they simply acquired their name because their reckless behaviour could only be attributed to the influence of drugs.

One of the stories told about the Assassins is that they were trained in the use of arms, then drugged and taken to a breathtakingly beautiful garden. According to an account by Marco Polo, who travelled through Persia in 1273, the garden was 'the largest and most beautiful that ever was seen, filled with every variety of fruit. In it were erected pavilions and palaces the most elegant that can be imagined, all covered with gilding and exquisite painting. And there were runnels too, flowing freely with wine and milk and honey and water; and numbers of ladies and of the most beautiful damsels in the world, who could play on all manner of instruments, and sung

[sic] most sweetly, and danced in a manner that it was charming to behold. For the Old Man desired to make his people believe that this was actually Paradise. So he had fashioned it after the description that Mahommet gave of his Paradise, to wit, that it should be a beautiful garden running with conduits of wine and milk and honey and water, and full of lovely women for the delectation of all its inmates. And sure enough the Saracens of those parts believed that it was *Paradise!*'[45]

Only those whom the leader intended to be his 'Assassins' were allowed into the garden. Afterwards, they were drugged again and taken back to the palace, where they were told that when they killed one of the enemy, they would return to paradise: 'And thus there was no order of his that they would not affront any peril to execute, for the great desire they had to get back into that Paradise of his. And in this manner the Old One got his people to murder any one whom he desired to get rid of.'[46]

For thirty years, Hasan's Assassins performed countless murders, picking off the Turkish leaders and their Arab allies one by one. Eventually, no-one in a position of power dared to venture outside without wearing armour under their robes. The Assassins would murder their victims in the open, and would often themselves be killed immediately afterwards. But they doubtless looked forward to their sojourn in paradise. Whether or not the legend of the garden is true, the Assassins certainly believed that, if they died, they would immediately be transported to everlasting bliss – of which they had already had a tantalizing taste.

In 1972, Colin Wilson, best known for his book *The Outsider*, wrote *Order of Assassins* – about murderers as outsiders in society. If only briefly, drugs allowed the outsider to become one with the world and experience divine unity. Charles Manson, for example, in a constantly drugged state, claimed to be both God and Satan. However, while drugs gave many a glimpse of heaven on earth, they gave others hell.

In Australia in 1961, a forty-year-old yoga teacher, Anne Hamilton-Byrne, founded a movement known, like Charles Manson's group, as The Family. Again like Manson's group, LSD doses reportedly formed a central part of the movement's practice. Members went through 'clearings' whereby altered states of consciousness were induced with injections of LSD. Some followers were even admitted to a mental hospital by movement-friendly doctors, and legally injected with drugs. Under the influence of the drugs, followers came to view

Anne Hamilton-Byrne as their saviour – not only could she solve all their emotional problems, she was also their route to salvation.

Before long, a chapel was built at the group's Ferny Creek headquarters and Anne Hamilton-Byrne would make grand entrances to the sound of Beethoven's *Ninth Symphony*. Although Hamilton-Byrne has now disappeared – she is thought to be living in Hawaii or Europe – her followers continue to receive tape-recorded sermons from her, and in 1990 her devotees in Victoria were still meeting twice weekly at the Ferny Creek headquarters. 'She could charm the very birds from the trees,' said her former husband according to a newspaper report. 'But she couldn't do anything without the use of a needle.'[47]

Despite the horror stories which emerged from countless drug experiences, many continued to hope that chemicals might provide a route to salvation. In 1967 Arthur Koestler, while condemning the serious risks of LSD, dreamt of the development of a drug which would enable 'the break-through from maniac to man'. Though humanity 'might be repelled and disgusted by the idea that we should rely for our salvation on molecular chemistry instead of spiritual rebirth,' he said, '. . . I see no alternative.' Moreover, he added, 'It is not utopian to believe that it can and will be done.'[48]

Meanwhile, drug rehabilitation programmes themselves began to take on a mystical twist – and even became full-blown religions.

The Church of Synanon is the most obvious example. Founded in Santa Monica in 1958 by Charles Dederich, a member of Alcoholics Anonymous, it began as a verbally confrontational therapy group but developed into a religion with Dederich as the guru. Members had to shave their heads, and such was their submission to Dederich that when he commanded that married couples should change their partners, 230 couples filed for divorce.

Alcoholics Anonymous itself provides a spiritual path. Bill W, founder of the organization, despairing of his addiction, experienced a revelation: 'All at once I found myself crying out, "If there is a God, let Him show Himself!" Suddenly the room lit up with a great white light . . . It seemed to me in my mind's eye that I was on a mountain and that a wind, not of air, but of spirit was blowing'.[49] The forces of shared belief and group cohesiveness have become central to AA. L. Ron Hubbard's Church of Scientology, founded in 1954, also has a drug rehabilitation programme, Narconon.

Others have moved away from drugs – although not from

psychedelia. In 1981 Genesis P. Orridge founded the Temple ov Psychic Youth (TOPY) and formed the band Psychic TV. A correspondent of Charles Manson and *Junkie* author William Burroughs, as well as a keen student of Aleister Crowley, P. Orridge believes in bringing about social transformation through personal transformation. Members of TOPY, which has centres in Europe and the United States, are organized into 'tribes' and psychedelia is one the many esoteric subjects they study.

In Britain, P. Orridge was one of the prime forces behind Acid House, a movement which began in a London club called Heaven and culminated in the so-called second Summer of Love in 1988. Paisley patterns and Smiley badges were resurrected from the 1960s and followers spoke of blissed-out 'mystical experiences' on the dance floor. Acid House was fuelled by Ecstasy, or MDMA, a drug which includes hallucinogenics and amphetamine. But P. Orridge himself is anti-drugs, having first-hand knowledge of those 'taken in' by them.

According to P. Orridge, the world will be transformed into heaven on earth through a committed search for self-realization – and drugs just provide the inane, 'self'-destroying happiness Huxley portrays in *Brave New World*. Like Timothy Leary, P. Orridge believes 'the only real revolution takes place inside people's heads',[50] but unlike Leary he advocates the use of non-chemical magic. Sex magick is used – and so are dancing, music and a whole myriad of ideas and techniques from the personal growth movement. 'I just have a fundamental feeling that the human race is here to evolve and is capable of becoming something relatively interesting and special,' he says.[51]

FIVE | BE ALL YOU CAN BE

C ountless acid apostles believed they were swallowing the chemical formula which alchemists had been searching for since before the third century BC – the elixir which would ensure immortality. As Alan Watts put it in 'The New Alchemy' (1960): '. . . in every experiment with LSD one of the first effects I have noticed is a profound relaxation combined with an abandonment of purposes and goals, reminding me of the Taoist saying that "when purpose has been used to achieve purposelessness, the thing has been grasped". I have felt . . . free to look about me as if I were living in eternity without a single problem to be solved'.[1] Then, legal clampdowns, the news that LSD could addle your brain, and numerous drug-related deaths put an end to the psychedelic explosion.

The search for the philosopher's stone had been going on for centuries. The Taoists of China were especially keen alchemists. Somewhere in the eastern hemisphere, it was believed, lay the Isles of the Immortals, an earthly paradise where voyagers could eat the food of everlasting life. The Emperor Shih Huang Ti is said to have sent out fleets of ships to track down the heaven's whereabouts.

One way or another, most religions offer their followers immortality. In Christianity, the Son of God himself went on record as saying, 'Verily verily I say unto you. He that believeth in me hath everlasting life.' Members of the Eternal Flame, a group founded in the early 1960s, have dabbled with both Taoism and Christianity, but they have gone beyond searching, beyond belief or faith, and have discovered a paradise which, they say, is 'the greatest human potential ever'. The charismatic triumvirate who head the group are not talking spiritual immortality, or the transcendence of the soul. They are talking flesh and blood immortality, a heavenly, immortal, everlasting Be-In.

'Death is unhealthy – a useless custom – a bad habit – a grave mistake. The belief that death is inevitable is the major cause of sickness, violence and war,'[2] the Flame's leader, American Charles Brown, known as Chuck, was preaching in the late 1980s. The true war which should be fought, he teaches, is that within the cells of the body. By getting the body's immortal cells to fizz and multiply, they will triumph over the death enzymes in DNA. For Chuck, 'Physical Immortality' is the second coming, the awakening of the Christ in the body of every human being. Some two decades earlier, Timothy Leary was expounding his belief that 'the language of God is the DNA code'; that the 'intermediate manifestation of the divine process which we call the DNA code has spent the last two billion years making this planet a Garden of Eden'.[3]

As a minister in the Episcopalian church, Chuck had himself been deeply involved in the death culture before experiencing enlightenment in 1960. Following the experience, he began to spread his message, earning his way playing country and western songs in bars.

Later, he was joined by BernaDeane – first his accompanist, now his wife – and Jim Strole. The three of them – Chuck, Bernie 'n' Jim – live together as one body – an earth-bound expression of the Trinity. For Immortals, as members of the Eternal Flame are known, there is no male and female as ordinary earthlings know it. It is their slightly androgynous quality – a state which Norman O. Brown recommended – which, if anything, marks the Flame out from mortal folk; that, and their 'liveliness'.

At a meeting in London a willowy, wild-eyed Immortal stalks the stage wielding a microphone. 'I love you all. You are my lovers,' he exclaims. His fellow Immortals applaud, call out, jump up and down, hug one another. It is important for Flame members to meet up and hug one another. It keeps the cells moving. Not surprisingly, then, Immortals tend to live near each other, some in communities. They need other Immortals to help them hunt out their death programmes, they say. The largest community, numbering some two hundred Immortals, is in Scottsdale, Arizona. Every so often members of the Flame gather there at the Paradise Holiday Centre for an Immortal convention. Death has occasionally struck down Immortals unable to conquer their cultural programming in time – those who have experienced Immortality intellectually rather than in the body. There have also, however, been Lazarus-style resurrections.

In the late nineteenth century former British MP Laurence Oliphant and his wife brought spiritual life to unbelievers by lying down next to them and keeping them in a state of prolonged sexual excitement. The Flame follow much the same formula. Members tell how a long-term Immortal lay on her deathbed, apparently past saving. But when one of the leaders climbed into bed beside her, she made a miraculous recovery. Rather than being brought to spiritual life, she had been brought to Physical Immortality. 'The body is the most spiritual thing you have,' say Immortals.

During the late 1980s, the Flame began to spread like wildfire – maybe because those born into the 1950s' youth movement and raised in the counter-culture of the 1960s were beginning to stare the Great Reaper a little closer in the eye.

Back at the London meeting, an attractive woman called Eterna takes the mike. As she sweeps aside her hair before speaking, it is startling to notice her advanced years. When she was seven, says Eterna, she was made to kiss a dead lady. 'I thought, what did she do to bring this on herself?' The question begs no reply. The Flame know the answer – the woman chose death. She created it herself – just as the wheelchair-bound woman at the meeting chose her disability.

'The cells have a bias towards life. The mind has programmed the body to die. When the mind stops arguing the cells start moving,' explains UK leader Paul Massey – which also explains the abuse which greets new members of the Flame who attempt to rationally question their new-found Immortality. 'I hate your ego. I hate your mind! Let go of your spiritual ego and melt!' screams a veteran at a puzzled Flamelet. The woman hesitates, the angels pass . . . it is a life-and-death moment. A sigh of relief escapes the Immortals as the young woman crosses the stage to Paul and hugs him. The immortal cells are on the move again.

Many Flame members are rebirthers – a therapy with a spiritual input which through breathing techniques and bodywork aims to put clients in touch with the birth experience. 'You merge with your breath, flowing, glowing, soaring, relaxing profoundly, your mind melting into your spirit, surging, awakening your inner being and the quiet sounds of your soul . . .' writes 'father of rebirthing' Leonard

Orr.[4] Like the Flame, Orr teaches that from conception human beings are exposed to – and become addicted to – negative programming. He and his protégé Sondra Ray, now a New Age leader in her own right and the founder of Loving Relationship Trainings (LRT), are working towards Physical Immortality with the help of Indian guru Babaji. Sondra's latest book sports the title *How to be Chic, Fabulous and Live For Ever*.

For a British LRT coordinator, Physical Immortality is like 'living in a concept', something akin, but far superior, to 'My mind to me a kingdom is . . . That it excels all other bliss'.[5] Whereas positive thinking in the style of the Rev Norman Vincent Peale (see Chapter Six) stems from the rational mind, tending merely to repress the negative, Sondra Ray teaches Immortals to acknowledge and release the negative while immersing themselves in the new. Acknowledgement is a key word in the personal growth movement; affirmations also help. 'I am safe and immortal right now,' they might say. Or, 'So long as my life urge exceeds my death urge I can choose to live as long as I like.' It was Leonard Orr who introduced the Flame leaders to Britain in 1988. One of the trio's first venues was Glastonbury – the 'immortal city' of Arthurian legend.

Immortality was given another slant by Carl Jung (1875–1961) who has had an immense influence on today's New Age movement, not least because of his belief that men and women are essentially spiritual beings. Alchemy is generally believed to have given rise to modern-day chemistry. But for Jung, alchemy dealt with the human psyche and was the precursor of psychology – the gold alchemists sought was the transformation of consciousness into a godlike state. Through identifying the transformative power, man became a type of redeemer.

It was Jung's line of thinking which gave rise to humanistic psychology, which in turn gave rise to the Human Potential Movement. Coming after the Freudians and behaviourists, the humanistic psychologists are known as the 'third force'.

In 1948, *Walden Two*, a novel by B. F. Skinner, a leading behaviourist, was published. In the book, members of the community undergo carefully controlled conditioning which guarantees their survival and happiness. Much of Huxley's *Brave New World* was modelled on the thinking of an earlier behaviourist, Ivan Pavlov, and, like *Brave New World*, *Walden Two* wavers on the line between a dystopia and utopia. The leader of the community in the novel, Frazier, has 'no truck with philosophies of innate goodness – or evil, either, for that matter'.[6] The modelling of human behaviour is everything, he believes, and given a perfect, controlled environment, the individual will be perfect. 'I've had only one idea in my life – a true *idée fixe*,' says Frazier. 'To put it as bluntly as possible – the idea of having my own way. "Control" expresses it, I think. The control of human behavior . . .'[7] The emphasis is on a highly structured environment, positive reinforcement of behaviour, science and experimentation. Several communities modelled on *Walden Two* sprang up in the United States, among them Twin Oaks in Virginia.

Skinner believed that the so-called freedom of man is simply an illusion, to protect him from his lack of knowledge of himself and the world. 'There is no place in the scientific position for a self as a true originator or initiator of action,' he wrote.[8]

The humanistic psychologists, on the other hand, believe mankind's birthright is for each individual to recognize the full potential of his or her 'self': 'The greatest attainment of identity, autonomy or selfhood is itself simultaneously a transcending of itself, a going beyond and above selfhood',[9] wrote Abraham Maslow (1908–1970), the leading figure in the field. Maslow's work focused on 'healthy' individuals – people who had achieved what can variously be called self-fulfilment, full humanness, authenticity or self-actualization. Self-actualized people, said Maslow, realize their potential, achieve 'acceptance and expression of the inner core or self'[10] and experience fleeting moments of their higher natures, 'peak experiences in which time disappears and hopes are fulfilled'.[11] They are able to live in their inner psychic worlds of experience and emotion and 'enjoy it to such an extent that it may be called Heaven'.[12] Although Maslow believed that self-actualization is easy, he estimated that only one per cent of the adult population achieved it – mainly because culture had taught them that man's intrinsic nature is evil.

Maslow's work, which repeatedly stressed the life-enhancing nature of mystical and religious experience, developed into what became known as the 'fourth force' – transpersonal or spiritual psychology. The term transpersonal psychology was first used by psychedelic experimenter Stanislav Grof in the late 1960s; another of its exponents was American John Lilly who was busy investigating altered states of consciousness in a sensory deprivation tank. What they were all concerned with was existential psychology – that man, set down in an alien universe, has to be enabled to create himself, create his own reality and somehow give meaning to his life. While many existentialist writers concentrated on the bleakness of such an outlook, Maslow stressed the redeeming quality of love.

The 1980 film *Altered States*, directed by Ken Russell, sets the scene. The hero, played by William Hurt, sets out on a quest for self-discovery and 'significant religious experiences' through isolation tanks and hallucinogenic drugs given him by an American Indian tribe. 'Ever since we dispensed with God we've got nothing but ourselves to explain this meaningless horror of life,' says the hero. A sceptical friend describes him as a 'Faust freak', selling his soul to find a greater truth, and his wife claims that 'human life doesn't have great truths. We are born in doubt, we spend our lives persuading ourselves we are alive and one way we do that is by loving each other . . .' Undeterred, the hero regresses to the ultimate origins of self via a number of ape-like creatures and strange gooey substances and eventually finds – nothing. On the brink of self-extinction, he is redeemed and re-embodied by his love for his wife. According to one reviewer, 'the picture has a dismal, tired humanistic ending'.

Lilly later went on to study with Oscar Ichazo, founder of Arica, the mystical system based on the work of Gurdjieff. Lilly, Grof and Maslow were all associated with the Esalen Institute, founded in 1961 at Big Sur, California by Mike Murphy and named after an Indian tribe. Maslow led one of Esalen's first seminars and Grof eventually took up residence there, moving away from LSD into a type of breath therapy based, like Leonard Orr's rebirthing, on a form of Indian yoga.

Born in 1930, Murphy was in his second year at Stanford University when he took a course in comparative religion. Soon after being introduced to Eastern thinking, he began to practise meditation and to study the works of Sri Aurobindo (1872–1950), the Indian spiritual leader, educated at Manchester Grammar School and Cambridge University. Increasingly, the Human Potential Movement was gaining impetus from Eastern influences.

While imprisoned by the British as a result of his involvement in nationalistic politics, Aurobindo had a profound religious experience. On his release he founded a community at Pondicherry in Southern India, committed not to 'the spirituality that withdraws from life, but the conquest of life by the power of the spirit . . . in which the veil between man and God shall be removed . . . [and] all of our action a sacrifice to the master of our action and an expression of the greater self in man'.[14] Apparently, through the form of yoga Sri Aurobindo developed, the 'ideal of divine humanity will . . . be accomplished, and the world will be transformed into the Kingdom of God.'[15]

In the late 1950s, Murphy spent eighteen months at the Aurobindo ashram and returned determined to explore the evolution of consciousness. Two years later, he visited Hot Springs, Big Sur, owned by his grandfather. At that time it was home to a Christian evangelical sect, as well as a number of artistic types. It seemed the ideal location for an American consciousness-expanding centre. The first seminar held there, in 1962, was called Expanding Vision. The decade which American sociologist Philip Rieff described as marking the advent of 'psychological man' was underway.

Murphy was interested in Aldous Huxley's ideas – in particular those he put forward in *The Doors of Perception*. Blake's poem, from which the title is taken, continues: 'For man has closed himself up, till he sees all things thro' narrow chinks of his cavern.'[16] Huxley was among the first of a long line of human potential gurus to visit Esalen.

While Esalen is still thriving, the Aurobindo ashram has become dis-spirited. Although it still attracts Westerners, the stated aim of bringing spirituality into life appears to have failed and given way to a po-faced self-righteousness in the face of a long-running bureaucratic squabble over ashram rights and ownership. The town is filled with ashram boutiques selling Western-style clothes and knick-knacks at Western-style prices. One old-timer, tucked away behind shutters and courtyards, speaks only with bitterness of the dream turned sour.

But at Esalen, conflict and the confrontation are enriching. From the start it was accepted that cleansing the doors of perception could prove an unpleasant, even traumatic, experience. After all, Blake had written that 'the way of excess leads to the palace of wisdom'.[17]

While Abraham Maslow talked of self-actualization and man's higher nature, Fritz Perls (1893–1970) took a more earthy approach to achieving the whole person. Perls lived at Esalen for several years during which he held court as the Institute's controversial guru. When Maslow asked him to prepare a paper for a conference on the language of existentialism, Perls sent in a poem:

I am not a lady perfuming her farts,
I am a scoundrel and a lover of arts.
I am what I am and I screw when I can,
I'm Popeye the sailor, man.[18]

Perls believed that the energy which goes into conflict can be used as a means for personal growth. The method he used to put his ideas into practice is known as gestalt therapy. Gestalt – the German word for form or configuration which carries with it the idea that the whole is more than the sum of its parts – had been used to describe a form of psychology since the early twentieth century. Through confrontational encounter groups, Perls developed a practical therapy from the idea, shocking clients out of their habitual thought patterns into a variety of self-realization, of living in the Now. One by one, students would take the 'hot seat' and be jolted into seeing themselves for what they were – often ridiculous figures.

British psychologist R.D. Laing (1927–89) also visited Esalen. In 1965 he set up Kingsley Hall, a therapeutic community in the East End of London which eliminated the boundaries of client/therapist and, following the tradition of other cultures, saw in madness an attempt to break through to a new vision. 'True sanity,' wrote Laing, 'entails . . . the emergence of the "inner" archetypal mediators of divine power, and through this death, a rebirth, and the eventual re-establishment of a new kind of ego-functioning, the ego now being the servant of the divine . . .'[19] Laing's community was eventually closed in 1970.

Thousands of seekers from all walks of life have visited Esalen – some, including successful business-people, dropped in to live there full time. It is impossible to guess how many of those visitors achieved self-actualization, a heaven on earth, but many saw their heaven in Esalen. Two of Perl's students entered another world through suicide, after having been jeered at while on the 'hot seat' for threatening to end their lives. Perls's gestalt prayer apparently summed up his reaction:

I do my thing, and you do your thing,
I am not in this world to live up to your expectations
And you are not in this world to live up to mine.
You are you, and I am I.
And if by chance, we find each other, it's beautiful.
If not, it can't be helped.[20]

The concept is similar to that of Zen, where students aim to make their everyday life a manifestation of the infinite, to achieve 'freedom from clinging'. In the words of Blake again:

He who binds to himself a Joy
Doth the winged life destroy;
But he who kisses the Joy as it flies
Lives in Eternity's sunrise.[21]

Alan Watts, who popularized Zen for Westerners with his numerous books and articles on the discipline, was another early visitor to Esalen, as was the Protestant theologian Paul Tillich (1886–1965). But Robert Heinlein, author of *Stranger in a Strange Land*, refused Mike Murphy's request to lecture at the Institute. Heinlein's science fantasy novel, first published in 1961, embodied many of the ideals and fears of the time. Its hero – Valentine Michael Smith, the Man from Mars – has a Zen-like 'capacity for enjoying the inevitable'.[22] This capacity is due to a Martian faculty known as 'grokking', which can be described as an ability to attune with life, or to swallow it whole. Humans, rather than grokking, tend to be taken in.

Mike Smith was born on the first space ship to land on Mars. The sole survivor of the voyage, he was raised by Martians but was brought back to earth by the second space ship to visit the planet. Because he poses a threat to the established order of earth, or Terra as it is known, he founds a community or 'nest' where he teaches earthlings how to 'grok' with life. Members of the community are all 'water brothers', seeing one another as being as important as themselves. There is a bucket of money by the door for anyone who needs some and sex is carried out through the mind as well as the body.

As he is being killed by the mob who refuse to hear his message, Mike says, 'Blessed is he who knows himself and commands himself, for the world is his and love and happiness and peace walk with him wherever he goes . . . Thou art God. Know that and the Way is opened.'[23] Heinlein's book had a profound influence on its millions of readers, some setting up their own communities of water sharers (see Chapter Eleven). It has even been suggested that Charles Manson's The Family was inspired by the Man from Mars' utopian community. The child of Manson's first follower was, apparently, named Valentine Michael Manson, and Manson, together with other Heinlein fans, attempted to do away with language and simply 'grok' the world and each other.

According to Manson, 'All words are without meaning,'[24] and 'No sense makes sense. You won't get caught if you don't got thought in your head.'[24a] The idea that language shapes reality became immensely popular in the 1960s, spreading out from the arena of philosophy and entering student and hippie street life. The advances in technology accounted in part for the change. According to Canadian professor Marshall McLuhan, the printed word was dead and a utopian Global Village, made possible by sophisticated communications, would arise.

Benjamin Lee Whorf (1897–1941) was one of several linguists to develop an interest in language from one in religion. Whereas the ancient Greeks believed that language was the means by which the universal, unchanging essence of reason was expressed, Whorf, writing in the Theosophists's journal, claimed that 'commitment to illusion has been sealed in Western Indo-European language'. However, through a deep understanding of language man could begin to achieve a 'culture of consciousness', leading him to a 'great illumination'.[24b]

Whorf, an admirer of Peter Ouspensky, was introduced to the Theosophists by Fritz Kunz, whose book *The Men Beyond Mankind* (1934) is a study of 'the next step in personal and social evolution' and looks forward to a 'New Age'.[25] Whorf was also impressed by gestalt psychology, which dates from about 1912, claiming that it had 'discovered an important truth about the mind', but that language was the barrier to its leading to a breakthrough in the understanding of human life. Three decades later, gestalt therapist Fritz Perls would conduct gibberish exercises in his encounter groups.

Many groups intent on introducing members to enlightenment – or a new version of reality – develop a jargon-laden in-language which conforms to that new reality. Notable among such groups is the Church of Scientology. A science fiction writer before founding his religion in 1954, L. Ron Hubbard (1911–86) – like Heinlein – was first published in the New York-based magazine *Astounding*. The exploration of inward and outward space went hand in hand. Manson is said to have dabbled in Scientology and picked up a number of the movement's phrases.

The Scientology bible – *Dianetics: The Modern Science of Mental Health* – is crammed with strange words and phrases. 'In dramatizing an engram, the aberee always takes the winning valence and that valence is not, of course, himself. If only one other person is present and the other is talking in terms of apathy, then the apathy is the tone value of the engram,' writes Hubbard. 'In reading this book, be very certain you never go past a word you do not understand,' instructs an Important Note at the beginning of the book. 'Don't go any further, but go back to *before* you got into difficulty. Find the misunderstood word and get it defined.[26] According to Hubbard, man 'chose between language and potential madness and for the vast benefits of the former he received the curse of the latter'.[27]

Once introduced to the broader reality of Scientology, followers of the movement might just be able to glimpse Hubbard's promised prize of a piece of 'blue sky' through the narrow chink of their cavern. Or they may simply lose touch with everyday reality. Rollo May, along with Abraham Maslow, one of the leading existential psychologists of the day, reviewed *Dianetics* in the *New York Times*. 'Books like this do harm,' he wrote, 'by their grandiose promises to troubled persons and their oversimplification of human psychological problems.'[28]

Hubbard, whose *Times* obituary described him as 'not, by any standards, a nice man, but . . . a highly influential figure among the myriad inventors of magical and religious systems who have appeared in modern times'[29] declared that Scientology 'gave scientifically-validated evidence of the existence of the human soul'[30] and that the true self was an all-powerful, immortal being known as a thetan. Once people cleared themselves of engrams – destructive and negative mental blocks – they would become these god-like beings. One can become clear of engrams through a Scientology practice known as auditing – go into any of the Scientologists' offices and you will find, after a completing a personality test, that you are in need of several hours of auditing – which is because 'anyone not released or cleared has upwards of two or three hundred engrams'.

'I recommend that you start now,' says one of the uniformly keen staff in the central London office. 'Don't let it fester. Now you know what's wrong in your life, it will get worse. It can only get worse. You must start changing it before it's too late . . . Terrible things have happened to you and you want to get rid of them before they grow and . . . get worse,' he says. 'I recommend,' he concludes, 'twelve-and-a-half hours, that's eight to nine sessions – of auditing.'[31]

For many, that introduction leads to several years', if not a lifetime's, involvement in Scientology.

The thinking is similar to that behind The Life Training, a 'mass therapy' founded by former Episcopalian priest Brad Brown. Brad teaches trainees a five-step technique known as the 'Clearing Process', in which they are told to re-experience their Lifeshocks and, after listening to their Mindtalk, tell the truth about the experience.[32]

Before entering the seminar room, trainees must agree to a list of rules. Certain words are forbidden, including any reference to a deity, but 'You may speak of such matters by referring to your experience'. Moreover trainees are told, 'When describing or referring to your feelings, do not use the words Good or Bad.'[33]

Scientology is not the only group to develop a science-fiction-inspired language. Universal Trainings, formerly known as Self Transformations, an offshoot of The Bellin Partnership, has described its seminars as 'intergalactic mystery tours'. One training offered by the group is described as The Cosmic Vortex. 'This workshop is an opportunity to see and experience the universe in a completely new light. It is a step through into another dimension, which can change your picture of the world forever',[34] reads the brochure.

Among the areas explored are 'apparitions of "gods", angelic beings, and nature spirits and UFOs'.[35] Graham Browne, who runs the courses, says their power is such that trainees may be cured of congenital illnesses – one woman found she no longer had to wear glasses, for example.

Such concepts are not limited to civilian life. In the 1970s, James Channon, a retired United States Army lieutenant colonel, created the First Earth Battalion – a 'concept army' of transformed individuals or 'Warrior Monks'. Once these futuristic soldiers came into being they would, he suggested, have 'the power to make paradise'. The only obstacle preventing these Monks from creating their heaven on earth, Channon claimed, was the 'language of the possible': 'Where those limits are ignored . . . people bend metal with their minds, walk on fire, calculate faster than a computer, travel to new places in their mind's eye . . . and see into the future. There are no limits in the Earth Battalion.'[36]

Channon, who has himself sampled more than a hundred 'psycho-technologies', was a regular participant in, and inspiration of, Delta Force activities. An informal group of some 300 US Army Officers, Delta Force was set up in the 1970s to look into numerous parapsychological techniques including, for instance, the ability of soldiers to leave their bodies and walk through walls. Armies are interested in winning – and the Human Potential Movement looked as if it had caught on to something which worked. As early as the 1950s, during the grey days of the Cold War, rumours circulated that the Russians had perfected a technique of affecting behaviour telepathically. Determined not to be out-psyched, the US Army began to investigate extrasensory perception, and later parapyschology – and later psychotechnologies. Anything which might produce results was worth a try. What civilians were using for enlightenment, the army was developing for markedly different ends.

In March 1982, Delta Force – which should not be confused with the antiterrorist unit of the same name – held its tenth conference. 'The role of a tribal elder is to keep the tribe's vision,' ran the conference report. '. . . And tell stories . . . A shaman tells stories too. Especially stories about mysterious powers and powerful mysteries. Our own tribal leader happens to be our senior shaman. This is his story about our tenth tribal gathering. It's a story about vision and fire. And Power.'[37]

One of the speakers at the conference was key New Age popularizer Marilyn Ferguson. Another leading figure in the New Age movement, Barbara Marx Hubbard, had previously addressed the Force. Marilyn Ferguson believes that mankind is about to undergo a 'paradigm shift' – a change in consciousness – and be transformed into a godlike being. In the battle to effect such a transformation, the mind is the enemy. Speaking at the conference, Ferguson advised delegates who experienced difficulty in overcoming the rational mind to attend one of the many 'enlightenment seminars' on offer to turned-on America.

The findings of the conference were later presented to three generals – one was sceptical, one open-minded and the third, General Thurman, was enthusiastic. The following year, Delta Force was disbanded. But in 1985 the Army Research Institute asked the National Research Council (NRC) to assess a field of techniques designed to enhance human performance. The Committee on Techniques for the Enhancement of Human Performance was founded. At dinner on the first evening of the Committee's first conference, General Thurman was the key speaker. And it was General Thurman who helped to devise the hugely successful slogan 'Be all that you can be' for a US army recruitment campaign. The same slogan would doubtless be equally successful as a rallying cry for the Human Potential Movement.

The psychologists from the NRC were asked to look into altered mental states and a variety of parapsychological processes such as remote viewing and mind-over-matter skills – including the capacity to turn machines on and off at distance. They were also asked to examine neuro-linguistic programming (NLP), a system which has been widely used by the army, as well as by the business world for sales and management training – and by leaders of today's New Age seminars. The technique aims to access the programming function within individuals at a deep level, bypassing normal forms of communication. A recent NLP best-seller in the US is called *Unlimited Power*.

NLP can also be used to model in infinitely minute detail the behavioural characteristics of individuals, in order that the 'modeller' might acquire their attributes. It is rumoured that Hitler and Mussolini are studied by those seeking leadership qualities. NLP is, in a sense, a form of psychotechnological alchemy – imagine Dr Frankenstein as a psychiatrist rather than a surgeon.

The report which finally emerged recommended that NLP, subliminal learning and altered states of consciousness should be examined further. Although the committe found 'no scientific warrant' for the existence of parapsychological phenomena, it felt that monitoring by the army of the field would be prudent and suitable.[38]

One of the enlightenment seminars that Marilyn Ferguson recommended to delegates at the tenth Delta Force conference was Werner Erhard's est, which has been described as the LSD of the Human Potential Movement – explosive and potentially life-transforming. (See Chapter Six.) Est was renowned for its strict rules – in particular the lack of toilet breaks – and numerous former 'esties' have felt that the experience was, like LSD, psychologically harmful.

Erhard is effectively handing trainees an existential philosophy, with the deification of self as the final building block. 'Werner has discovered higher truths; ways to lead humans to ultimate reality,' said one of the guru's sidekicks. 'Heidegger, in his attempt to redefine philosophical inquiry, is the closest we have to Werner.'[39] Martin Heidegger (1889–1976), an existentialist, believed that man creates himself by choosing his character and his actions.

'You're the *source* and creator of all your experience,' says an est trainer in Luke Rhinehart's account of a typical est training, ''You're a God, but what you, the individual entity bouncing around inside the big universe you've created, what you do is totally out of your control. It's total nonsense. Total paradox. You are the source of all your experience and you don't have the least control. All you can do is choose what happens. When you learn to *want* what you get, you know what? You get what you want. From now on you'll *always* get what you want, always . . . as long as you want what you get.'[40]

Heaven on earth, indeed. At the same time, there is a remarkable similarity here with the leader of Aldous Huxley's *Brave New World* who says that 'the secret of happiness and virtue [is] liking what you've *got* to do'.[41]

In Dostoevsky's *The Devils*, Kirilov argues with Stavrogin:
'All's good.'
'All?'
'All. Man's unhappy because he doesn't known that he's happy. Only because of that . . .'
'But what about the man who dies of hunger or the man who insults and rapes the little girl – is that good too?'
'Yes, it is. And he who blows his brains out for the child, that's good too. And he who doesn't blow his brains out, that's good too. All's good . . . They are not good . . . because they don't know that they are good. When they find out, they won't rape a little girl. They have to find out that they are good, for then they will all at once become good, every one of them. . . . He who teaches that all are good will bring about the end of the world.'[42]

According to Erhard, 'Of all the disciplines that I studied, practised and learned, Zen was the *essential* one . . . it created space . . . And it built up in me the critical mass from which was kindled the experience which produced *est*.'[43] Some of the shock tactics employed in Erhard seminars, such as verbal abuse and disorientation techniques, have been likened to the methods a Zen master might use.

Luke Rhinehart, est graduate and student and teacher of Zen, devised a game known as 'die-ing' or 'dice living', described in his 1971 novel *The Dice Man*. There, to sidestep the problem of choice and indeterminism, a disillusioned psychologist devises a game whereby he runs his life by the roll of a die. Einstein, when faced with the indeterminism of quantum physics, announced 'God does not play dice',[44] but gradually, the psychologist allows the die to run his life. 'If that die has a one face up, I thought, I'm going downstairs and rape Arlene . . . a one means rape, the other numbers mean bed, the die is cast. Who am I to question the die?'[45] By turning over his self-responsibility to the die, the player can experience loss of self, or de-identification. Eventually, the die becomes God. 'You must never question the wisdom of the Die. His ways are inscrutable. He leads you by the hand into an abyss and, lo, it is a fertile plain . . . There is no compromise: you must surrender everything.'[46]

An amalgam of such ideas informs Erhard's seminars. Trainees cannot be taught the philosophy, they must experience it, experiencing also, *en route* to enlightenment, a variety of psychotechnologies designed to shock them out of their 'mechanicalness'. Like philosopher mystic Gurdjieff, Erhard teaches that 'Man is a machine': the mind consists of a stack of records 'that the mind interprets as necessary for survival . . . This stack operates quite *mechanically*, quite automatically, quite moronically as a matter of fact'.[47] For Erhard, 'Mind is at the root of all the trouble'[48] – a discovery he claims to have made through Scientology.

According to Gurdjieff, 'Rules are the alarm clock that wake the sleeping man', and like Gurdjieff's pupils, Erhard's trainees are expected to comply with numerous seemingly pointless rules: 'You can't keep agreements, and your lives are so messed up you don't even *know* that you can't keep agreements . . . But if you choose to stay, then you're choosing to keep the agreements and to experience the anger and nausea and boredom I've just described to you . . . you'll get it. It will blow your minds . . .'[49]

Trainees 'get it' when they stop being run by belief systems – or their stack of records. 'Getting it' is an achievement similar to the 'grokking' of Heinlein's Mike, the Man from Mars. When Mike finally understands the concept of God he says, 'The word is God . . . *Thou art God!* . . . Thou art God . . . That which groks'.[50]

'The mind is a linear arrangement of multisensory total records of successive moments of now,' says the est trainer.[51] In Heinlein's *Stranger in a Strange Land*, the Man from Mars is asked who started the world. In reply, Mike says 'A *nowing*. World is. World was. World shall be. *Now*.' ' "As it was in the beginning, so it now and ever shall be, World without end —' " says his baffled host. 'You grok it!' Mike replies.[52]

Alongside the New Age movement to deify mankind and live in the now, a scientific breed of alchemists is exploring the field of cryonics – a method of draining and deep freezing bodies (current rate in the region of £60,000) and heads (£20,000) which will be reanimated when science catches up with them. One subscriber to the great deep freeze explained that 'My definition of immortality . . . is ending the death sentence that we have on us now.'[53] It is considered likely, however, that following the freezing process, the individual will have no memory. The question troubling many people in the field is that of whether a body without a memory is a person; whether someone truly living in the now can actually be said to exist.

Another problem with deep freeze immortality is, of course, its price tag. But then the relationship between money and paradise has always been uneasy.

SIX | THE PROSPEROUS SELF

For millions of Americans, heaven on earth in the 1980s was a 1200 acre plot in North Carolina known as Heritage USA. The dream-child of televangelist Jim Bakker, Heritage USA was a crazy fantasy park taking as its theme a cheery cartoon Christianity. The place teemed with biblical symbolism from a 'real-life' Upper Room – scene of the Last Supper – to a 163-foot water slide which shot hysterically happy holidaymakers into the cleansing waters of the Holy Spirit.

But the dream was to hasten Bakker's downfall. The former small-town preacher and his wife Tammy Faye sold slices of heaven on earth to their flock – lifetime partnerships which entitled them to a quota of free nights in paradise for the rest of their lives. The money rolled in, but heaven, it transpired, didn't run to sufficient accommodation for all the partners.

Though heaven on earth was short on rooms, it didn't lack a wealth of worldly delights including a miniature village inhabited by bearded gnomes, roller-skating rinks, a mini train, shopping malls and fast food joints. Among the innumerable knick-knacks on sale were a Tammy Faye make-up line and dolls which sang gospel music when you pressed their tummy buttons.

The Bakkers were engagingly up-front about their spending habits and many of their disciples revelled in their reckless shopping sprees. When Tammy Faye announced she hoped to buy her husband two giraffes for his birthday, they were charmed. When they heard of her air-conditioned dog-house, Jim's fleet of cars, their vast and many houses, they rarely questioned whether the money might be better spent.

In Bakker, millions of Americans had found a saviour who gave them licence to enjoy. For many, the catharsis was considerable. Over and over again the New Testament insists that money itself brings neither happiness nor heaven. 'It is harder for a camel to pass through the eye of a needle than for a rich man to enter the kingdom of God' (Matthew). 'The love of money is the root of all evil' (Timothy). 'Lay not up riches on earth' (Matthew). 'Consider the lilies of the field' (Matthew). To Bakker's disciples, money was a sign of God's love.

The difficulty of finding heaven through riches is not peculiar to the Christian tradition: myths and folk tales, too, continually emphasize that riches bring misery. Midas, the legendary king of Phrygia, is threatened with starvation after Dionysus grants his wish that everything he touches is turned to gold. And the goose that laid the golden egg ended up dead.

But Bakker was the proponent of a doctrine known by detractors as 'name it and claim it'. With an engaging enthusiasm, he and Tammy Faye introduced the Gospel of Prosperity to the countless viewers who tuned in to their *Praise The Lord* or *People that Love (PTL)* TV shows. The message was simple – and was lifted straight from the pages of the Bible: Ask, and it shall be given you. Whatever they wanted, God would provide: a new car, new kitchen or new job – whatever it took to make them happy. It worked for Jim. All he had to do was to pray on television and millions of dollars, or 'love offerings', flooded in. The amount of cash people gave was a measure of their love for God. And the amount of cash people received was a sign that God loved them.

In 1987, news of Bakker's affair with one of his flock, Jessica Hahn, began to filter out. Together with the growing rumours of financial scandal, Bakker realized his days were numbered. Determined to keep his ministry from the clutches of televangelist Jimmy Swaggart, who had denounced him as a cancer that needed to be excised from the Body of Christ, Bakker handed over the reins of *PTL* to Jerry Falwell.

A fundamentalist Baptist, Falwell strove to curb the excesses at Heritage USA. In 1979 he had founded the right-wing religious group the Moral Majority which reigned throughout the 1980s, hand in hand with president and former film star Ronald Reagan. Then, in 1989, Falwell announced the Moral Majority's demise.

The televangelists promised money would appear like magic and until the scandals of 1987–88 it did – for them, at any rate. But by the end of 1989, Jim Bakker had been found guilty on twenty-four charges of fraud and conspiracy and sentenced to forty-five years in prison; Heritage USA had been bought by a developer from Toronto and now belongs to another televangelist; evangelist Oral Roberts had lost credibility after announcing that God would take his life unless he raised several million dollars; and Jimmy Swaggart had been defrocked.

Swaggart was himself found to have a proclivity for the services of prostitutes. 'Another of the shameless buggers got whacked last week,' wrote Hunter S. Thompson. 'Jimmy Swaggart, a fifty-two-year-old howler from Baton Rouge known in some quarters as "the Mick Jagger of TV evangelism", got nailed in a nasty little sting operation down in New Orleans and was forced to resign his $245 million-a-year ministry.' Comparing Swaggart with Bakker, Thompson commented, 'It reminded a lot of people of that naked lunacy that blew Gary Hart out of the '88 presidential race.'[1]

In Britain, 'Restoration' churches, aimed at restoring God's kingdom on earth, flourished. One of the movement's most prominent proponents, Michael Bassett, said, 'God will make you rich and prosperous in all areas of your life – spiritual, emotional, social and financial.'[2] His critics call him a 'faith preacher of the prosperity gospel'.[3]

The 1980s have already gone down as the decade of materialism – if not of greed. Money, it seemed, could buy paradise, and certainly for many it bought ready-packaged lifestyles. But while money was everything, it was also nothing – as the junk bonds or Black Monday stock market crash readily displayed. Showmanship and salesmanship were prized qualities.

Though the word televangelist wasn't coined until 1981, overt marketing of the prosperity gospel had been around for some time. At the turn of the century, Billy Sunday and Dwight Moody had cheerfully announced themselves God's salesmen and claimed the key to making money was to get converted, get the right attitude, go out and get a job, and work diligently.

All this was a far cry from sixteenth-century Protestant reformer Martin Luther's (1483–1546) attitude to money. For him, material gain was a side effect of worship and devotion – you worked hard in order to please God, not yourself. As far as money was concerned: 'So our Lord God commonly gives riches to those gross asses to whom He vouchsafes nothing else,'[4] he said. Calvin's (1509–64) message was much the same – work glorified God, and provided a discipline which reduced the opportunities for sins of the flesh. Prosperity might indicate you were one of the elect, chosen to enjoy life everlasting in heaven, but it by no means ensured it.

Televangelism itself took off in 1950s America. Meanwhile, in Britain, newly instated commercial television began to churn out utopian pictures of the ideal family – mother deliriously looking after the children with the latest wonder product and father returning home each evening, tired after his heroic quest at the office. One particularly telling television advertisement from the 1950s promises salvation through a soap called Puritan. 'It takes Puritan and elbow grease,' the housewife declares.

The 1950s was the decade in which the here and now became increasingly important. The world had already born witness to the carnage of Hiroshima, decimated one summer's day in 1945 by the first atom bomb. According to psychiatrist Robert Jay Lifton, 'Hiroshima victims could be said to have experienced a genuine confusion between the state of death and that of life.'[5] Arthur Koestler (1905–1983), guru of the human condition, claimed that 'From now onward, mankind has to live with the idea of its death as a species . . . It would perhaps not be a bad idea if we all kept a second calendar, at least in our minds, starting with the year when the new Star of Bethlehem rose over Hiroshima.'[6] Then, on January 30, 1950, the go-ahead was given for the development of the H-bomb. Throughout the decade, the West was constantly reminded, with H-bomb tests and public debates, that it was dealing with the concrete possibility of Armageddon. In 1956, America's first airborne hydrogen bomb explosion took place in the northern Pacific. Lifton tells how a science writer described 'this rising supersun' as 'the symbol of the dawn of a new era in which any sizable war had become impossible'. The 'great iridescent cloud and its mushroom top' would, apparently, 'continue shielding us everywhere, until the time comes, as come it must, when mankind will be able to beat atomic swords into ploughshares, harnessing the vast power of the hydrogen in the world's oceans to bring an era of prosperity such as the world has never even dared dream about'.[7]

Even the H-bomb was a prophet of prosperity. Increasingly, however, people sought instant heaven in the miracle of money – whether through premium bonds, bingo, TV quiz shows or prosperity theology. TV dinners were invented, credit consumerism took off, and the words 'In God We Trust' were stamped on America's coinage.

The 1950s also gave birth to the Organization Man, bred to belong to the workplace and examined by William H. Whyte in his 1956 book of the same name. And there was always the spectre of George Orwell's *1984*. In 1952, Norman Vincent Peale's *The Power of Positive Thinking* was published, shooting rapidly up the bestseller lists. The self was capable of anything said Rev Peale. All you had to do was set your sights on money and success, and the world would be yours: '. . . by channelling spiritual power through your thoughts, you can rise above obstacles which ordinarily might defeat you . . . you will become a more popular, esteemed, well-liked individual.'[8] It was heady stuff, putting heaven within the grasp of everyone.

Catherine Ponder, 'the Norman Vincent Peale among lady ministers'[9] joined the nondenominational California-based Unity ministry in 1956 and began to churn out books in praise and pursuit of prosperity. Among them is the 'Millionaires of the Bible' series which reveals the 'prosperity secrets' of Moses, Joshua and Jesus. Her ministry now reaches throughout the United States and to forty-seven other countries. All you have to do is to 'Open Your Mind to Receive', she says.[10]

The year after Rev Peale's bestseller appeared, Victor Paul Wierwille founded The Way, a nondenominational Christian organization selling itself under the banner Christians Should Be Prosperous. The Way teaches members that they can be winners in all areas of their lives. In the 1980s the movement became known by detractors as 'the yuppie cult'. Every Way recruit is encouraged to go through a course known as the Power For Abundant Living which, according to one of the group's leaflets, 'Increases Prosperity, disciplines the mind by believing, Maintains health, Establishes and maintains a positive attitude'.[11] The final lesson in the course is speaking in tongues.

Those fully committed to the movement become members of The Way Corps after attending a training programme which is, apparently, 'financially an opportunity for the family of the corps participant. If the family does not maintain at least the suggested level of corps donations the participant should seek support for the corps program from additional sponsors'.[12] Members of The Way Corps are encouraged to record how they spend every minute of the day on Redeemed Time Analysis forms containing one column entitled 'How I spend my time' and another, 'How I can improve'.

Based in Ohio, the group has branches and 'twigs', as they are called, throughout the world including in Zaire, Argentina, Australia, New Zealand, Germany, Venezuela and Scotland. The Way believe 'the deliverance of the Book of Acts is happening NOW'.[13] In the 1980s the message of a forthcoming, prosperous heaven on earth helped to make it 'the fastest growing cult in America'.[14] 'I'd rather be a cult than a denomination,' retorted one of the movement's leaders.[15]

In a handbook for ambassadors of The Way, members are advised to 'work Dale Carnegie's book *How to Win Friends and Influence People*, applying the principles to witnessing'. Dale Carnegie's book, written in 1938, has sold more than fifteen million copies. Its message, quite simply, is that of its title. 'This book can easily be worth its weight in gold to you,' its promotional blurb promises.

The Way is supervised by the Bless Patrol, and a kit list issued to students entering The Way's training college at Emporia, Kansas, included 'rifle or shotgun (handgun also an asset)' and 'military dress uniform'. In the late 1970s members of The Way received weapons training from the Kansas National Guard. Survivalism often goes hand in hand with the prosperity ethic.

In 1953, the same year The Way was founded, Fuller Brush salesman turned evangelist Billy Graham stormed England and Scotland, drawing audiences in excess of two million. 'I am selling the greatest product in the world,' he declared. Science fiction writer L. Ron Hubbard founded his Church of Scientology, a belief system created from a blend of therapy and strange forces from far-flung planets. 'If a man really wanted to make a million dollars the best way to do it would be to start a religion,' he said.[16] Sure enough, Hubbard soon became a millionaire while many of his followers became penniless paying for 'auditing' sessions to clear themselves of their mental blocks. Others worked full time for the church receiving little pay, and feeling under constant threat of being declared 'Suppressive Persons' if they voiced complaint or left the movement.

Two books which appeared in 1957 – Douglas MacGregor's *Human Side of Enterprise* and Ayn Rand's novel *Atlas Shrugged* – both dealt with the survival of the self. The former, taking the humanistic approach, emphasizes the importance of the self being given room to develop at work, and the latter champions the cause of 'self'ishness. For Ayn Rand, life was a progress towards excellence, which could be measured by the amount of money each individual made. Some supporters set up an Ayn Rand Institute, relieved to have discovered a personal success ethic.

In north America, the 1950s ended to the tune of Harvard mathematics professor Tom Lehrer singing 'a carol to all we most deeply and sincerely believe in – money'. Meanwhile, many people were beginning to wonder quite what they would do with the leisure money would buy them. Indeed, a 1950s poll of an American union showed that although its members thought work was boring, it was less boring than doing nothing. The heaven they were being offered was simply one where nothing ever happened. H.G. Wells had provided a solution to the problem in his 1901 utopian novel *The First Men in the Moon*. There, workers were drugged into a state of coma whenever their duties were not required.

Walt Disney (1901–66) stepped into the breach in 1955, creating Disneyland, a fantasy world 'dedicated to the ideals, the dreams, and the hard facts that have created America . . . with the hope that it will be a source of joy and inspiration to all the world'.[17] Each year, Disney's theme parks provide millions of visitors with a taste of a utopian fantasy land. The thousands of staff at Disneyland have to enter that dream, become citizens of utopia: 'You can dream, create, design and build the most wonderful place in the world . . . but it takes people to make the dream a reality,' says a staff brochure. While emphasizing the importance of people in the dream, the Disney empire developed a type of automaton which is almost more real than the original, using a technique called audioanimatronics. According to Umberto Eco, writing of Disneyland, 'In addition to enjoying a perfect imitation, one takes pleasure in the persuasion that the imitation has reached its apogee and that now the reality will always be inferior.'[18]

Disney went further. In the mid-1960s he dreamt up EPCOT – the Experimental Prototype Community of Tomorrow. When he first broke the news of EPCOT to the press, a reporter described Disney as resembling a 'born-again Christian at a revival meeting'.[19] EPCOT, said Disney, would be 'like the city of tomorrow ought to be, a city that caters to the people as a service function . . . It will be a planned, controlled community; a showcase for American industry and research, schools, cultural and educational opportunities. In EPCOT there will be no slum areas because we won't let them develop. There will be no landowners and therefore no voting control. People will rent houses instead of buying them, and at modest rentals. There will be no retirees, because everyone will be employed according to their ability. One of our requirements is that the people who live in EPCOT must help keep it alive'.[20] Disney's dream was not to materialize, however. EPCOT opened in 1982 as 'a cluster of space-age pavilions, each representing a resource deemed vital to the future of mankind (imagination is allocated its own pavilion) . . . and a collection of national pavilions'. Apparently, 'the cultural stereotyping is predictable . . . The German pavilion boasts a beerhall . . . The United Kingdom, which shows no visible content of anywhere other than England, is the quaint, picture postcard town of a bygone age that never was'.[21]

At the other extreme to Disney's EPCOT vision, there is the nightmare millionaire's holiday camp depicted in the 1973 film *Westworld* where visitors are turned upon by robots. The fear of the disappearance of the real and authentic found expression in the revolt against the workplace. In his *The Greening of America*, which appeared at the end of the 1960s, Charles Reich claims that organizational demands had 'substituted something artificial for something real'.[22] The problem was that 'for most Americans, work is mindless, exhausting, boring, servile and hateful, something to be endured while "life" is confined to "time off"'.[23] But the theme parks were even confining 'time off' to mechanization and the unauthentic.

Reich describes the 'new generation' as seeing industrialized work as 'one of the chief means by which the minds and feelings of people are dominated in the Corporate State. It is work, unrelenting, driven, consuming, that comes between the professor and his students, the lawyer and his family, the bank employee and the beauty of nature. Consciousness III [the name Reich gives to the new, transformed way of life he sees arising] regards freedom from such work, making possible the development of an individual's true potential as a human being, to be among the greatest and most vital forms of liberation'.[24] Underlying Consciousness III is 'an exalted vision of man . . . not part of a machine, not a robot . . . living as fully as he can, using to the full his unique gift, perhaps unique in the universe of conscious life'.[25]

In the 1960s, numerous members of the counter-culture sought freedom from the capitalistic, 'self'-destroying system in communes – several of which had names such as Paradise or Unity. Most attempted to establish a new work ethic – one which was 'not to be confused with the "Protestant work ethic" in which work is regarded as an onerous burden which must be borne in the name of heavenly rewards, social good, or, more materialistically, deferred benefits', insisted one communard but 'one in which work is valued for itself, indeed becomes a form of leisure'.[26] Many attempted to reassess the meaning of value, measuring it not in terms of money but in terms of the energy needed to accomplish a task.

These new approaches and attitudes to work were largely confined to the counter-culture. But by the 1980s, many of those who had dropped out to 'find' themselves in the 1960s suddenly found themselves with mortgages and families. They might well still have believed 'Love is all you need', but now many found it necessary to learn to love a rich outer as well as inner life. And having already got the hang of loving themselves – sometimes by standing naked in front of a mirror and intoning 'I love you' – many had come to realize they deserved nothing but the best. Various gurus began smoothing over the transition for them, enabling them to square their designer lifestyles with spiritual enlightenment.

'Pleasure is the subjective experience of the love of God,'[27] taught New Age leader Sondra Ray at a self-religion seminar held in the mid-1980s. At Ray's Loving Relationships Training, trainees listened to tapes about money, rehearsed prosperity affirmations and were taught that 'Enlightenment is the certain knowledge of the absolute truth: thought is creative'.[28] According to one trainee, 'The implication was that if you wrote long enough prosperity affirmations, you would get rich'.[29]

'The materially poor can never become spiritual,' said Bhagwan Shree Rajneesh – he of the twenty-seven Rolls Royces – adding, 'Capitalism is not an ideology, it is not imposed on the society, it is a natural growth. Capitalism simply gives you the freedom to be yourself, that's why I support it.'[30] The mainstream church was meanwhile seen to regard business and industry as 'mucky and squalid'.[31]

According to futurologist Christine MacNulty, who forecasts social trends, former Prime Minister Margaret Thatcher appealed to a new social group known as the 'meta inner directed' who view capitalism as a means for individual growth. Margaret Thatcher's reign was inaugurated in May 1979, just in time to welcome in the 1980s. Across the Atlantic, Ronald Reagan was helped into his presidential seat in 1980 by the Moral Majority, and the two reigned side by side to the accompaniment of the gospel of prosperity throughout the decade.

In the 1980s, then, heaven came through dropping in to the

mainstream rather than dropping out. No longer was it a question of either/or. This was the era, as so many New Age leaders put it, of both/and. 'Take a Holiday For The Rest of Your Life' urged the brochure for a success seminar founded in 1980, continuing, 'We're told that we can't have our cake and eat it too. Ha! Why not buy two cakes, eat one and keep the other?'[32]

Whereas for the televangelists loving God makes you rich, for proponents of the New Age loving your self makes you rich. But the self-religion gurus were not entirely divorced from the Christian evangelists. After the televangelism scandal, Robert Schuller, inheritor of Norman Vincent Peale's mantle, was left leading the spiritual TV ratings. With its blend of positive thinking and spirituality, his weekly television programme *The Hour of Power* continues to attract more than one-and-a-half million viewers in the United States and is also shown on satellite television throughout Europe. In addition, Billy Graham's gospel has certain affinities with that of Werner Erhard – above all, the profound sense of 'self'-responsibility. It seems that 'the Billy Graham theory of morality [is] that the victim is responsible for the sins visited on him . . . Blacks are to blame for racism, the North Vietnamese brought on the destruction of their country . . . it all flows from the doctrine that sinners created Hell'.[33] Erhard's remark, frequently cited by his detractors, that the Vietnamese babies created the napalm that fell on their heads can be seen to belong to a tradition.

The self-religions focused on enabling the individual to find their true 'self' so that they could become enlightened members of the capitalist mainstream, and while enjoying all its benefits, help to transform it. By taking their inner paradise into the office, so it was reasoned, big business itself would become the engine room of utopia.

With the introduction of self-religions to the workplace in the form of management trainings, the office itself became an arena for enlightenment. Heaven on earth was found not through money, but through applying the principles of the self-religions to work. As with the Protestant work ethic, money was often a by-product. But in the New Age, money is not a cause for guilt; instead it is to be enjoyed as a manifestation of abundance.

Salesmanship, positive thinking and spirituality all went into the 'self-religions', with the added input of philosophy and Eastern mysticism. Disciples learnt that they were the seat of ultimate power, that they created their own reality. Converts broke through the barriers of the mind to a utopian state where self ruled supreme.

Two of the most renowned self-religion gurus – Americans Werner Erhard and John Hanley – were both salesmen before turning their skills to enlightenment: Erhard dealt in used cars and encyclopaedias, and Hanley in toilet cleaning services. Part of Erhard and Hanley's novitiate was spent at William Penn Patrick's Leadership Dynamics Institute and Alexander Everett's Mind Dynamics. Both organizations, which folded in 1973, ran high-intensity courses using sometimes bizarre techniques to hone the salesmanship of trainees.

In 1971, Erhard, born Jack Rosenberg in 1935, experienced enlightenment when sitting in his car by San Francisco's Golden Bridge: 'I experienced Self *as* Self in a direct and unmediated way. I didn't just experience Self; I became Self . . . It was an unmistakable recognition that I was, am, and always will be the source of my experience . . . I was whole and complete as I was, and now I could accept the whole truth about myself. For I was its source. I found enlightenment, truth, true self all at once. I had reached the end. It was all over for Werner Erhard.'[34] That same year, Erhard held his first course – Erhard Seminars Training, known as est, in California. Three years later, John Hanley founded Lifespring.

The early 1980s were busy years for the self-religion gurus. Est, which had attracted a good deal of criticism for its controversial methods of spreading enlightenment, was transformed into the Forum, Transformational Technologies was founded and Programmes Ltd took off.

Less confrontational than est, the Forum offers 'a breakthrough for people – into a new dimension of possibility unavailable in our common practice, common knowledge or common sense . . . The Forum promises to produce an extraordinary advantage in your personal effectiveness and a decisive edge in your ability to achieve'.[35] Several other courses and seminars including Excellence, Accomplishment and High Performance were introduced. Not surprisingly, the Forum attracted people interested in getting on in life and some Business Forums – directed specifically at the commercial world – were held.

Transformational Technologies, on the other hand, was a means of introducing breakthrough and transformation to the corporate world by franchising the Erhard technology to management consultants. According to one enthusiastic TT franchise, 'In est people sat around and thought about themselves. With [TT] they sit around and think about the company. And you can even go to the bath-room'.[36]

Companies which have used Erhard's technology include NASA, Rover, and Procter & Gamble. It was, apparently, an Erhard acolyte who thought up merchant bank Shearson Lehmann's slogan 'Com-mitment, Integrity, Vision'. In Britain, half the staff of shipping Company Cunard Ellerman have experienced Erhard trainings. Some say their new-found ability to create reality enabled them to save the company more than £1 million. Others say the 'saving' was achieved simply by selling off rolling stock and that Erhard's trainings split the company into converts and sceptics.

In Britain, est-graduate Robert d'Aubigny, born Fuller, founded the now-disbanded Exegesis. It was, he said, 'probably one of the only live religions in a sense . . . but it's not a religion because it's alive'.[37] The seminar was, he claimed, about 'creating an environ-ment in which an individual can experience for herself or himself the truth of his existence . . . once experienced, there is a total transformation in the process of living'.[38] Many Exegesis graduates came to look on the blue-eyed, velvet-voiced d'Aubigny as a guru: 'I didn't mind what I did so long as it was with Robert,' said one.[39]

An Exegesis trainer hints at what it takes to experience total transformation: 'After you've been humiliated enough, and after you've bled enough, after the walls are covered with your blood you'll say "this must be the one: anything that hurts as much has got to be the truth".'[40]

In 1981 Programmes Ltd, a telephone sales company informed by d'Aubigny's philosophy and staffed at first by Exegesis graduates, was founded. The company offered a complete lifestyle, both dur-ing and outside working hours and, according to one Programmes employee, its intention was 'to transform business in this country as much as possible'.[41] Indeed, the company was founded under the slogan 'The business of transformation and the transformation of business'.[42]

'In the Exegesis seminar, you end up having a religious experience of consciousness – that attracted me to working in Programmes,' said a former employee. 'It was a bit like joining a monastic order.'[43]

D'Aubigny taught that ' . . . despair, jealousy, grief, fear, anger – all of these are negative things, arise from an experience of feeling separate – wars, poverty, all of these conditions arise out of that one simple superstitious idea that we're a speck of protoplasm that's separate from the rest of the milieu'.[44] By putting enlightenment on the production line, by discounting history and society and instating an indigenous company culture, the sense of unity was regained.

D'Aubigny's philosophy, like that of Erhard, seeks to induce a profound sense of self-responsibility into apprentices, to the extent that they begin to believe in their own magical powers. Failure indicates a lack of enlightenment. If a telephone line is engaged it is because the caller is 'not in'. If an employee's bus breaks down on the way to work, it is the employee's responsibility. 'Throughout all my time at Programmes I wasn't a minute late,' said one former employee.[45]

Programmes Ltd received numerous accolades – and most of the company's clients were thrilled with the results it achieved for them. So Programmes started taking its philosophy out into the business world in the form of management trainings – to companies including British Telecom, Clydesdale Bank and airline company British Midland.

As well as organizations such as Erhard's empire and Programmes, the 'enlightenment' movement has spawned hundreds of individual management consultants who are now selling success through transformation to the business world. In 1982, a group of New Age enthusiasts founded the Business Network – sometimes referred to as 'Angels in Pinstripes'. Its aim was 'to act as a forum and discussion point for all those who feel that business should be nourishing not only to the wallet, but also to the mind, the emotions, body and the spirit'.[46]

The consultants within the Network have, between them, spread their gospel at firms including Olivetti, Courtaulds, Cathay Pacific, Esso and British Gas. 'We offer a fitness course of the spiritual,' says Network co-founder Francis Kinsman. In 1984, members of the Network organized a seminar on the future of business, drawing representatives from American Express, Shell, BP, Whitbread, Ford and British Rail. When planning the seminar, Network members attuned themselves to the task in hand assisted by a crystal, candle and paying-in book. One of the aims of the seminar was to oversee the shift from 'Organization Man to Human Organizations'.

A Network sub-group, Financial Initiative, aimed to 'restore the spiritual dimension to financial transactions',[47] by running seminars which helped members and other interested entrepreneurs to let go of their 'blocks' about making money, enabling them to redefine it as 'a means of exchange and a store of love'. Then, it was hoped, they could 'conduct their lives in such a way that the creation of wealth becomes as natural and intrinsic a function for them as their own heartbeat'.[48]

In America, hundreds of companies – including General Motors and General Electric – have taken part in 'organizational transformation' and the movement has also taken off throughout Europe, particularly in Sweden and Holland.

Londoner Ben Bartle claims to have created the term 'prosperity consultant' in the early 1980s. Formerly a management consultant, he describes his new line of work as a combination of personal growth, prosperity and business. 'Prosperity is about having a feeling, a sense of abundance,' he says, adding that one of his clients increased her income sevenfold within six months of her first consultation.

As well as counselling individuals, Bartle holds seminars called Creating Your Dreams. 'Over the years I have come to the firm belief that I can create anything,' he says. 'I think it's possible we will get to a time when money doesn't exist. But for now we should accept the money system and enjoy it.' Through the use of a variety of manifestation techniques such as creative visualization and affirmations, he aims 'to prevent clients from sabotaging themselves'. 'I am lovable' is one of his preferred affirmations.[49] Australian-based prosperity lecturer Lionel Fifield also advises clients to practise affirmations. 'Abundant money, big financial surprises and rich appropriate gifts now come to me under grace in perfect ways for my personal use and I use them joyfully and wisely' is one he recommends. And another: 'I am the result of my thinking. My thinking makes me rich, well and happy now.'[50]

'My aim is to make all IBM's managers see themselves as God,' said one consultant in the mid-1980s.[51] The same consultant is convinced the workplace of the 1990s will become 'an arena for people to be empowered'. According to another management consultant, Roger Evans, of Creative Learning Consultants, courses like his are going to be a growth area in the 1990s: 'The hard management side of the 1990s is how to empower PEOPLE. Organizations will be a basis for people to be empowered.'

In October 1990, the Findhorn Foundation, an international spiritual community based in a remote part of Scotland, held a week-long course on Intuitive Leadership: Inner Listening for Outer Action.

Interest was such that 100 people had to be turned away, while the 250 who did attend the seminar included managers from top companies throughout Europe. The seminar focused on the need for a 'deeper spiritual quality to be drawn forth from people within an organization'.

Another conference held in the first year of the 1990s was called Joining Forces: Working with Spirituality in Organizations. A joint venture between the Centre for the Study of Management Learning, University of Lancaster and Transform, a management consultancy rooted in the teachings of former Theosophist Rudolf Steiner (1861–1925), one of the workshops ran under the title 'Management: What! A *Spiritual* Foundation?!!'

Whether the workplace will indeed become a training ground for a self-enlightened heaven on earth, or whether most employees will continue to see the office simply as a necessary evil *en route* to earning utopia is still unclear.

Timothy Leary believes that in the future, work will take place in Virtual Reality, a hi-tec heaven currently being developed in California's Silicon Valley. While sunning herself on some southern beach, the twenty-first-century businesswoman will step into the world of work through a three-dimensional computer-based reality, discuss a problem with colleagues, then turn off the computer and listen to the waves lapping on the shore.

Some New Age enthusiasts are attempting to get rid of money altogether and instead follow a barter system; others are predicting the end of materialism. But courses in money-making continue to flourish. Several seminars teach trainees to create Treasure Maps by cutting pictures of what they desire out of glossy magazines and pasting them down on pieces of card. Their utopias are created with scissors and sticky gum.

SEVEN | LIVING GODS

The bus clatters through the barren landscape, radio blaring, cramped passengers overflowing their seats and spreading into the aisles. It is the last lap in a journey which leads to Prasanthi Nilayam, the Abode of Highest Peace – the birthplace, and home, of God. Over the years, while some had been seeking out the god of money, others had sought – and claimed to find – the divine in human form.

As far as the eye can see, the land is relieved only by awkward volcanic protuberances rising eerily from the featureless plains. Difficult though it is to believe anything can lie at the back of this beyond, a brochure from Bangalore promises that 'this Godman turned the remote village of Puttaparthi into a world where thousands of people throng every day to have a glimpse of Him; seeking his advice, help and blessings . . .' In 1990, more than half a million devotees turned up for his sixty-fifth birthday celebrations.

The trail to Puttaparthi had been laid all over South India: in hotels, restaurants, on the streets, Sai Baba's name or picture would materialize, as if from nowhere. Later, his followers would say it was a sign.

Sai Baba was born Sathyanarayana Raju in November 1926, the year Sri Aurobindo, the Indian guru followed by Mike Murphy of Esalen, saw a beam of light flash from the heavens and strike earth in the region of Puttaparthi. He is, say his millions of followers, an avatar – an incarnation of God – who has taken on the form of man to help them through the Kali Yuga, the age of wickedness, into an era of everlasting peace and bliss.

The story of Sai Baba's childhood seems to meet with traditional

Indian expectations: a snake – the sign of Shiva – was found curled up in bed beside him; he was fond – like Krishna – of playing pranks; he confounded his teachers and performed numerous miracles. But despite these oddities, Sathyanarayana seemed a fairly standard child, materializing sweets for his schoolfriends and acting in plays based on the stories of the Hindu gods. Then, at the age of thirteen, he was transformed, collapsing first into a fit and then losing consciousness for several hours. When the boy came round he was a different being; his personality had changed entirely and, as well as suffering violent mood swings, he would launch into protracted bouts of religious teaching. Some have tried to explain such occurrences by describing them as epileptic fits; others refer to them as attacks of divine madness.

Sathyanarayana's family was convinced he had become possessed by evil demons and attempted to have him exorcized. Eventually, he announced that he had become Sai Baba, an Indo-Muslim saint from Shirdi in Maharashtra who had died twenty-two years earlier. His parents found little comfort in this latest claim and took him to a devotee of Sai Baba of Shirdi who lived in a neighbouring village. Sceptical at first, the man was eventually persuaded to put aside his doubts when Sathyanarayana materialized endless supplies of *vibhuti*, or sacred ash. Later, when someone demanded further proof, the boy threw handfuls of jasmine flowers into the air; when they landed, they spelt out SAI BABA.

The air in the bus is thick with the sickly scent of jasmine. The journey seems interminable. At length, nearing Puttaparthi, the landscape mellows, the rocks give way to grass and there, on a hillside, lies the glittering white wedding cake – Sai Baba University. Below it nestle more schools and colleges and, enclosed by a high white wall, the ashram itself.

Outside the barricade, a jungle of Westernized shops spills into the road, their owners jostling to attract the new shipment of business. But behind the walls, calm descends, disturbed only by the noise of digging machines up by the dormitories – Sai Baba's following is ever on the increase: almost 100 countries were represented at his 1990 world conference and in Britain alone there are more than 100 Sai Baba study groups. Solemn devotees pace up and down the level walkways beside the long, low administrative buildings. Behind them, and in stark contrast, lies the sugar-pink temple – where God lives in an upper room.

The ashram staff, like extras from Dr Kildare in their immaculate white jackets and trousers, quietly enforce the many rules: no speaking between unmarried men and women, no smoking, respectable clothing, no following of Baba substitutes . . . Everywhere, there are Westerners – from Australia, Germany, Italy, Hong Kong, New Zealand, the United States, United Kingdom. A picture of Sai Baba hangs in the registration office, beneath it are inscribed the words: 'Though I am omnipotent and found everywhere, you can find me installed wherever my glory is sung.'

It wasn't until 1963 that Sai Baba announced he was God incarnate, an avatar of the supreme deity – like Christ or Krishna, say his followers. By then, he had already attracted thousands of devotees, the majority Hindus. Later, as more and more Westerners joined his movement, he became known as the Universal God.

Sai Baba teaches that there is only one caste – the caste of humanity; there is only one language – the language of the heart; there is only one God – who is omnipresent; and there is only one religion – the religion of love. According to British devotee Lucas Ralli, 'To me you can find God in any form because God is the totality. Sai Baba never tells anyone to change their religion. Buddha, Christ, Muhammad and Sai Baba – all are the One.'[1]

Baba's miracles – and he is the first to admit this – are the initial attraction for many of his followers. The tales are endless – of healings, of portraits that drip honey, and of materializations. At one time he regularly used to vomit up Shiva lingams – large phallic-shaped rocks – and Lucas Ralli tells how he and his wife saw him produce food out of thin air for twenty-five of his devotees. One of the most unusual materializations to date is a small wooden cross with a figure of Jesus nailed to it. The cross is, allegedly, made from the same material as the cross of Christ's crucifixion. But experts are sceptical of its authenticity: it has never been tested adequately by qualified scientists and Jesus is shown with the nails piercing his palms rather than – following the practice of New Testament days – his wrists. Besides, say the doubters, if Sai Baba can materialize objects so easily, why doesn't he materialize some money for the thousands upon thousands of India's poor? 'So why didn't Jesus feed the five thousand on a more regular basis?' counter Sai Baba's devotees.

Despite the controversies, Baba's disciples continue to be delighted by his miracles but it is, they say, his capacity for infinite love that wins them over. A German woman reverently displays a ring engraved with her initial which Baba materialized on her birthday – without having been told her name: 'He is God, he is another Jesus Christ, helping mankind through the Kali Yuga', she says. The woman, a journalist, had come to the Abode of Highest Peace to write about Sai Baba. Now, she never wants to leave.

A lively twenty-two-year-old Londoner tells how her father was brought back to life by Baba after a heart attack. 'He is love, he is God, he is everything,' she says. She and her sister hope to stay at the ashram for a year or so. They spend their days studying Sai Baba's teachings along with those of other religious leaders, attending study groups and prayer meetings – and gossiping. The atmosphere inside the dormitory is that of a girls' boarding school – one whose inmates are swooning gracefully over their latest film idol. The walls are hung with pictures of Sai Baba, his books lie scattered on the floor – *Words of Jesus and Sai Baba* is one of the titles – and the sisters huddle together with friends from the nearby Sai Baba university, comparing notes, munching biscuits and talking always of their *swami*. Although there is a certain amount of rivalry for Sai Baba's affections, he has, they say, taught them the meaning of endless love.

'There is only one Yoga discipline that matters,' Sai Baba has said. '– not the Hatha Yoga of the conditioned body, or the Raja Yoga of the orderly mind, but the Prem Yoga – Prem meaning the highest aspect of love, loving the Divine Self, the God Self.'[2]

Today's Sai Baba devotees are not wide-eyed and love-beaded hippies, nor disillusioned materialists: the sisters still enjoy wearing beautiful clothes and can reel off the names of the best hotels and shops in Bangalore. Introduced to Sai Baba by an aunt, they are not rebelling against their family – they hadn't even wanted to come here, the last thing they were looking for was a spiritual guide. But during their first meeting with Sai Baba, they realized they were in the presence – and, more than that, actually talking to – God.

As dusk settles, the ashram shops – all with their separate entrances for men and women – are in full swing. An English family gathers round the Milky Way ice-cream parlour, a German disciple doggedly circles a monument to the world religions, chanting under her breath. Other women, draped in becoming robes and scarves, loiter beneath the trees. Paradise? Or a spiritual holiday camp?

That day, Sai Baba had left Prasanthi Nilayam for his summer home at Whitefields, called there by an Indian government official who sought his advice on state affairs. 'I miss him so much. When is he coming back?' an Australian woman wails. Antonio Craxi, brother of the former Italian Prime Minister, is one of Baba's followers and his children attended the Sai Baba school.

The next morning, hundreds of devotees pile on to luxury coaches – not for them the rickety local service – to follow their saviour to Whitefields, a stone's throw from Bangalore. Before leaving the ashram, sachets of sacred ash, materialized by Sai Baba, are handed out to followers. Laboratory analysis has shown the *vibhuti* to be nothing more than the ash from burnt rice. But that doesn't phase Sai Baba's followers – God, after all, works in mysterious ways.

The Whitefields courtyard is awash with disciples, gathered there for a meeting, or darshan, with Baba. His staff allot seating space with scrupulous even-handedness. Cohorts from various different countries sit together, spiritual scouts in their Baba-emblazoned neckerchiefs. Grouped at the front are the physically handicapped, including several wheelchair-bound Western children brought here by their mothers. In the centre stands a velvet-covered throne, on its arm a single rose placed on a white napkin. Then, as excitement mounts, the chanting and singing starts and lollipops are thrown to the waiting masses.

'There is a tremendous energy level in his presence,' says Lucas Ralli. 'I feel totally different when I am near him. Even in the bright sunlight I can see his aura. When you are in his presence it is an experience very difficult to describe. You have probably been waiting desperately for an interview, but when you get into the interview room your mind goes blank. You forget everything. You may have ten questions to ask him, and after he has spoken to you for a few minutes, you will find the questions are all answered.'

Two years after Lucas Ralli was first drawn to Sai Baba, something happened. 'It was on my second visit and at first he was all smiles. Then, suddenly, he totally ignored me – it's known as being "put in the repair shop". My wife told me to sit down until I received a message, and then I got it – just one word . . . surrender. Ten years later, I have still failed to surrender totally. If I had, I would be a better person . . . In the West, it is very difficult to surrender everything to God. From my limited experience, surrender is the best way to inner living, to living in tune with the infinite and finding peace of mind.'

Eventually, way across the courtyard, the tiny figure of Sai Baba emerges from beneath an archway. Clad in a long saffron robe, his head framed with a top-heavy halo of thick dark hair, he approaches the waiting crowd, sometimes raising a hand to circle it in time with the chanting, sometimes pausing to gaze about him. Several women begin silently to weep.

Slowly – painfully slowly – he draws nearer, eventually reaching the waiting crowds. Some attempt to surge forward, an ocean of waving hands seeking to touch his robe, his feet, his sandals. But the hovering white-coats are there to hold them back and gather in the envelopes containing messages of love, pleas for healing, questions on everyday problems and life-and-death matters. Twice, Sai Baba pauses to place a hand on kneeling disciples who sob uncontrollably. His head barely moves but, half-smiling, his eyes flicker from side to side, occasionally pausing to unearth some hidden core with the briefest glance.

Whatever the truth behind his claims to divinity, Sai Baba can certainly hold a crowd. Some say he has used the power to manipulate his followers. Others say that whatever he does is just fine; it is a method of testing the devotee. And besides, who are we to judge God? Now and again devotees might become disillusioned; often, they become increasingly determined to follow God's – Sai Baba's – guidance along the route to higher consciousness. 'Being near him is like being in heaven,' says a young Australian.

Sai Baba stands out among today's Eastern gurus as the only one to have attracted a wide Western following without leaving the East, and indeed barely moving from his homeland. Western interest in the East had been awakened in the nineteenth century, in part by the teachings of the Theosophical Society and the appearance of Swami Vivekenanda, the prophet of Vedanta at the World Parliament of Religions in Chicago in 1893. Vivekenanda wanted to spread a universal spirituality, to make 'a European society with India's religion'.[3] But it wasn't until the late 1960s that the Eastern masters made a concerted Westward push. The timing was perfect. 'The psychedelic at-one-ment had been a chemical preview of what could be attained forever with Yoga,' said one commentator of the times. 'Yoga was beyond LSD.'[4]

Several of the incoming gurus preached a 'No Drugs, No Sex' gospel, among them Maharaj-ji, 'the boy guru', who inherited the spiritual mantle of his father in 1966 when he was just eight years old. Maharaj-ji Senior had staunchly avoided gurus in his own youth, preferring the teachings of the social reform-cum-vigilante movement the Arya Samaj (Society of the Noble) with whom the Theosophists had teamed up for several years towards the end of the nineteenth century and who aimed to return Hinduism to its roots. In time, however, Maharaj-ji Senior encountered a path to bliss through a guru and eventually formed the Divine Light Mission to spread his route to enlightenment.

Maharaj-ji Junior made his first world tour when he was fourteen, establishing centres throughout Europe and the United States. 'I can show you God,' he said, 'because I have realized him!'[5] The offer, together with his pledge to establish world peace within a generation, attracted thousands of followers worldwide. Their youthful leader – God incarnate as they proclaimed him – promised them 'Utopia in action. The kingdom of heaven established on earth'. Utopia would be ushered in at 'Millennium '73', a massive celebration at the Houston Astrodome. In that same year, Maharaj-ji announced, New York would be destroyed by an earthquake. Despite being well clear of the earthquake site, the Texas event turned out to be less popular than planned, although it still attracted 20,000 followers.

While urging his devotees to give up drugs and sex, the young Guru Maharaj-ji appealed to 1960s flower power, turning up in London in a Rolls Royce plastered beyond recognition with a thick carpet of blossoms. Before long, he began to acquire a taste for a jet-setting Western lifestyle, including aeroplanes, fast cars and an American wife. His mother was far from happy, and many Indians switched their allegiances to her and another of her sons. Outraged, Maharaj-ji took her to court where, during the trial, the Divine Light Mission attempted to deny their leader had ever been God incarnate. The family in-fighting created an atmosphere far from utopian. One visitor to the movement's Hardwar ashram described it as 'somewhere between a heaven and a prison camp'.

But before long Maharaj-ji was back in the driving seat, touring the world in his jet and initiating more followers into the 'Knowledge', his four-fold route to enlightenment which includes looping the tongue down the throat to taste the divine nectar and experiencing the vibration of the Holy Name. In the early 1980s, his movement became known as Elan Vital, and still has thousands of members.

Rajneesh made no bones about the frequency with which he changed his name and status. Though adopting the title Bhagwan

(Lord or Blessed One) in 1971, he declared, 'Calling myself Bhagwan is just a device, I can drop it at any moment . . . If a few of my sannyasins [devotees] start blooming, I will stop calling myself Bhagwan; the device will have worked.'[6]

Born in Madhya Pradesh, central India, in 1931, the son of a cloth merchant, Rajneesh attained enlightenment aged twenty-one. By the end of the 1960s, he had left his post as Professor of Philosophy at the University of Jabalpur and had begun to conduct meditation camps, focusing on a cathartic technique known as dynamic meditation. Later, he was to announce that 'therapy plus meditation is equal to religion'.[7]

In 1970, Rajneesh began to initiate his growing number of followers into 'Neo-Sannyas', or discipleship. Before long, thousands of Westerners began flocking to his ashram at Poona, near Bombay. 'It is impossible to find a man who is not carrying a dream of utopia,' said their master, '. . . of a world which is better, more human, more beautiful, more loving; a world without conflicts, wars, discriminations, a world sensitive, compassionate, understanding. Every human being carries in some corner of his consciousness the dream.'[8]

The ashram provided the dream in action – offering hope and meaning to the well-heeled and beautiful from all corners of the world through a synthesis of Western psychology, Eastern mysticism and contempt for authority. Priests, personalities and politicians were to be done away with. 'He tried to bring a synthesis to the modern Western spiritual seeker and India, to make everything as clear as possible to as many as possible and as easily as possible,' says a sannyasin, or follower. 'Finding him was like finding paradise.'[9]

Dressed in flowing robes, Rajneesh's sannyasins confronted their deepest hopes and fears, laughed and cried while meditating, sat dreamily by the ashram's beautiful fountains, watched the water play, danced, screamed to attain a blissfully mindless state aptly called 'No Mind', listened to the gentle strumming of guitars, and adored their master.

Much of Bhagwan's teaching was in line with that of the Human Potential Movement: 'Osho is saying be whole, be total, be all you can be,' says a sannyasin. 'It was very appealing to find someone who understood the Western psyche as well as he did. Esalen's teachings were beginning to seem dry. I had tried Arica, I had been looking for a master . . . When I saw Osho there was an immediate knowing in me that what I was looking for he had. It was a deep feeling of stillness. Now I had to find how to discover that within myself. Knowing him, the search for the master was finished, and the path of discipleship began.'[10]

Several leading figures of the Human Potential Movement made their pilgrimages to the ashram. Among them were Gerda Boyesen, founder of Biodynamic Therapy, a development of Wilhelm Reich's teachings, Richard Price, founder, with Michael Murphy, of Esalen, Bernie Gunther, a body-centred therapist who gave workshops at Esalen, Paul Lowe, co-founder of Europe's Esalen-modelled therapy centre Quaesitor and Michael Barnett, another European group therapy leader and author of *People not Psychiatry*. Richard Price later repudiated the 'authoritarian, intimidating, violent'[11] methods used in the ashram's encounter marathons, recounting examples of limbs being broken in the disciples' efforts to break through to enlightenment. But many sannyasins were prepared to take the risk: 'I have always known that discipleship is not a safe process,' says one. 'If it is real it is dangerous.'[12]

'Anything goes' was the slogan governing Rajneesh's route to enlightenment. 'The moment you become predictable you become a machine . . . mind is a robot,'[13] he taught, along the lines of Gurdjieff. But Rajneesh claimed to be 'Gurdjieff *plus* Ouspensky. That way, nobody can stop my work. I am continuously moving in the world of no mind and in the world of words and books and analysis. Gurdjieff worked on himself and Ouspensky worked in the library. I am continuously working in both'. But while the Russian mystic claimed 'Life is only real then, when I AM', Rajneesh said, 'Just knowing this much, that "I am" – is not enough. It is not much knowing. You have to go into your inner being to explore the vast blissfulness and the peace and the silence and your divineness, your godliness. But don't get lost into the inner. The outer is also divine, the outer is also immensely useful . . . The outer and inner should be like two wings: with one wing you cannot fly like an eagle into the sky; you need both the wings.'[14] The mediocre mind-state mankind had settled into was, said Rajneesh, a result of the world having denied and rejected its potential saviours – including himself. To combat this, he preached the need for a new man and woman. Selected students would be trained at a university dedicated to meditation and deprogramming and the resulting meritocracy would constitute an enlightened elite.

Ideas of meritocracy appear to have gone to some of the sannyasins' heads. In 1981, Rajneesh moved his whole ashram to Oregon in the United States. 'Oregon was all about creating an alternative society, a kind of spiritual El Dorado,' says a sannyasin.[15] But warfare – largely verbal, some physical – broke out between the community, incorporated as the 5000-strong city of Rajneeshpuram, and Antelope, the neighbouring town. 'It was like a western wagon train with us inside and them out, backed by various born-again Christians in power,' says one former Rajneeshpuram resident.[16]

Ma Anand Sheela, then Rajneesh's right-hand woman, attempted a takeover of the town council and eventually resorted to lacing a local salad bar with salmonella at the time of the elections to prevent opponents from voting. Sheela also became bitterly jealous of Rajneesh's personal doctor, Dr George Meredith, or Devaraj, and tried to poison him. Eventually, the authorities caught up with her, she was imprisoned and, in the furore, Rajneesh was also shut away for several days. Many of his disciples believe he was given a plutonium sandwich while in jail. Eventually, he was deported. To some, this signalled the end of Rajneesh and his sannyasins, but by 1987 they were back in Poona and the ashram was once again thriving.

In 1988, Rajneesh inspired his sannyasins to found a World Academy of Creative Science, Arts and Consciousness – the 'prelude to a World Government'. The Academy would 'be a chance for governments to be free of the Nation-State and its obsession with science-for-death-type programmes. The aim was to totally transform the pivot of scientific research to peaceful, life-affirming work'.[17] Its influence has been minimal. Some notable scientists did indeed become involved, but on discovering the Academy was fathered by 'sex guru' Rajneesh, backed out.

According to Rajneesh, 'The dream of human beings living in peace and love as an organic unity is against all politics, against all those who are in power. It is against all the so-called religions, because if you succeed in creating a dream here and making it a reality, who is going to bother about their heaven and hell and god? . . . all the powers are against any utopia, any freedom for the human heart, any love, they don't want the world to become a paradise, because then they will be out of employment, and nobody is ready to lose his bread and butter. So as you grow old, you slowly, slowly start thinking that utopias are utopias, and you start compromising with the society. But there are a few crazy people like me who go on dreaming in spite of the society, in spite of the whole world. And howsoever difficult the dream seems to be to materialize, still my heart says there is not harm in making another effort. Perhaps one day, if not in my life, then in the life of future human beings, utopia will become a reality.'[18]

In January 1990, Rajneesh died. It is a problem which confronts all living gods at one time or another, creating a situation which, unless the deity is resurrected, can lead to bitter in-fighting over who is to be successor. Some believed that Paul Lowe, who had set up shop in Switzerland as a channeller of spirits from the beyond, might attempt a comeback, or that Sheela, now released from prison and living in Germany, would reappear on the scene. As yet, the coast is clear.

The same cannot be said of the furore following the death of the Indian guru Muktananda in 1982. Before leaving the planet, the Perfected Being appointed a brother and sister as his successors but soon after taking control, the brother became convinced the sister had hired assassins to do away with him. Bitter fighting broke out between the two factions.

Muktananda had attracted thousands of Western followers, including visits from California Governor Jerry Brown and singers James Taylor and Carly Simon. Ram Dass, formerly psychedelic disciple Richard Alpert, Harvard colleague of Timothy Leary, accompanied Muktananda on his first United States tour in 1970.

Some years earlier, Muktananda had been visited by 'the most spiritually developed Westerner I have come across' – Franklin Jones. Like Rajneesh, he too is said by his followers to be bridging the gap between East and West, but Franklin Jones was born and raised an all-American boy, the son of a real-estate agent. Apparently, Jones arrived on the planet an enlightened being but relinquished his advanced spirituality so that he might find out how to transcend the limitations facing the average human being and so learn how best to serve Westerners.

To regain enlightenment, he had to experience the setbacks and disillusionments of an ordinary seeker. That way, he would be able to speak to his future devotees with absolute clarity. After taking Muktananda as his guru, Jones progressed to Nityananda, Muktananda's own guru who by then had left his body. From Nityananda, he moved up to the Hindu goddess Shakti, the Divine Mother, whom he calls 'Ma' and who is, he says, his constant consort and companion.

In 1970, Franklin Jones re-realized Perfect Divine Enlightenment in a temple in Hollywood. Then, in 1974, Heart Master Da Love Ananda, as he later became known, gave his 'First Great Teaching Demonstration'. Known as 'Garbage and the Goddess', it was a way of excess, a Dionysian romp, 'without doubt one of the most humanly exuberant, Spiritually Powerful, and maddeningly heart-Distracting Demonstrations of Divine Siddhi [Spiritual Power] ever shown on Earth'.[19]

While his disciples consumed vast quantities of junk food – egg-bacon-cheeseburgers, French fries and milkshakes, Heart Master Da 'was transforming the landscape and His Residence into a "Loka" or Spiritual realm of Ecstasy, so that they [the disciples] sat snarling and jerking and blissfully falling face-forward into their delicately seasoned Chinese soup'.[20] According to a devotee, 'He got down from his chair and got in with the people. He taught them the freedom to explore any area of experience they wanted. He taught them the lesson of life – you can't become happy, you can only be happy – and it can only be a bodily understanding.'[21]

Heart Master Da teaches that everyone feels diseased and longs to become whole. The big joke, he says, is that they are indeed at ease, and Free, they just don't realize it. Once they break through to an awareness of their Prior Freedom, they can become responsible for their lives.

'I saw in him someone who was completely happy and free,' says a devotee. 'And the knowledge that I had come across someone on the planet who was completely free awoke in me an incredible sense that I had come home. To find enlightenment you need someone who is there already and it was obvious to me that he was my guru. When I first met him there was no question – it was whole body recognition. My whole world slipped round 360 degrees; it all seemed so obvious. He was born to do transcendental blessings.' According to another devotee, 'I am completely sure in terms of my own experience that he is an incarnation of the divine . . . When you look at him there is nobody home. He simply IS.'

Heart Master Da later took on the name Sri Da Kalki, Kalki being the final avatar who will lead mankind out of the Kali Yuga – in Hindu cosmology, the world cycle dominated by Kali, goddess of destruction. 'When I looked at him my heart went out,' says a devotee. 'There was this tremendous light coming from his eyes as if he was looking from infinity to infinity. It completely overwhelmed me – he gave me a vision of God in that moment. Any doubt I ever had was washed away. Without saying a word, he drew me in to this tremendously sweet relationship with him – my body was filled with all these sweet, blissful energies.'

Sri Da Kalki believes that only the most extraordinarily rare beings can become enlightened without surrendering to a truly enlightened master. As yet, however, only a few of his devotees have become at all advanced in surrendering to their guru. According to one, 'As a Western person, I had no idea at all of the function of a Spiritual Master. I wanted to take what was given and do it all myself . . . I had no idea what it meant to surrender to the Guru and be receptive to His Help.'[22] Another devotee says, 'My surrender is at the point that I have taken him on as my guru but I still spend most of my time resisting him.' Nevertheless, Sri Da Kalki accepts the rejection of his devotees believing that the ego will always be at war with the guru. 'He never gives up on us, and yet we have done so much to offend him,' says one of his followers.

The same devotee found that, after taking only the first steps in surrendering, 'Extraordinary things started to happen. I began to have psychic experiences, out-of-body experiences, and to see all the heart awakenings happening on and on. But those experiences don't make you happy. Forgetting yourself makes you happy.'

Sri Da Kalki is very critical of people who feel they can 'guru themselves' and become 'god realized by their own willpower', says a devotee. As well as giving his followers various spiritual disciplines, he instructs them in all areas of their lives – from how often they floss their teeth to what they eat. He also recommends that they visit him in person at least once a year at his Sri Love Ananda ashram in Fiji. As yet, it is only on retreats, in the presence of their heart master, that most devotees are capable of totally forgetting themselves. 'The feeling was incredible – of intense love and happiness,' says one. 'By contemplating him, just being in front of him, I felt incredibly ecstatic, intensely happy.'[23]

Devotees are, apparently, drawn to Sri Da Kalki through 'divine distraction'. He currently has a thousand disciples, largely in Britain, America, Australia and Holland. His mission is to draw as many people as want him into a god-realized state – but to become god-realized takes immense dedication – followers must give everything. What devotees have to learn is to relinquish even the most subtle egoic motives so that they might achieve union with the ever-present state of Freedom, or 'God'. Only Sri Da Kalki can 'awaken him or her to His own Condition of ecstatic unity with the Divine of Love Incarnate'.

Pure and simple hero worship was a feature of the nineteenth century – when admiration was turned 'from a virtue into a religion'. In 1841, Thomas Carlyle in his *Heroes and Hero Worship* had described great men as the 'lightning out of Heaven' that kindled the dry dead fuel of 'languid Times, with their unbelief, distress, perplexity'.[24] People were looking for a messiah – and Carlyle provided them with Odin, Goethe, Napoleon, Samuel Johnson . . . so that mankind might offer 'heartfelt prostrate admiration, submission, burning, boundless, for a noblest godlike Form of Man'.[25]

Towards the end of the century, Frederic Harrison led his fellow English Comtists in the Religion of Humanity. 'We worship . . . we submit ourselves reverently to Humanity,' he said.[26] Founded by Auguste Comte in 1851, the Religion of Humanity extolled freedom, enlightenment and progress and was intended to be a sober, rational and, above all, manly religion. According to Harrison, 'Religion, with Auguste Comte, means the perfect unison between man's intellectual convictions and his affective nature – both being devoted to a wisely ordered activity.'[27] The aim was that followers should become 'conscious of Humanity as a power, with an infinite past, with an incalculable extent in the present, and with a limitless future, far transcending the individual'.[28] To that end, Comtists advocated a New Calendar, so that instead of, for example, October 27, 1889, they would say 'the 20th day of the month Descartes . . . the day of the great naturalist Buffon'.[29]

Comte had also compiled a list of Great Men suitable to be worshipped and his followers held pilgrimages to their homes or tombs so that they might offer 'that religious consecration which befits a genuine pilgrimage by filling our minds with reverence for the immortal spirit whose footsteps we were seeking to trace'.[30] Today, pilgrims to Elvis Presley's former home feel much the same. And some have claimed post-death sightings of him, too.

But how much better to have a divine living hero. Throughout history, numerous people have set themselves up as messiahs. In the twelfth century there was the Breton Christ, as well as Tanchelm – who so entranced his followers that they would drink his bath water. In the early twentieth century George Baker – later known as Father Divine – set himself up as God, established a mission called 'Heaven' in New York, and surrounded himself with attractive young women helpers known as angels. And Sun Myung Moon of the Unification Church has styled himself the 'New Messiah'.

How many of these divine beings would pass the rigorous tests set forth by the American-based research project Understanding Cults and Spiritual Movements in the late 1980s is uncertain. According to their guide, the ideal guru should be modest, come from a recognized tradition, promote democracy in his followers, and try to ensure that they are all stable and happy people. Bhagwan's view on such a guide is: 'Was Gautam Buddha, was Moses an appointed master? Was Jesus appointed by someone? These are things which blossom of their own. It is not a government bureaucracy where you are appointed. If a master is appointed by somebody else, he can be dis-appointed any moment.'[31]

Jiddu Krishnamurti, chosen by the Theosophists to be the 'messiah of the New Age', had to dis-appoint himself. In his opinion, seekers should find their own path to paradise. Though for some seekers heaven will continue to be found only through, and around, their divine guru, for most the East returned the self to Western man – and said that *it* was God.

EIGHT | EASTERN PROMISE

O n January 12, 1990, thousands of meditators around the globe settled down in front of their satellite screens and tuned in to their guru's message, beamed to them from his World Capital of the Age of Enlightenment in northern India.

The Maharishi Mahesh Yogi's statement for the new decade was one of hope and optimism: 'The age of ignorance and suffering is going to be over very soon. Everyone will soon begin to enjoy heaven on earth,' he had promised a few days earlier.[1] Now, heaven on earth was 'inevitable': 'The dawn of world peace, the upsurge of freedom everywhere, the opening of borders and relaxing of boundaries, and the blossoming of a new international patriotism demonstrate that world consciousness is undergoing a fundamental transformation.'[2]

According to the Maharishi and his followers, heaven on earth would materialize as a direct result of Transcendental Meditation (TM), a technique practised by some three-and-a-half million people worldwide since its introduction to the West nearly thirty years earlier. The man who had organized Maharishi's first world assembly, held in London's Royal Albert Hall in March 1961, was none other than Leon MacLaren, leader of the School of Economic Science. In time, a split developed between Maharishi and MacLaren. But the guru had been given his opening.

Many Eastern religions teach that paradise, or a divine bliss-consciousness, can be achieved in the here and now. Few, however, have gone to the lengths of Maharishi to translate the teaching in such literal and well-publicized terms. The Maharishi was one of the first gurus to transport the wisdom of the ancient Hindu scriptures

Westwards in a form which would appeal particularly to the young. His mission had an inauspicious start – a story engrained in TM folklore tells how he turned up at Delhi airport unaware he needed a passport. But his unworldliness was soon cured: despite predictions from many onlookers that he would disappear from the world scene with 'a giggle and a puff of smoke', the guru now heads a worldwide multi-million dollar operation with activities ranging from diamond trading to holistic health cures.

Born in 1911, Maharishi Mahesh Yogi graduated in physics from Allahabad University in 1940 before studying under the Shankaracharya of Jyotir Math in northern Indian, Brahmananda Saraswati, known as Guru Dev (1869–1953). Before he died, Guru Dev chose a much younger disciple than Maharishi to succeed him as spiritual leader of his Himalayan ashram. Whether through pique or pragmatism, Maharishi turned his sights elsewhere and founded the Spiritual Regeneration Movement of India. The method by which such a regeneration was to be achieved was Transcendental Meditation, an ancient technique for attaining a new level of consciousness which Guru Dev had rediscovered from Hindu scriptures.

In 1958, the Maharishi – pictured always with a flower in his hand – made his Westward journey. At first, times were hard. But in 1967, The Beatles and other youthful glitterati latched on to him. TM had been neatly packaged for Westerners: the exotic figure of the Maharishi with his flowing hair and robes provided Eastern promise, while the technique itself – 'easy, effortless and completely natural' – offered Western promise: quick results. Moreover, the wisdom of the ancient Hindu scriptures, the Vedas, was draped in a scientific language easily digested by, if often completely incomprehensible to, the Western mind.

TM markets itself as a self-help technique the benefits of which, claims the movement, have been verified by more than 450 research studies. Like many New Age movements, however, it fails to put newcomers entirely in the picture. While going out of its way to play down its spiritual nature, no one is initiated into the technique without taking part in a worship ceremony.

Some fundamentalist Christians believe that Transcendental Meditators are quite literally 'in the dark' over the practice: though ignorant of what they are doing, they are, they say, being lured towards the devil by following Hindu teachings. Nonetheless, millions of

Westerners took up TM and were introduced to new horizons of being.

The Maharishi loosely follows the ninth century philsopher Shankara's form of non-dualistic or advaita Vedanta. Advaita Vedanta teaches that there is only one true reality in the universe – Brahman, Eternal Being, or what Westerners might call cosmic consciousness. What we take to be reality is in fact the reality we impose upon it, and the relationship between Brahman and the world as we see it is known as maya. Once we fully realize the unity of self and the absolute – Thou Art That, as it is put in the *Upanishads* – we achieve liberation. Eternal Being can be reached through mystical experience, through intuition or through meditation. Shankara explained that the personal God was part of the great illusion – along with the self, part of the lower reality. Deities could, however, be worshipped as a step towards the higher enlightenment. Shankara's opponents accused him of being a crypto-Buddhist.

If they so choose, meditators can search out the Shankara's wisdom from the Maharishi's more widely available teachings. Through TM, meditators are told they can tap into the 'unified field' and find 'unity in the midst of diversity' – something akin to Eternal Being; they will experience maximum levels of creativity or 'bliss consciousness', a godlike self-realization; they will transcend the thinking process to the source of thought, the level of no thought, realizing that the world as commonly perceived is illusion. Only the One is real. And all this can be achieved simply by sitting quietly for twenty minutes morning and evening.

Some meditators go on to study the TM Sidhi programme which teaches the technique of yogic flying: trainees sit cross-legged and attempt to levitate, which in practice means hopping about on mattresses. Flyers claim to have scientific evidence that their hopping has helped to reduce violence in the Lebanon, resolve strikes and bring down the Berlin Wall. 'Extensive scientific research has shown a dramatic decrease in negativity and improved positive trends in society wherever groups of people – as little as the square root of one per cent of the population – practise the TM-Sidhi programme in one place,' the movement claims.[3] For proof, simply turn to one of the many charts and diagrams the organization churns out.

In 1975, Maharishi inaugurated the Age of Enlightenment from his International University in Switzerland. Five years later, British Transcendental Meditators founded an 'ideal community' at Skelmersdale in Lancashire. Some 500 meditators live there and the community has a school, health centre, shops and dozens of businesses. Known as European Sidhaland, residents meet daily at the Maharishi Golden Dome to conduct 'coherence creating' meditations.

In his New Decade sermon, in January 1990, the Maharishi was not simply promising heaven on earth as a mystical concept. He and his movement are determined to bring it about in reality through the Heaven on Earth Development Corporation, which has headquarters in Malibu, California. The Corporation 'offers a consulting service to individual home builders and to developers of whole communities who want to create ideal living environments'.[4] The principles for planning and constructing their ideal homes and towns are laid out in the Maharishi Sthapatya-Ved, a body of knowledge based on ancient teachings, and 'are now being applied in planned communities on every continent, called Maharishi Cities of the Immortals'.[5]

The Cities of Immortals will be free from stress, pollution, crime and noise. Buildings and interiors will be constructed to 'ideal' proportions, paving the way for maximum quality of life, and transport will be provided by the Maharishi Electric Car, a 'state-of-the-art automobile being built by the Electric Chariot Division of Maharishi Heaven on Earth Development Corporation which will help eliminate the growing danger of air pollution from combustion engine exhaust'.[6] Each country will eventually blossom into a rich and beautiful city of gardens with spacious pavilions and tree-lined boulevards. As for the details, 'Our homes should be celestial, highly artistic homes worthy of Heaven on Earth,' says a spokesman for the World Centre for Sthapatya-Ved. 'Using good materials is not enough. All the surfaces should be richly carved inside and out. The artists and the architect should work together to create a formidable, magical piece of art, stunning to the senses and fulfilling to the heart.'[7]

One of the first sites chosen for a City of Immortals was the Soviet town of Leninakan in Armenia, destroyed by the 1988 earthquake. Citizens would be housed in Golden Domes and would meditate together to create coherence and stability in the region. Implementation of this plan would 'transform Armenia from one of the most troubled and tense regions of the world into an ideal society that will serve as a model for Maharishi's world initiative to create Heaven on Earth'.[8] Together with American magician Doug Henning, star of many a magic show, the Maharishi is now planning to build a $1 million theme park – Vedaland – next to Walt Disney World in

Orlando, California. Central to the park will be a 'levitating' temple which will hover several feet above a lake. Visitors will learn that there is more to reality than meets the eye, and will leave with the impression that they are one with the universe. Among the planned pleasure rides is a trip on a flying chariot which will grow smaller and smaller until it disappears into the molecular structure of a rose.

Over the years, many of Maharishi's followers have become disillusioned with the price-tag he puts on heaven. Meditators can buy in to Heaven on Earth for between $300,000 and $1 million a home.[9] And some businesses, which in the 1980s were introduced to TM through the Maharishi Corporate Development Programme, have complained that the organization overcharges. Former Beatle Ringo Starr said the Maharishi's ashram in Rishikesh reminded him of a spiritual Butlin's Holiday Camp. Some followers turned to other gurus, among them Beatle George Harrison who took up the cause of Abhay Charan De Bhaktivedanta Swami Prabhupada (Prabhu to devotees).

Born in 1896 in Calcutta, an astrologer is said to have predicted that at the age of seventy, Prabhu would 'cross the ocean, become a great exponent of religion, and open 108 temples'.[10]

Sure enough, in 1965, Prabhu stepped aboard the *Jaladata* and set sail for America. His first temple was in a former giftshop on Second Avenue in Manhattan's East Village. 'Matchless Gifts' was the sign hanging above the door. Prabhu quickly gathered a following from among the seekers of the day and founded the International Society for Krishna Consciousness (ISKCON) – usually known as the Hare Krishnas.

Prabhu's followers worship Lord Krishna, an avatar of the great Hindu god Vishnu, and trace their roots back through the sage Caitanya Mahaprabhu (1485–1533) to a time when the world was, allegedly, ruled by one government and one religion. Caitanya taught that God could be realized through bhakti (devotion), or loving adoration. According to ISKCON, Caitanya 'swept aside the stifling restrictions of the hereditary caste system and made it possible for people from any station of life to achieve the highest platform of spiritual enlightenment . . . He was not an ordinary human being, but an incarnation of the Supreme Personality of Godhead, Lord Krishna Himself, appearing as a great devotee of the Lord'.[9a]

Like Maharishi's followers, Hare Krishnas believe that repetition of the Hare Krishna mantra will bring about transcendental consciousness – for Maharishi's followers it is union with the Absolute, for Prabhu's followers it is Krishna Consciousness. According to Ragunath Das, formerly US hippie Richard Torretti, 'Before coming to Krishna Consciousness I was going completely crazy, searching for higher truth, fooling around with anything I could find. The chanting was just something else to give a try. I was both curious and in distress. We all were at the time.'[11]

Quick to tune in to the times, Prabhu described Krishna Consciousness as like a room full of LSD. Certainly, his followers were fascinated with what appeared to be another opportunity for surrendering the mind and 'tripping out'. One of the early adverts for Prabhu's meetings ran under the headline

STAY HIGH FOREVER
No more coming down
Practice Krishna Consciousness
Expand your consciousness by practising the TRANSCENDENTAL SOUND VIBRATION

'Simply practice what I have taught you and your life will be perfect,' taught Prabhu,[12] holding out before his devotees the promise that, even in the midst of the Kali Yuga, a golden age could appear – a heaven on earth.

'Society at the moment is falling to pieces,' says a British Krishna devotee. 'But when Krishna is awakened in the hearts of everyone through the practice of devotion, in the hearts of all society's leaders, then there will be peace. Once the leaders become aware that everything is God's property rather than trying to steal and exploit it, we will have the Golden Age. Through the sublime chanting, transcendental consciousness will be revived.'[13]

According to Prabhu, followers of Shankara's school of Vedanta are atheists – or, alternatively, he says, 'Sankaracarya is supposed to be an impersonalist who preached impersonalism, impersonal Brahman, but it is a fact that he is a covered personalist.'[14] The personality of Krishna is of vast importance to devotees. As Ragunath explains, 'Whereas Catholicism, the religion I was brought up with, just talked about the mystery all the time, the Krishna devotees were able to explain in great detail not only who God is but what He looks like, where He lives, what He likes and doesn't like. It was wonderful to come upon this God who was so real. Then I saw the ancient literature and knew that this wasn't just a fly by night religion. It was genuine and solid, just like Krishna. Some people came from India and performed tricks – Prabhu just presented the absolute truth as it is in all times and all places.'[15]

Not surprisingly, the favourite Vedic text of Hare Krishnas is the theistic *Bhagavad Gita* or 'Song of the Lord', which emphasizes the belief in a personal God through whose worship man can find release from the cycle of rebirth: 'Give me thy mind and give me thy heart, give me thy offerings and thy adoration; and thus in thy soul in harmony, and making me thy goal supreme, thou shalt in truth come to me.'[16] According to Prabhu, 'In this verse it is clearly indicated that Krishna consciousness is the only means of being delivered from the clutches of this contaminated material world.'[17]

Towards the end of the 1960s, some of Prabhu's followers set up an ideal community in West Virginia. Called New Vrindaban, after Krishna's birthplace in India, the community would be based on Vedic ideals and provide a model for the world. The devotees aimed to be self-sufficient, cooking over a wood fire and even covering the kitchen floor with cow dung in imitation of an Indian village home. Today, the community has become a tourist atraction – but has also been expelled from the main ISKCON movement. The centrepiece is a vast temple, the Palace of Gold, its dome and walls sheathed in shimmering gold leaf.

It was the temple and community the Hare Krishnas built at the original Vrindaban, a small village near Delhi, that Prabhu himself described as 'heaven on earth'.[18] The guest house there is a large, impressive building, its rooms filled with Western devotees and the hum of chanting. Even devotees from the Soviet Union now come to Vrindaban – before *glasnost*, many were interned in psychiatric hospitals.

Three young women – one English, one Norwegian, one Finnish – sit in reception eating peanuts. They have just returned from a barefoot pilgrimage, begging food on the way, and display their blistered feet. Later, they chat about previous reincarnations – who was a chariot driver, who a doctor – occasionally breaking off to prostrate themselves on the floor when a renounced devotee walks by; Prabhu's former masseuse, now an iridologist in the States, pauses for a chat. His daughter lives at Bhaktivedanta Manor in England, a glorious eighteenth century manor house donated to the movement by George Harrison.

Padmalochan, a Puckish, British-born devotee of seventeen years'

Mme Helena Petrovna Blavatsky
(1831–91), founder of the
Theosophical Society and
matriarch of the New Age.

Inside the Theosophical Society's
headquarters at Adyar, Madras, the wall
plaques bear witness to the movement's
commitment to discovering the Truth within
all religions. The pair of compasses, the
symbol of Freemasonry, point to the
affiliations between the two groups.

The Theosophists' chosen Messiah Jiddu
Krishnamurti with leading members of the
society, Charles Leadbetter and Annie
Besant, who nurtured their protégé to
prepare him for his cosmic role.

Unhappy with the path marked out for him by the Theosophists, Krishnamurti attempted to shrug off his divine status. Undeterred, thousands of devotees continued to hang on his every word.

Countless fantastical stories grew up around the Institute for the Harmonious Development of Mankind, the consciousness research centre founded in 1922 by Russian philosopher-mystic G.I. Gurdjieff (*c.* 1873–1949).

Despite being labelled the wickedest man in the world, the 'Beast 666', Aleister Crowley (1875–1947), carved himself a place in London society. Always keen to provoke controversy, he appears here at a literary lunch seated next to an effigy of murderer Charlie Peace.

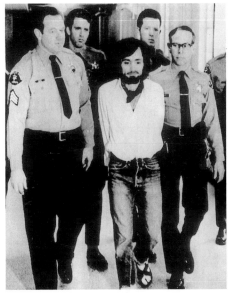

Diminutive mass murderer Charles Manson struck horror into the hearts of millions with his carefully orchestrated Tate-Labianca slayings. Together with reports of the absolute control he wielded over his followers (The Family), the Manson Murders helped bring an end to the Swinging Sixties.

Televangelist Jim Bakker, together with his wife Tammy, brought religion into millions of living rooms – and sensation into millions more as the cameras relentlessly documented their downfall.

The Abode of Highest Peace near Bangalore attracts thousands of Westerners. Home to living god Sai Baba, visitors report countless miracle cures and materializations effected by their swami.

Hounded from his township in America, the controversial and charismatic 'free love guru' Bhagwan Shree Rajneesh return to India, allegedly poisoned but no less perky.

The Maharishi Mahesh Yogi (left) introduced Westerners to Transcendental Meditation. By blending mysticism and flower power with 'scientifically-validated' evidence of TM's benefits, he hit upon a winning formula.

Vrindaban, Krishna's birthplace near Delhi, holds a special place in the hearts of Hare Krishnas. They have built a splendid temple there, and a sanctuary in honour of Prabhupada, their founder.

At his ashram in southern India, Fr Bede Griffiths seeks to bridge the gap between Eastern and Western spirituality. Services in the small chapel include readings from both Hindu and Christian teachings.

Druids celebrate the summer solstice at the ancient monument of Stonehenge. Their use of the site provoked a row with certain conservationists who wanted public access to the stones restricted.

The Shakers, or United Society of Believers in Christ's Second Coming, were founded in the nineteenth century. The movement's following has dwindled because members must practise celibacy, while their strict lifestyle attracts few new recruits from outside the organization.

Natural charisma and the gift of oratory helped black radical Malcolm X turn the Nation of Islam into a mass movement. Usually known as Black Muslims, the Nation of Islam was led by Elijah Muhammad (seated left).

The Ku Klux Klan is an ugly blend of nationalism, protestantism and racism. Members dream of a utopia open only to those of the 'correct' race, creed and colour.

More than two thousand couples were blessed at the Unification Church mass wedding in Madison Square Garden in 1982. The event was presided over by the Rev Sun Myung Moon and his wife. Before getting married, Moonies are supposedly cleansed of Original Sin.

Hitler would often borrow the stage props of religious life to endow his ceremonies with a mystical quality. Most notable for this were the Nuremberg rallies, of which the 1938 event is shown here. They were intended to heighten emotion so that participants and onlookers happily surrendered themselves to the supreme power of the Nazi Party.

standing, throws himself in a chair, tired after his job of looking after the community's cows. Before coming to Krishna Consciousness, Padmalochan was a Hell's Angel. 'I think it was through being with a group of people who had some philosophy of life that eventually drew me towards Krishna Consciousness,' he explains. 'I had begun to experiment with LSD but then came across a group of devotees, tried the chanting and liked that more.'

He goes on to explain his arrival in India, by seemingly magical circumstances. 'I wanted to go to India but didn't have the money. Then a very strange thing happened. One day, a young Sikh came up to me in Oxford Street and said he had dreamt he was going to meet me and that he was going to help me go to India. A few days later, he came to the temple, gave me a ticket and said, "The flight's tomorrow morning." So the next morning I flew to Delhi.' Such occurrences are, apparently, commonplace among Krishna devotees.

Padmalochan plans to spend the rest of his life in India. 'There is something about this place. People here have been praising Krishna for thousands of years. It's a type of paradise.'[19] When his duties with the cows are finished, Padmalochan walks the countryside, stopping off to give spiritual advice to the neighbouring villagers. At Vrindaban, the 1960s tradition appears to have reversed itself. Now, the Westerners are the gurus, the Indians the seekers.

Behind the guest house lies the Gurukula, or Guru School, where several children, mainly from England and America, are instructed according to Vedic principles. One of the teachers, a young American woman, has moved to live permanently with the community. Formerly a teacher in the United States, she came to Krishna Consciousness after becoming disillusioned with the apparent hollowness of the American way of life. Krishna, she believes, holds the meaning and the truth. Next week, she is marrying another devotee. A woman's role within the movement might appear subservient, she says, but their marriages last.

At Hare Krishna temples throughout the world, devotees get up before dawn to chant and worship Krishna. At Vrindaban, the ritual has an added quality. Wrapped in shawls in the cool Indian dawn, devotees hurry down the stone flagged walkways to the as yet unfinished satsang or shrine to Prabhupada and form a ghostly gathering before his golden statue. After praising Prabhu, they make their way to the main temple to worship Krishna with dancing, chanting and banging of drums. The temple is a large, three-domed building with a black and white marbled floor, ornate colonnades and a sacred tulsa tree reaching upwards from the middle of the courtyard. Several local Indians join in the worship, but it is led by Westerners and at the entrance a temple guide displays photographs of Prabhu with the Queen of England, Prabhu with Margaret Thatcher, Prabhu with the Pope.

'Wherever I shall go now, this policy of important men being invited to talk with me about our Krishna Consciousness movement shall be implemented,' Prabhu once told a disciple[20], duly attracting the interest of pop stars such as John Lennon, George Harrison and Donovan.

But money used for the furtherance of Krishna Consciousness is spiritual. And by extension, the display of wealth is spiritual, too. Such thinking lay behind Prabhu's plan to build a spiritual capital of the world at the birthplace of Caitanya Mahaprabhu near Mayapur. Far removed from the simple community he envisaged at New Vrindaban, this would be a monumental, ornate creation with pillars of silver, gold and jewels, marble floors, electric fans and lights, and modern toilets and showers. Dominating the entire city would be a magnificent Temple of Human Understanding. Eventually, the city would provide homes for a population of 50,000. Visitors would quickly become Krishna devotees, 'chanting and dancing in ecstasy'. By the mid-1980s, the Spiritual City contained two enormous guest houses, ornamental gardens, fountains, parkland, a school, endless offices – and the beginnings of the temple.

After Prabhu died in 1977, his movement lapsed into a period of chaos and controversy. He had appointed several successors believing that they would thereby be provoked to 'transcendental competition' and so spurred to ever-greater efforts. But the 'transcendental competition' took on an earthbound nature. Alexander Kulik, a temple leader in California, was convicted on charges of distributing heroin, and Thomas Dresher pleaded guilty to murder of another Krishna devotee in an internal battle.[21]

Britain had been left in the hands of James Immel. In 1982, however, he was thrown out of the movement after declaring he was God and substituting doses of LSD for prasadam – a gift, often food, which has been offered to the deity. After his expulsion, Immel set up a hippie commune in California known as the Golden Mountain Sanctuary, devoted to enlightenment through free love and drugs. In 1987, another former Krishna devotee sawed off Immel's head with a butcher's knife, afterwards claiming, 'I had to kill him because he was evil. He's ruined a lot of people's lives. He deserved to die. I believed that as long as he was alive there was no hope for the world. The head is off the beast. The same spirit that was in Rasputin was moving in Immel.'[22]

Such events did little to endear the Hare Krishnas to the establishment but gradually the organization is finding its feet. 'I was into the London music scene, drinking, taking drugs. Then I heard the chanting, liked it, and learnt more about the movement,' says Simon Murphy, a twenty-two-year-old who has just been initiated into the movement and received his new name, Sri Hari Das. 'That world didn't make me happy. With this movement, I can help bring about the Golden Age.'[23] It is 1990, but it might just as well be the 1960s except for one detail – Sri Hari Das's parents are at his initiation ceremony, and his father has himself taken up chanting. Whereas in 1969 George Harrison and John Lennon helped popularize Krishna Consciousness through their music, in the 1990s Boy George is bringing the movement recognition through a song backed by chanting Krishna devotees.

Prahbu's first Western followers, who had begun to gather round him in 1966, came from the Paradox restaurant, a New York haunt for Zen students and devotees of macrobiotics. A diet based on Eastern teachings, macrobiotics became for many a total way of life – and its developer, George Ohsawa, acquired a large Western following. Zen was made widely available to the West in the late 1940s by Japanese scholar Daisetz T. Suzuki and was popularized by Alan Watts. Gary Snyder and Jack Kerouac, the former of whom had studied under a Zen master in Japan, developed Zen-like principles into what became a youth cause – the Beats. In his *Beat Zen, Square Zen, Zen*, Watts describes the Beat mentality as 'a younger generation's nonparticipation in "the American Way of Life", a revolt which does not seek to change the existing order but simply turns away from it to find the significance of life in subjective experience rather than objective achievement . . . '[24]

The aim of Zen is non-attachment, leading to a full loss of self and thus *satori*, or sudden, spontaneous enlightenment. Its beauty is that *satori* is happened upon through ordinary, everyday life rather than through the deliberate effort of renunciation. The Rinzai Zen school – the form most popular in the West – presents students with Koans, enigmatic texts whose 'solution' lies beyond the bounds of rational throught, aiming thereby to jolt the mind from its programming.

The *Upanishads* also emphasized the importance of a state which transcended the rational mind: 'He comes to the thought of those who know him beyond thought, not to those who imagine he can be attained by thought. He is unknown to the learned and known to the simple.'[25] Gurdjieff, too, stressed the importance of becoming childlike, and Jesus had said, 'Except ye be converted and become as little children, ye shall not enter into the kingdom of heaven.' But for those who had entered into the Eastern mind-set, the words 'be converted' were anathema. Today, numerous workshops are held to help trainees recapture the timeless quality of childhood.

Certainly, Zen had innumerable quasi-followers who used the philosophy as an excuse for rejecting the older generation's values. Henry Miller, describing such discarded standards in his 'Beat Bible' *Tropic of Capricorn*, published in 1957, wrote: 'Everything was for tomorrow, but tomorrow never came. The present was only a bridge and on this bridge they are still groaning, as the world groans, and not one idiot ever thinks of blowing up the bridge.'[26]

Eastern thinking did not see time as belonging to the Western Judaeo-Christian tradition – as a linear progression through a world separate from God, to an afterworld heaven, or hell. In the Eastern tradition, time is not real, the world as we see it is not real and it is not slowly evolving towards perfection; it is perfect every moment, if we could but realize it. Heaven is ready and waiting, Paradise exists in the timeless and universal Now, the eternity of every moment. Many Beats and hippies were accused of seeking 'instant gratification'.

One block to attaining *satori* was habituation: Zen students talk of seeing something for the 500th time in the same way they saw it the first time – the world fresh-made each moment. In 1960, two psychiatrists at the University of Tokyo fitted a group of Zen priests and disciples with electrodes, hooked them up to machines and played a repeated clicking sound to them – once every fifteen seconds. Whereas a control group quickly became dulled to the sound, eventually showing no response to it whatsoever, the Zen masters responded to the click just as strongly each time.[27] Rather like Gurdjieff's followers, Zen students aim to keep fully awake and to eliminate all the machine-like preconceived notions of themselves and the world.

The Beats came and went, but the thinking went on. Composer John Cage and psychoanalyst Erich Fromm were both Zen enthusiasts. Fromm dreamt of an ideal 'One World' which would be inhabited by the New Man. John Cage's music of silence occasionally attempted to demonstrate the isness of nothingness – the void that is nirvana. Martin Heidegger, who said that Zen was the same as his existential philosophy, inspired Werner Erhard.

Like Zen, Sufism works outside a framework, relying on individual experience rather than on a set of rules. Through the Sufi dance, dervishes [dancers] are supposed to become one with the unity of all things. 'I have put duality away,' wrote the thirteenth century philosopher-poet Rumi, 'I have seen that the two worlds are one, One I seek, One I know, One I see, One I call.' Or as the Eastern-entranced poet Yeats asked: 'How can you tell the dancer from the dance?'

Today, company bosses are being taught the 'whirling dervish', the ecstatic Sufi dance believed to have been introduced by Rumi. Apparently, the dance will help them reconnect to the 'Divine in everything'. On his travels, Gurdjieff met up with members of this mystical Islamic sect and it is said that through him the first Sufi dancers were introduced to Britain, although it was not until the 1970s that their wisdom was made readily available to Westerners through the works of Idries Shah.

IBM's top-ranking staff are being introduced to the Taoist *I Ching* or *Book of Changes* as part of an in-house course called 'Fit For the Future'. According to Tom Jennings, manager of IBM's Employee Development Training, 'The *I Ching* has a magical way of working. It helps employees understand themselves better. Some may see it as an aid to personal decision making, others as a challenge to their usual thinking. The Western mind has no regard for chance, whereas the Eastern mind looks to the unity behind everything. We try and make that connection.'[28]

While usually seen as a type of divinatory oracle, for Carl Jung, the *I Ching* showed that all accidents and coincidences are linked to the subconscious mind – the realm of unity, beyond that of cause and effect, where man and the universe are at one. Study of the *I Ching* helped Jung to develop his theory of synchronicity. The new physics, which emphasizes the interconnectedness of all matter, is also discovering worlds of similarity with the *I Ching*. Increasingly, Eastern wisdom is at the forefront of Western development.

In the 1920s, the field of quantum physics began to unearth the relation between Western science and Eastern philosophy. At around the same time, the Indian philosopher-poet Rabrindranath Tagore (1861–1941) announced that '. . . the world is not atoms or molecules or radioactivity or other forces, the diamond is not carbon, and light is not vibrations of ether. You can never come to the reality of creation by contemplating it from the point of view of destruction'.[29]

The new discoveries gained wide popularity in the 1970s with the publication in 1975 of Fritjof Capra's *The Tao of Physics*. According to Capra, the results of modern physics could lead us 'to the Buddha or to the Bomb'.[30] Eastern gurus also had their piece to say on the atomic bomb. Sivananda (1887–1963), founder of the Divine Life Society, claimed that 'Renunciation is the Atomic Bomb which instantly reduces the citadel of Desire and ignorance to ashes . . .' Then, playing on the Hindu word for the eternal within man – '*atman*' – he added, 'Become desireless, then you will know the formula for the manufacture of the Atomic Bomb.'[31]

Prajapati Brahma (1877–1969), formerly diamond merchant Dada Lakhiraj, warned members of his Brahma Kumaris movement: 'Remember this Iron-aged vicious world will soon get destroyed by nuclear war, natural calamities, civil wars etc. Therefore, BE HOLY, BE YOGI.'[32] Brahma Kumaris World Spiritual University (BKWSU), based in India but with headquarters in London and New York, has been affiliated with the United Nations as a Non-Governmental Organization since 1980 and has been active in organizing and sponsoring peace conferences. In 1987 the administrative head of BKWSU was presented with the United Nations International 'Peace Messenger' Award. The movement aims to bring about paradise on earth through a One World Religion and One World Government. Members practise Raja Yoga which involves meditating quietly until the Third Eye, or eye of wisdom, is opened.

Speaking through Prajapati Brahma, the God-Father Shiva announced, 'This world in the beginning was Heaven or Paradise in *Sat-Yuga*. It has passed through the cycle of *Treta*, *Dwapur* and *Kali-Yuga*. It has now become a veritable Hell or Devil World. Therefore, I have re-incarnated in the corporeal medium of Prajapati Brahma, alias "Adam" to give you, your God-fatherly Birthright of complete purity, peace and prosperity in the Heavenly Kingdom, Paradise or Golden-aged (*Sat-Yuga*) New World which I am now re-establishing.' He added, 'However, you can attain them only if you become vice-less through the knowledge and the *Raj-Yoga* which I am now teaching.'[33]

By 1982, Fritjof Capra could write that 'the awareness of the profound harmony between the world view of modern physics and the views of Eastern mysticism now appears as an integral part of a

much larger cultural transformation, leading to the emergence of a
new vision of reality that will require a fundamental change in our
thoughts, perceptions and values'.[34]

That same year, a conference on Western science and Eastern
wisdom was held in Bombay, organized by California's Institute of
Transpersonal Psychology. Fritjof Capra, Swami Muktananda and
the Dalai Lama were among those invited. Father Bede Griffiths, a
Benedictine monk who guides Saccidananda Ashram in India, a
centre dedicated to bringing Indian spirituality to the Christian
life, also attended the conference. Quoting American 'consciousness
researcher' Ken Wilber, Bede Griffiths says that we have to go beyond
the world of phenomena, towards the ultimate reality, the *atman*:
'In the early Upanishadic tradition,' he says, 'they went beyond all
phenomena to the transcendent Self and this is the vision the world
has lost . . . This is what we have to recover and relate, reintegrate
with Western sciences.'[35]

In the early Eastwards rush many Westerners were accused simply
of exploiting the lack of moral framework the East offered them – as
murderer Charles Manson once asked, 'If God is One, what is bad?'
Moreover, precisely because Eastern thinking presented humankind
with the possibility of making paradise, it also presented them with
a tremendous amount of self-responsibility which could result in
dislocation rather than non-attachment. The East was often simply
all too much for Western man.

According to Bede Griffiths, Westerners have been labouring under
the 'split universe' of Isaac Newton – a devout Christian, but one who
had 'discarded the ancient traditional wisdom of Christianity'. Today,
however, says Fr Bede, 'With science opening itself to the whole
mystical dimension of religion I feel that we are really entering into
what they call in America the New Age, a New Culture and a New
Way of Understanding Human Life.'[36]

According to Bede Griffiths, Christians need to turn to Meister
Eckhart, the great mystic of the fourteenth century, to discover a
transcendent reality. Eckhart's teachings were long viewed as heretical
– a problem Christians continually come up against when they seek
to realize the Kingdom of Heaven on earth. And if they turn instead
to the literal plain truth of the Bible, they are confronted with the
threat of Armageddon. It is, then, perhaps not surprising, that the
Christian quest for heaven on earth throws up some of the most
bizarre stories.

| WESTERN REVELATIONS

While the Maharishi Mahesh Yogi was cheerfully promising his followers heaven on earth, deep in Paradise Valley, Montana, Elizabeth Clare Prophet's devotees were putting the finishing touches to their Armageddon shelters. There, in the bleak landscape which sits so uneasily with its name, strange grey mounds began to rise up, the result of two years' back-breaking work by members of Prophet's movement – the Church Universal and Triumphant.

In October 1987, Elizabeth Prophet – Mother to her followers – had received a message from one of her many spirit guides: 'Ere twenty-four months have passed, be it known to you that this nation must have the capacity to turn back any and all missiles . . . where there is no defence you invite the bear into your haven . . . ere twenty-four months pass . . . there shall be a reckoning and a confrontation unless something is done . . .'[1] Clearly, it is not simply Mother's claim that she, rather than the Pope, is leader of the Catholic Church that makes her a controversial religious figure.

Church members were not caught off guard by Mother's apocalyptic message. Founded in 1958 by her now-ascended husband Mark Prophet, the group had bought their Paradise Valley site, on the banks of the Yellowstone River, in the early 1980s. Known as Royal Teton Ranch, the property later expanded to 33,000 acres. Coincidentally, the Bhagwan Shree Rajneesh helped stock the vast commune – when the Indian guru was hounded out of his Oregon township and driven from American soil in 1985, the Church Universal and Triumphant bought house trailers and kitchen equipment from his followers. Their commune equipped for everyday life, Prophet's followers were ready to start building for their post-Armageddon life in paradise.

The date of Mother's Armageddon keeps changing, but the threat and the aggressor remain the same: the bear is the Soviet Union; Mikhail Gorbachev, hailed by many New Age devotees as the 'avatar of the New Age' is for Mother the avatar of destruction. Though seeking to stave off the cosmic battle with her rabidly right wing political stance and staunch support of the Anti-Ballistic Missile programme, Mother nonetheless predicts the imminent cosmic carnage of nuclear war. The 1990s, she says, will be 'a time of troubles that has not been seen before'. And scripture, she adds, says 'head for the mountains'.[2] When the dust settles, Mother's elect will crawl blinking from their forty-odd steel and concrete homes – the largest big enough to house the movement's 700 staff – and glory in the 1000-year reign of Christ: heaven on earth.

Whereas in the Hindu and Buddhist tradition, heaven on earth can be achieved in the timeless here and now, in the Judaeo-Christian tradition, God tends to be viewed as working his purpose out through chronological time. The Church Universal and Triumphant, like many movements in the Judaeo-Christian camp, embraces the literal, historical outlook on the arrival of heaven on earth. It has a rich heritage to draw on.

Jewish apocalyptic prophets looked forward to a time when the hardships they suffered would be over. As the Book of Daniel puts it, 'I saw in the night visions, and, behold, one like the Son of man came with the clouds of heaven, and came to the Ancient of days, and they brought him near before him. And there was given him dominion, and glory, and a kingdom, that all people, nations, and languages, should serve him: his dominion is an everlasting dominion which shall not pass away, and his kingdom that which shall not be destroyed . . . And the kingdom and dominion, and the greatness of the kingdom under the whole heaven, shall be given to the people of the saints of the most High, whose kingdom is an everlasting kingdom, and all dominions shall serve and obey him.'[3] The Talmud, the Jewish interpretation of scripture, also makes it quite clear that one day, a messiah will arrive and establish the Kingdom of God on earth.

In the New Testament, the author of the Revelation of St John the Divine describes a vision in which the Anti-Christ will appear and cause havoc for several years, culminating in a fearsome battle at Armageddon. After the battle, in which Satan is overcome and cast into a bottomless pit, Christ will establish a kingdom for a 1000 years – the millennium. The citizens of this earthly paradise will be all those who 'were beheaded for the witness of Jesus, and for the word of God, and which had not worshipped the beast'.[4] At the end of 1000 years, satanic forces will make a final unsuccessful attempt to overcome God's kingdom, after which the dead will be resurrected. Those whose names are missing from the book of life will be thrown into a lake of fire and everyone else will live in the New Jerusalem, a magnificent city which will descend from heaven.

According to Revelation, 'The Lord God of the holy prophets sent his angel to shew unto his servants the things which must shortly be done. Behold, I come quickly . . .'.[5] The Gospels, too, were filled with hints that the second coming was in the offing: 'There be some standing here, which shall not taste of death, till they see the Son of man coming in his kingdom,' says Jesus in the Gospel according to St Matthew.[6] Not surprisingly, many early Christians took this to mean that the second coming was almost upon them – and they took themselves to be the future citizens of heaven on earth. Some worked themselves into a frenzy of self-mortification in preparation for the day of judgement. One such ascetic, a Phrygian called Montanus, announced in 156AD that the New Jerusalem was about to descend from the heavens on to his homeland and he and his followers called on all Christians to hurry there to await the descent.

Millennial expectations were not confined to splinter groups. Irenaeus, the second century Bishop of Lyon, looked forward to a return to the splendours of the Garden of Eden before the Fall. The garden would be populated by the righteous from both the dead and living, women would give birth to countless children, wine and grain would flow in abundance, no-one need work and everyone would live in peace and harmony. Irenaeus set the date of the millennium at 6000 years after the beginning of world history – a chronology which had wide acceptance at the time. According to Psalm 89:4, 'A day with the Lord is as a thousand years' and, since the seventh day would be a symbol of heavenly rest, this must be the 1000 years of Christ's reign on earth.

Augustine of Hippo put an official end to literal interpretations of heaven on earth in the fifth century. In his opinion, Revelation should be understood in purely symbolic terms: the millennium had already begun with the birth of Christ; all those who loved God and received His grace through the sanction of the Church were already in the nearest possible equivalent to an earthly paradise which, because of humanity's fallen nature, required rules and laws. Augustine's teaching became orthodox doctrine and the earthly paradise of Irenaeus was suppressed. Nonetheless, these two strands of thinking – one claiming that heaven on earth has already arrived for those who believe in Christ, the other that it is yet to come in the form of some blissful, edenic state, continue to exist alongside each other.

Nowadays, many New Age groups are turning for inspiration to the teachings and lifestyles of some of the earliest Christian sects and their Jewish counterparts, believing they display a purity and firmness of vision which has since disappeared. Like many of today's movements, these early groups thrived on a knife-edge of expectancy, predicting with unflagging determination the arrival of heaven on earth.

For members of the Church Universal and Triumphant, as for many other of today's New Agers, the Jewish Essene sect has an almost magnetic attraction. To Elizabeth Prophet they were, quite simply, a 'New Age community', whereas to Sir George Trevelyan, founder of New Age educational organization the Wrekin Trust, their lifestyle 'reflected the best of what we now know as Nature Cure or Natural Therapy, organic agriculture and transpersonal psychology, but set within a structure of worship and communion which fully recognized the sacredness and unity of all life in Earth and the Cosmos'.[7]

The Essenes lived on and around the shores of the Dead Sea from the mid-second century BC, numbering in the first century AD some 4000 members. Their lives were simple, even spartan, but they confidently awaited the arrival of heaven on earth, convinced that they, the sons of Light, would overcome the Roman occupiers of the Holy Land. As an excerpt from their War Rule puts it:

Shout for joy, O daughters of my people!
Deck yourselves with glorious jewels
    and rule over the kingdom of the nations!
Sovereignty shall be to the Lord
    and everlasting dominion to Israel.[8]

Then, in the war with Rome, culminating in the destruction of Jerusalem in 70AD, they disappeared.

In 1947, a Bedouin farmer discovered a bundle of documents at Qumran, a few miles from Jericho by the Dead Sea. Not realizing their worth, he used some of them to light his fire. Over the next ten years numerous documents and fragments, now known as the Dead Sea Scrolls, were unearthed. What was pieced together was a picture of an inner-circle Essene community of some 150–200 'men of perfect holiness' living in expectation of a future age – its particulars relayed to them by the 'Teacher of Righteousness to whom God made known all the mysteries of the words of His servants the Prophets'.[9]

Two of the Qumran documents, the War Rule and Messianic Rule, are specifically concerned with plans for the New Age which would be 'a time of salvation for the people of God, an age of dominion for all the members of His company, and of everlasting destruction for all the company of Satan'.[10] Their victory in the preceding war was assured for 'the King of Glory is with us together with the Holy Ones. Valiant [warriors] of the angelic host are among our numbered men, and the Hero of war is with our congregation; the host of His spirits is with our foot-soldiers and horsemen. [They are as] clouds, as clouds of dew (covering) the earth, as a shower of rain shedding righteousness on all that grows on the earth'.[11] While awaiting the new era, members of the community believed they were living in a 'House of Holiness',[12] a 'House of Perfection and Truth'.[13]

Piecing together and interpreting fragments of the Dead Sea Scrolls, often relying on intuition and visionary inspiration, has proved an absorbing pastime for many modern-day prophets, one of whom has described the Essenes' alleged conspiracy as the 'Jesus Initiative'.

With backing from twentieth century seers such as Edgar Cayce, writer Peter Lemesurier suggests that the community chose two of their number to conceive Jesus and then directed his role through life, determined that he should fulfil the prophecies of a future messiah and usher in heaven on earth. To play out his allotted role, however, Jesus had to suffer and survive his crucifixion. It would not be the first time someone had come through the ordeal, and Jesus would be helped by being given one of the Essenes' famed herbal potions – what most Christians believe to have been merely a sponge soaked with vinegar – which would slow down his pulse rate, making him appear dead.

Jesus's body would then be taken down from the Cross and, once safe in his tomb, the Essenes would treat and revive their patient. After three days, Jesus would come out of the tomb, dressed in kingly raiment, and his apparent resurrection would convince the people he was the true messiah. The Essenes would then overcome the Romans, and Jerusalem would become the holy capital of the world. Eventually the messiah would inaugurate the New Age, the era of bliss.

Things went according to plan: Jesus was nailed to the cross, given the Essene potion, appeared dead, and Joseph of Arimathea, an Essene sympathizer, dashed to Pilate and asked for the body. In his absence, however, the spear thrust of an unknown Roman soldier put paid to the 'Jesus Initiative'. This, however, is not the end of the story. Maybe, suggests Lemesurier, the Essenes had simply got their calculations wrong. Maybe the prophecy that Jesus would rise on the third day really meant that he would return in the third millennium. If so, the second coming is almost upon us.

According to Lemesurier, the ultimate messiah will achieve initial world sovereignty sometime between 2034 and 2039, and he will be 'what the Essenes always imagined him to be – Man at last come fully into his own through attunement with the Ultimate Reality . . . God's kingdom will, in effect, be a second Garden of Eden ruled over by a Second Adam – but, in this case, man *en masse*, working as a single entity'.[14] Heaven on earth will, in other words, be a transformation of man's consciousness – just as the majority of today's New Age prophets preach.

Other theories link the Essenes to the Grail legend via the Knights Templar and Joseph of Arimathea who, according to legend, brought the Holy Grail to Glastonbury. Elizabeth Prophet, tying herself in to the increasingly knotty thread of esoteric thought, claims to be a reincarnation of Queen Guinevere. Before moving to Paradise Valley, she and her followers lived at 'Camelot', a community in Malibu, California.

One of Elizabeth Prophet's preferred religious texts is the non-canonical Book of Enoch, several fragmented sections of which were found at Qumran, including the chapters on the last judgement, the destruction of Israel's enemies, the resurrection and the advent of the messianic age. 'Millennia ago,' Mother teaches, 'Enoch wrote a book warning his children about the Watchers – fallen angels who mated with the "daughters of men" and wrought deadly destruction upon the earth. Then Enoch's book was denounced in church and temple and lost for a thousand years.'[15]

Elizabeth Prophet has resurrected the book for her flock, putting forward the belief that the 'men' who hold the reins of power over the earth may in fact be embodied fallen angels and number among them members of the KGB, the Mafia, Church leaders, international terrorists and all those who take money and sex as their gods. It is the Watchers, says Mother, who murdered *Utopia* author Thomas More, who killed Thomas à Becket, who pump children 'full of marijuana, their death drug', who 'destroy the nations and the international community', and who introduced abortion and birth control. *'Voilà!'*, she exclaims '. . . for thousands of years the fallen angels have been propagating themselves and propping themselves up – up on the social and success cult ladder. From the original prototype, they have cloned and carbon-copied an oppressive – and godless – power élite.'[16]

From the beginning, Mother continues, it is these Watchers who have spoilt the dreams of God and man. Once, God sent the great flood to wipe out the evil giants, the children of the Watchers, but they weren't completely done away with for, before their final judgement, 'the angels return and hurl themselves upon the East . . . And they will march up to and tread under foot the land of His elect ones . . .'

'This,' says Elizabeth Prophet, 'seems a chilling prophecy of our own time . . . There is no date stamped on the prediction, but a few word changes in the right places would make it duplicate today's headlines.'[17]

Mother's favoured Book of Enoch contains a delightful description of the heaven on earth which will follow on the tail of the cataclysm: 'In those days all the earth shall be cultivated in righteousness; it shall be wholly planted with trees, and filled with benediction; every tree of delight shall be planted in it. In it shall vines be planted; and the vine which shall be planted in it shall yield fruit to satiety; every seed, which shall be sown in it, shall produce for one measure a thousand; and one measure of olives shall produce ten presses of oil. The earth shall be cleansed from all corruption, from every crime, from all punishment, and from all suffering; neither will I again send a deluge upon it from generation to generation for ever. In those days I will open the treasures of blessing which are in heaven, that I may cause them to descend upon earth, and upon all the works and labour of man.'[18] It is to this earthly paradise, then, that Mother's devotees can look forward when they are holed up in their Armageddon shelters.

Like Elizabeth Prophet, Mani, the third century founder of Manicheism, set great store by the Book of Enoch. Mani incorporated a blend of Zoroastrianism, Christianity and Buddhism into his system, believing that all religions were based on the same universal truth. In his view, the world was dominated by warring forces of light and dark, or good and evil, and it was each individual's duty to do their best to release some of the sparks of light which had become embedded in matter, allowing them to return to their divine source.

Ideas stemming from Manicheism, or Manichaeanism, seem to have influenced the tenth–eleventh century Bulgarian-based Bogomils as well as the twelfth–fourtheenth century Cathars or Albigensians. The Cathars were vegetarians, studied the Jewish Kabbalah, and believed in the strict dualism of matter and spirit. Running through all the movements was a belief in Gnosis, in the possibility of gaining a personal knowledge of God.

The Gnostic belief in divine knowledge was often believed to put adherents beyond the laws of man – and so beyond the moral code. Many mainstream religions leapt to the conclusion that Gnostics must therefore indulge in all manner of licentious goings on. While some certainly did (see Chapter Three), others lived a life of simplicity, dedicated to achieving the inner personal experience of God through purity and self-restraint.

While Elizabeth Prophet's Church Universal and Triumphant is one example of a New Age movement influenced by the beliefs of these early Jewish and Christian sects, another twentieth century movement which has evolved from the same corps of thinking is the Universal White Brotherhood. The two groups exemplify how radically different movements claiming the same heritage could – and can – be.

Based at Sèvres outside Paris but with centres throughout much of the Western world, the Universal White Brotherhood is inspired by the Master Omraam Mikhael Aivanhov (1900–86). Born in Bulgaria, Aivanhov had an 'experience with the light', a type of divine illumination, when he was fourteen years old and before long became a disciple of the Bulgarian Master Peter Deunov. A clairvoyant, Deunov was well aware of the coming troubles and in 1937 sent Aivanhov to France. There, Aivanhov developed the teaching further, taking divine inspiration as his guide.

According to Norman Frizell of the Dove's Nest, a small Brotherhood community in England, the Universal White Brotherhood is firmly rooted in a tradition reaching back through the Bogomils to the Essenes. It incorporates elements of Christianity, Judaism and Hinduism but is headed by Christ.

Aivanhov's teachings point up what, through the ages, has turned the mainstream Church against Gnostic thinking. In an address to a gathering of his followers he said, 'If you were really very strong and able to resist all those influences, if you were capable of transforming the impurities that you pick up, you could do whatever you please with impunity'.[19]

The Brotherhood focuses on 'the one central question of man and his growth in perfection' finding backing from the quotation from St Matthew's Gospel, 'Be ye therefore perfect even as your father which is in heaven is perfect.' Through such efforts, 'the Kingdom of God may be established on earth'.[20] Again like the Gnostics, Aivanhov teaches his followers that, 'If they identify with the physical body (the form), they will never develop their spirit which is eternal, immortal and omniscient, a spark of God Himself.' On the other hand, those who develop their spirit 'are working for the Kingdom of God and the coming of the Golden Age'.[21]

Aivanhov was never specific about when the golden age would occur, but did warn the Brotherhood they would have to go through a period of trouble – known enigmatically as 'the events' – beforehand. 'We are working to create the Kingdom of God on earth,' says Frizell. 'We have to start on ourselves, to find the God within us and bring it out. We may not become perfect in this life, but if we follow Aivanhov's teaching, we will attain it in a later incarnation.'[22]

For Aivanhov, 'Christ is a Cosmic Principle . . . a solar spirit.' He believed that, 'It is the sun that will open our eyes to the "new heaven" . . . A new light is dawning . . . and it will create such harmony and unity amongst men that the whole earth will be one family, and brotherliness and peace will reign throughout the world.'[23]

Each year, up to a thousand members of the Universal White Brotherhood gather at the 'Bonfin', a property near Fréjus on the French Riviera. There, they assemble each morning on a rocky hilltop plateau for dawn meditations. Likewise, in their scattered communities, the Brethren rise before dawn each morning in summer to meditate and watch the sun rise. According to Greek sources, the Essenes rose before dawn and prayed to the rising sun. Certainly, in early Christian times, Jesus was often identified with the sun god, and running throughout the many Gnostic movements was the belief that particles of light had become imprisoned in the world and should be liberated and returned to the divine world of light.

'By getting to know the sun more intimately, in his sublime mani-
festations of light, heat and life, human beings will also come closer
and closer to the Deity, and the earth will become a Garden of Eden
where all men will live together as brothers,' said Aivanhov.[24] This
Edenic paradise will be 'the Age of Aquarius', ushered in and overseen
by 'one religion: the religion of light, warmth and life, the religion of
the sun'.[25]

After their sun meditations, members of the Brotherhood say
prayers and, like members of Gurdjieff's Institute for the Harmonious
Development of Mankind, perform spiritual breathing and physical exercises. Whereas Gurdjieff's exercises were intended to break
down the performer's mechanicalness and bring about individual
enlightenment, according to Aivanhov: 'When we do these exercises
all together we form a tremendously powerful collective force . . .
The more numerous we are, and the more keenly aware we are,
while doing these exercises, that we are creating currents of love
and harmony, the more we can be sure that beneficial waves will
sweep over the whole of mankind.'[26] The practice seems similar to
that of the Maharishi Mahesh Yogi's TM programme, which teaches
that if a set proportion of the world perform the technique, the effect
will be universal harmony.

Before meals, which are eaten in silence, the Brotherhood sing
four-part songs in Bulgarian, composed by mystic Peter Deunov. All
their daily activities, down to brushing their teeth, are based 'on the
science of the harmonious and balanced development of man's many
faculties'. 'It is a difficult teaching, at times, and Aivanhov could be
very demanding,' says Frizell. 'He is always pushing you to achieve
perfection in everything you do.'[27]

According to Aivanhov, heaven on earth will be a type of internal
transformation, 'mankind's mentality will change and humanity will
develop a new way of looking at things and behaving'. Again in
the Gnostic tradition, Aivanhov rejects dogma and teaches that, 'The
religion taught by Jesus was perfect . . . But it has been so deformed
over the centuries, that nowadays it is an artificial culture-medium
swarming with the germs of every kind of fermentation.'[28]

It was the same line of thinking that sparked off the Reformation.
The Roman Catholic Church had, until the sixteenth century, reigned
supreme in the West, gathering to itself the right to lay down doctrine
as well as immense power and wealth. There had been breakaway
movements from time to time, but none was so far-reaching as that of

the German Martin Luther. The atmosphere generated by his rebuttal of centuries of accepted doctrine inspired others to lay claim to the Truth, and innumerable movements sprang up, claiming they were God's chosen bearers of the light. For too long, it seemed, they had been governed by an over-privileged and corrupt clergy. And to top it all, while the laity were having to pay increasingly high taxes, the clergy – many of whom were wealthy aristocrats – were almost entirely exempt from taxation.

Among the many movements to arise from the ferment was that of the Anabaptists whose fascinating story Norman Cohn tells in his *The Pursuit of the Millennium*. Formed in the early sixteenth century and divided into some forty different groups, the Anabaptists were loosely united by their belief in the need for adults to be re-baptised – from which they earned their name – and their ideal of living together like members of the early church, in brotherly love and equality. Many, however, came to see themselves as superior to all those who remained un-re-baptised – and both Luther and the Roman Catholics came to view them as agents of the Anti-Christ. As a result, countless Anabaptists were persecuted and killed; the Anabaptist interpretation of the slaughters was that the last days must be drawing near. Heaven on earth was imminent.

The more the Anabaptists were trodden down, the more their leaders raised their hopes with millennial prophecies. The townspeople of Munster in north-west Germany had suffered more than most from taxation and were primed for a religion which held before them the vision of a promised land, governed by the principle of equal distribution of wealth. Blessed with an inspirational preacher, Munster began to throng with Anabaptists, who soon heard the war cry of Anabaptist Jan Matthijszoon, a former baker from Haarlem in Holland. His divinely-inspired mission, he claimed, was to cleanse the earth of the ungodly. In 1534 Jan Bockelszoon, a disciple of Matthijszoon, arrived in town. Before long it was announced that Munster would become the New Jerusalem – and the rest of the world would be destroyed.

Eventually, the Anabaptists gained control of the town council, the Lutherans and Catholics were driven out into the bitter weather and their legacy was obliterated in a mass burning of books. The townspeople were reaching fever pitch – and beyond – in expectation of the apocalypse, falling foaming to their knees in the streets and shrieking out their visions in apoplectic frenzy. Matthijszoon arrived on the scene, and the unbaptised crawled on their hands and knees begging his forgiveness. For those who remained unforgiven, death was the penalty. The town was soon under siege from the Catholics; but the Munster Anabaptists mounted an effective propaganda campaign, claiming they were living in joy, equality and brotherly love. The poverty-stricken Anabaptists in neighbouring provinces were happy to believe heaven lay just a few miles away.

When Matthijszoon set foot on a divine mission outside the city walls, he was instantly killed and Bockelszoon took over the kingdom's reins. Death became the penalty for everything down to lying and quarrelling – and quarrelling broke out in full force when Bockelszoon instituted polygamy. 'Go forth and multiply' said the Bible – and the men were instructed to balance out the excess number of women by taking several wives, Bockelszoon himself ending up with more than a dozen.

In 1534 Bockelszoon was proclaimed King of the New Jerusalem, the messiah whose coming was foretold by the Old Testament prophets. As executions became an almost daily event, and as Bockelszoon lived in greater and greater luxury, the remaining townspeople were buoyed up with ever-mounting visions of the millenium. Soon, troops surrounded and blockaded the town. Within a few months, food had run out and the people of Munster were reduced to eating dogs, rats and even the bodies of the dead. Still, they were told, Christ would return – and the corpse-like living were ordered to dance and celebrate his imminent arrival.

Eventually, Bockelszoon allowed some of the townspeople to leave Munster – though promising them they would be eternally damned. The men were instantly killed and the women, reduced to crawling around between the town and the surrounding troops eating grass, begged to have their lives ended likewise. On June 24, 1535 one of the exiles showed the besiegers a secret route into the city. The 200–300 surviving Anabaptists were promised safety if they gave in peacefully, but, after laying down their arms, were massacred. Bockelszoon and other leaders were lead about the neighbouring German towns on chains, then returned to Munster and tortured to death.

The carnage at Munster put an end to the Anabaptists' militant drive. But their original ideals of brotherly love and equality have inspired movements which exist today, including the Baptists, Quakers and Hutterian Brethren. Some of the Hutterian Brethren live in imitation of the early Christians of the first 200 years AD in

Bruderhof Communities in England, Germany, the United States and Canada, awaiting with 'urgent longing and hope' for the day when 'all men and women on this Earth will . . . live in true justice and brotherhood under the rulership of God'.[29]

Noel Stanton, founder of the Jesus Fellowship Church which has its roots in the Baptist movement, is today attempting to build the kingdom of heaven in a small English village. His 'New Creation Christian Community' has some 600 members who attempt to follow the lifestyle adopted by the Christians in Jerusalem in the first days of the Church. Property is shared and any wages are handed over to the communal purse. Nonetheless, or perhaps consequently, the Community has built up a successful business empire – a move seen by Stanton as taking resources from the world to further the work of the kingdom.

With the wealth generated by the Community's commercial enterprises, the Jesus People, as they are known, can outbid others for properties, enabling God, they believe, to replace the existing world with his chosen one. The walls of New Creation Farm are covered with slogans such as 'Pray for more celibates' and, under the banner 'Love, Power and Sacrifice', teams of followers, known as the 'Jesus Army', tour Britain seeking out new residents for the kingdom of god.

Another Baptist, the American William Miller, gave birth in the nineteenth century to Adventism. According to his calculations, the second coming would occur sometime between March 1843 and March 1884. Excitement mounted, but the kingdom of heaven failed to descend. Then one of Miller's followers set a new date for October 1844 – but again nothing happened. The non-event became known as the Great Disappointment and a disillusioned Millerite offshoot developed into the Seventh Day Adventist Church. As time went on, more and more offshoots were spawned.

In the twentieth century, Herbert W. Armstrong (1892–1986), founder of Adventist offshoot the Worldwide Church of God (WCG) saw his organization as God's church of the last days, identical to the Philadelphia Church of Revelation: 'Because thou hast kept the word of my patience, I also will keep thee from the hour of temptation, which shall come upon all the world, to try them that dwell upon the earth. Behold, I come quickly: hold that fast which thou hast, that no man take thy crown . . . and I will write upon him the name of my God, and the name of the city of my God, which is new Jerusalem, which cometh down out of heaven from my God . . .'[30]

Armstrong told his followers that they would survive the destruction of the last days by being transported to caves in the Jordanian desert in January 1972. Many members planned their lives around the event, selling up their houses in expectation. Nothing happened. Some disillusioned members left the movement, but there are always newcomers, keen to believe that heaven on earth is at hand.

In July 1989, the WCG's *The Plain Truth* magazine, which has a circulation of some six million worldwide, announced: 'The prophecies of the Bible show that the world is destined once more to explode in violence and cruelty, under the heel of a military, economic, political and religious power that the Bible labels "Babylon the Great" . . . – many of us alive today may see it in *fact*. Ominous signs show the "end time" may not be far off.' One of the ominous signs of 'humanity's insane rush towards self-destruction' is the advance of technology and modern medicine: 'So it shouldn't be surprising that like Frankenstein's monster, humankind's new technology is about to turn on us.'

Following the widescale devastation, Jesus Christ, 'the greatest newscaster' of all time will return 'to establish a *new government* over all others. A government devoted to right education based on the immutable Word of God – a government devoted to implementations of policies that really are for the good of all humanity. It's more than a dream. It's the reality of the future.' What humanity must continue to believe in is that: 'The world tomorrow – that paradise we announce in the pages of *The Plain Truth* – will soon be ushered in!'[31]

What will heaven be like? 'It is a magnificent, splendor-filled place . . . It is in fact this earth! Not the polluted, befouled, ruined planet we see all around us today but a beautiful, clean, properly governed world, free of sin and evil . . . Yes, there are splendid and awesome things in store for this earth and for those who shall inherit it forever.'[32]

The early nineteenth century saw a mass influx of Europeans to the United States and Joseph Smith (1805–1844) offered the resulting displaced souls a national identity, the belief that they were God's chosen ones. God, said Smith, had revealed to him that the Garden of Eden had been situated in Missouri, that Christ had visited America sometime after his resurrection – where he had delivered the Sermon on the Mount – and that America was to be the centre of God's future purposes.

Joseph Smith claimed that he had discovered a number of golden plates inscribed with a language he called Reformed Egyptian. The translation of the plates resulted in the *Book of Mormon*, published in 1830. That same year, Smith founded the Church of Jesus Christ of Latter Day Saints in New York State. These plates had, said Smith, belonged to descendants of the Lost Tribes of Israel who had disappeared at the time of King Zedekiah in around 586BC but had, according to the *Book of Mormon*, crossed to the New World. The tribe died out in 421AD, but the last members, the prophet Mormon and his son Moroni, hid the golden plates as a record for posterity.

In 1843 Smith introduced polygamy to his religion. Controversy broke out, Smith was jailed and armed men broke in and killed him. The practice of polygamy was outlawed in 1890, but most of Smith's teaching has remained intact and has drawn thousands upon thousands of followers, centred on Salt Lake City, Utah.

Latter Day Saints believe that before Jesus ushers in the millennium, Mormons will gather in an American Zion and Jews will gather in Jerusalem. Then, with Christ's second coming, there will be a massive physical transformation of the planet: the continents will join together, mountains will be levelled and valleys raised. Earth will be transformed into a Garden of Eden where the weather will always be fine and the righteous will live in peace and harmony. Cities will be built, crops planted, harvested and eaten, industries and education expanded. At the end of 1000 years, Satan will tempt the righteous for a short period before the final judgement. The renewed earth will be a sea of glass and fire, inhabited by those who are deserving of celestial glory, the highest level of whom will become like gods.

Another movement which surfaced in the nineteenth century was Zion's Watch Tower Tract Society, or the Jehovah's Witnesses. Its founder, American Charles Taze Russell, born the son of a clothes store owner in 1852, cheerfully set about predicting dates for the Christ's second coming. Using a complicated series of mathematical equations, he initially came up with the year 1874. As on his first sojourn on earth, Christ would preach for three-and-a-half years before establishing heaven on earth – a paradise populated by Russell's followers – and then return to heaven with the 144,000 of his inner elite, a number taken from Revelation.

But the awaited date came and went – with the faithful few dressed in white robes in expectation of their transportation to heaven – and nothing happened. Despite this display of their leader's fallibility,

Russell's movement continued to grow. Then, using calculations involving complex measurements from Egypt's Great Pyramid, Russell hit upon 1914 as the date when Christ's kingdom would be established in the heavens. By then, the movement had about 15,000 members and 55,000 followers.

Two years later, Russell died. He was succeeded by Joseph Franklin Rutherford, a circuit judge, who soon poured scorn on Russell's fascination with Pyramid calculations and set about turning the group into an efficiently run, well-advertised movement. Since the 1930s, the Jehovah's Witnesses have been proclaiming 'Millions Now Living Will Never Die', that Armageddon will happen in our lifetime and give rise to the New World, the New System or the New Order.

The year 1975 became the date set for the apocalypse. Again, nothing happened. But the predictions continue. According to a Jehovah's Witness publication of 1985, 'Mankind is now facing "the final part of the days" . . . Now, you are beginning to see what God's Kingdom is. It is a government in heaven, its King is Jesus Christ, and he is joined by 144,000 people from the earth. It will rule over faithful mankind on earth and will have the power to bring peace to the earth.'[33] In 1990 the Witnesses announced that 'the Bible is no supporter of any of the now growing number of doomsday prophets and movements that point to the stroke of midnight on New Year's Eve, 1999, as the end of the world. However, present world events clearly show that the time of the end of this dark, wicked system of things is "well along" and that Christ's millennium has "drawn near" . . . Jehovah's Witnesses are willing and able to help you be among those who will enjoy the blessings of the coming grand Millennium.'[34]

Along with many other Christians, Jehovah's Witnesses, of whom there are some four million today, feel that the deliberate intention to create an earthly paradise is morally wrong. The coming of the Anti-Christ will bring with it a living hell – chaos, murder, all possible evils. At the same time, it will herald the second coming and the Kingdom of Saints and is therefore anticipated by some with relish.

Being bound to submit to God's divine plan for the arrival of Armageddon, Jehovah's Witnesses are forbidden to have any truck with politics. According to a Witness pamphlet, *The Government That Will Bring Paradise:* 'King Jesus will "strike the nations . . . and he will shepherd them with a rod of iron". . . . Consequently, Jehovah's

Witnesses, although they pay their taxes and obey the laws of the land, do not get involved in politics.'[35] Far from celebrating *glasnost*, Witnesses say, 'It would appear that the nations that were formerly belligerent and suspicious of one another are now moving cautiously toward a situation in which they will be able to declare world peace and security. Therefore, from still another angle, we know that the day of Jehovah's judgment upon false religion, the nations, and their ruler, Satan, is near.'[36] As backing, they quote Thessalonians: 'For when they shall say, Peace and safety; then sudden destruction cometh upon them . . . and they shall not escape.'[37]

The New Age, on the other hand, celebrates *glasnost*, seeing it as a move towards 'one world'. Jesuit priest Pierre Teilhard de Chardin (1881–1955), one of the most influential New Age figures, looked forward to global unification through the emergence of a new form of Chistianity, brought about by an evolution of consciousness.

Somewhat in the manner of the thirteenth century mystic Joachim of Fiore, Teilhard prophesied a conspiracy of men and women who would trigger a 'critical contagion of change' for mankind as a whole. We are now in the transitional period but, 'There is for us in the future not only survival but superlife,' he wrote. In Joachim's Third Age, the Age of the Spirit, the whole of mankind would live in love and freedom. Using calculations taken from the Bible, he predicted the culmination of human history would take place between 1200 and 1260AD and would be ushered in with the help of a new order of spiritual monks.

It all seems light years away from members of the Church Universal and Triumphant, holed up in their Armageddon shelters. But there is a connection. Elizabeth Prophet's movement was apparently founded by 'the Ascended Master El Morya of Darjeeling, India' – and El Morya is none other than that same ascended master who spoke to Mme Helena Blavatsky, founder of the Theosophical Society. The Theosophists' Koot Hoomi – Kuthumi to Elizabeth Prophet – is also a regular Church adviser. And to the Church Universal and Triumphant Kuthumi is none other than St Francis (c 1181–1226) – who, according to a breakaway group of Franciscans, inaugurated Joachim's age of the spirit.

St Francis is looked up to by New Agers not only because of his spirituality, simple love of Christ and tolerance of other religions, but also because of his love of nature and insistence on the sanctity of all creation. It is, say many New Agers, the usual Christian teaching of mankind's superiority towards and dominance over nature which makes them turn away from that religion. Far from seeing Christianity as ushering in heaven on earth, they see the Christian attitude as helping to destroy the world we have.

TEN | GREEN SPIRITUALITY

In a small village in southern England lives a family of witches. Their presence there is not so unusual, for the village is within a short journey of Glastonbury and close to other ancient sacred sites. Witches, pagans and mystics tend to gather in the area. The family are part of a growing movement which aims to demystify witchcraft and reclaim it as a natural, nature-loving religion. The parents, 'Fay' and 'Leo', are both members of Britain's Green Party and most of the spells they conduct are for planetary healing. Their nine-year-old son is, they say, 'great at doing little healing spells with stones and flowers'.[1]

On an everyday basis, the family seek to live 'as close to the earth as possible, in as best a way we can', getting by financially on odd jobs, tarot readings and healings. Their home is sparsely furnished, yet they are happy with it – but for the fact that its concrete foundations stifle the earth's energy. They eat simple food, drink homemade wine and have built a natural fridge in the back garden, digging into the earth and building up the walls with stones. It has been partly a matter of necessity: when their consumer undurables break down, they cannot afford to replace them.

Sometimes, Fay and Leo will conduct spells sitting naked by candlelight, especially to celebrate the sabbats – seasonal festivals – and full moons. Most days, Fay will go into her Inner Realm, where she will communicate with her spirit guides, which usually appear to her as animals.

It is not easy for the family to speak out, as stories attributing ritual child abuse to witches periodically sweep the country. But to their kind, persecution is nothing new. Both Leo and his son have experienced memories of being burnt at the stake in previous lives – supposed victims of the medieval witch hunts, conducted by the Church in continental Europe and in Britain largely by the State. According to Fay and Leo, however, harm is done by those who are out of tune with nature and use their natural powers unknowingly – not by those who attune themselves to the natural energies.

Leo and Fay are both refugees from Christianity – though they have no quarrel with Jesus, whom they see as a loving, gentle peacemaker. Christianity, however, they believe, has taught humanity to dominate nature rather than to live in harmony with it. Fay can reel off the relevant verses from the Bible – 'And God said, Let us make man in our image, after our likeness: and let them have dominion over the fish of the sea, and over the fowl of the air, and over the cattle, and over all the earth, and over every creeping thing that creepeth upon the earth . . .' (Genesis 1:26); and –

What is man, that thou art mindful of him? . . .
For thou hast made him a little lower than the angels,
And hast crowned him with glory and honour.
Thou madest him to have dominion over the works of thy hands;
Thou hast put all things under his feet:
All sheep and oxen,
Yea, and the beasts of the field;
The fowl of the air, and the fish of the sea
And whatsoever passeth through the paths of the seas.
O Lord our Lord,
How excellent is thy name in all the earth! (Psalm 8)

Many proponents of the New Age also agree with the pagan diagnosis of the planet's suffering. And indeed to many, of whatever religion, the environmental crisis is concrete evidence of the approaching apocalypse. As some ecologists give us fifteen years to save the planet, as national newspapers mock up terrifying pictures of drowned cities on their front pages, and as books with titles such as *The End of Nature* fill the shelves, there seems to be plenty of evidence for their anxiety.

In his 1971 book *This Endangered Planet*, Richard Falk predicts that 'a disaster of catastrophic proportions is likely to occur in the 1990s'. The disaster, he suggests, might take the shape of induced earthquakes or large scale pollution of oceans, rivers, forests and skies. In this event, he says, the twenty-first century will be an 'Era of Annihilation'. On the other hand, if humanity gets its act together, the 1990s will be the 'Decade of Transformation' and, 'as awareness crystallizes and as mobilization proceeds, the transformation of world order will begin to occur'. If such a transformation transpires, the twenty-first century will be the 'Era of World Harmony'.[2]

However, if former British Green Party spokesman David Icke is to be believed, the former scenario will arise. In 1991, two decades on from the year Falk made his predictions, Icke announced the onset of earthquakes and other natural disasters, culminating in the end of the world – an event which, he said, would probably occur in 1997. In his self-proclaimed role as channel for the Christ Spirit, Icke will do his best to avert such a catastrophe.

Rather than relying on the Christ Spirit, Falk suggested that survival universities or colleges of world ecology should be established in order to help usher in the era of world harmony. A number of such colleges have sprung up, some on an *ad hoc* basis, others on a more ambitious scale, such as Schumacher College in Britain – the 'new International Centre for the Study and practice of Spiritual and Ecological Values'.

But according to some survivalists, only a powerful central government will implement the changes necessary for a sustainable future, and in some 'green' camps survivalism has even acquired a paramilitary fervour.

While some see the dangers of totalitarianism lurking in the survivalist mentality, others are equally discomfited by the approach which suggests that the only answer to the impending catastrophe is to tackle the problem on the level of global consciousness – that is to attune to, and transform the situation. This, say detractors, is equivalent to licensing inaction. It is, however, a solution with which both pagans and New Agers agree – though not to the exclusion of outward action. Unless human beings recognize their unity with all creation, they say, there is no hope for the planet. Pagans and New Agers clearly have much in common – and indeed many New Agers are themselves pagans – but some pagans believe the New Age lacks a grounded quality, losing itself in esoteric pursuits rather than rooting itself in nature. And, points out Fay, some aspects of the New Age are simply commercial enterprises – the boom in crystals, for example, simply exploits the earth's resources, she says.

When Fay first came across witchcraft she was put in touch with John Score, known as 'M', a former Royal Air Force flight lieutenant who had turned to witchcraft and retired to the New Forest. Feeling immediately at home with her new religion, Fay tested out a coven but decided instead to become a solitary or hedge witch – something akin to the village wise woman of olden times. Like 'M', she prefers to think of witchcraft as 'wisecraft'. Some witches call themselves wiccans, which they say derives from the Old English for wise (wis) or for witch (wicca). According to Fay, it is increasingly common for witches to practise their craft alone and to do away with the razamatazz of coven life which, say many witches, can all too easily degenerate into an excuse for dressing up in bizarre outfits and acting out erotic fantasies. No real witch would have anything to do with such goings on, they say.

'M' played an important role in what is known as the 'pagan revival' of the 1970s and 80s. In 1971 he helped to found the Pagan Front, now the Pagan Federation, a London-based networking organization which provides information on the numerous pagan groups. Paganism takes as one of its key principles: 'Love for and kinship with Nature, participation in the cosmic Dance of Goddess and God, Woman and Man, rather than the more customary attitude of aggression and domination over Nature, or suppression of the female principle.'[3]

While the Pagan Federation was finding its feet in Britain, the Pagan Way took off in America, influenced by, among others, 'M'. The Pagan Way provided an opportunity and a set of principles for like-minded nature lovers to get together in groves, or groups. When some members wanted to get involved in more esoteric mysticism, other groups were formed. Although the Pagan Way no longer exists, its principles are still followed by numerous neo-pagan groups.

The three main principles of neo-paganism are polytheism, pantheism and animism. Trees, flowers and stones all have their own spirits, and the Divine is immanent in all nature. Seeing God in everything, as identified with nature, borders on the Christian heresy of pantheism, conflicting with the orthodox Christian view of God as transcendent and so distinct from his creation. While many Christians argue that pantheism 'lowers' man to the level of beasts, nature lovers often argue that only human beings are capable of true depravity.

For pagans, life is woven together into an interconnected and interdependent whole and it is through paganism that mankind can re-enter that unified world – one from which, say many pagans, most Westerners become alienated after childhood. The poet and Christian mystic Thomas Traherne (c 1636–74) describes the process: 'Certainly Adam in Paradise had not more sweet and curious apprehensions of the world, than I when I was a child . . . Eternity was manifest in the Light of the Day, and something infinite behind everything appeared . . . The city seemed to stand in Eden, or to be built in Heaven. The streets were mine, the temple was mine . . . The skies were mine, and so were the sun and moon and stars, and all the World was mine; and I was the only spectator and enjoyer of it. I knew no churlish proprieties, nor bounds, nor divisions: but all proprieties and divisions were mine: all treasures and the possessors of them. So that with much ado I was corrupted and made to learn the dirty devices of this world. Which now I unlearn, and become, as it were, a little child again that I may enter into the Kingdom of God.'4

Pagans would say it is possible to retain the wonder and oneness of childhood throughout life, and that Traherne's Christianity had heightened his alienation from the kingdom. Many pagans work as therapists, and a movement known as 'deep ecology' has emerged which aims both to empower the individual and heal the planet. According to one New Age workshop '. . . many of us close off to the pain of the world and thereby disempower ourselves from experiencing our own wholeness as human beings and from taking effective action to help the planet'.5

In 1970, Otter Zell, high priest of the California-based Church of All Worlds, experienced a vision in which he saw earth as a single vast creature which had emerged from a single cell. Zell called this being Terrebia. Eventually, he said, when man shrugged off his alienation from Terrebia by achieving telepathic union with it, humanity would evolve to a new stage of being. One way to bring about this evolution, said Zell, is to become involved in the ecology movement. In 1975, he heard about the work of British scientist James Lovelock, developer of what came to be called the Gaia Hypothesis, and the two corresponded briefly. In Greek mythology, Gaia is the earth goddess.

The Gaia Hypothesis suggests that the world, like the human body, is a single, self-regulating system and that the planet, together with everything on it, is a living entity. Conventional wisdom, on the other hand, suggests that the planet and life thereon evolved in separate ways and that living entities were compelled to adapt to planetary conditions. The Gaia Hypothesis has had a profound effect in ecological circles, offering scientific credibility for a new vision of reality. The ecologically-minded tend to believe that if humanity reclaims its relationship to the planet, as part of one living whole, we might see an end to the ecological crisis. Shortly after learning about Lovelock's work, Zell changed the name of his visionary earth from Terrebia to Gaea.

The Church of All Worlds was the brainchild of a group of Heinlein fans. In his novel *Stranger in a Strange Land*, Robert Heinlein's hero, Martian-born human Valentine Michael Smith, forms a Church of All Worlds devoted to a full appreciation or 'grokking' of the divine in everything. In its early days, the Church was organized into small groups or nests – just as in Heinlein's novel.

Zell was also interested in the ideas of humanistic psychologist Abraham Maslow, one of the key inspirational figures in the Human Potential Movement. For a time, his Church teamed up with an organization called Fereferia to explore not human potential but what Fereferia's founder, Fred Adams, called 'eco-psychic' potential.

Adams dreamed up Fereferia in the late 1950s. In this utopian society, the dehumanizing technological advances of man would be scrapped and life would once again be rooted in nature. With a number of hand-picked members, Adams formed a group of Fereferians who aimed to live by 'eco-psychic' principles, seeking at all times to relate to nature and the earth. The global Fereferia they dreamt of would support some ten to twenty million inhabitants, whittled down from today's figures by birth control and natural disasters. The survivors would be divided into communities of roughly 1000, and live off fruits and berries, nuts and vegetables. Instead of cities there would be cultural centres where people would come together to worship and celebrate nature.

Like other neo-pagans, many modern-day Druids work to heal humanity's alienation from nature. London-based Philip Carr-Gomm, chief of the Order of Bards, Ovates and Druids (OBOD), explains that Druidry, rather than being a religion, is 'A particular way of working with and understanding the natural world. It puts forward various philosophical schemes which can be helpful to people in steering themselves through life.'

'One of the problems people have today is that they feel alienated,' he explains. 'Psychotherapy aims to heal this feeling of separation. But people also feel alienated from the earth. Druidry provides a way to reconnect to a sense of oneness.'[6] According to Carr-Gomm, Druidry offers humanity a way out of the industrial wasteland we have created by exploiting nature, and into a new age of naturalism.

As a teenager, Carr-Gomm learnt the ancient wisdom of Druidry from previous OBOD chief Ross Nicholls, then headmaster of an exclusive London crammer. How many of Nicholls' students picked up the wisdom along with their more run-of-the-mill studies is uncertain. But a blurred photograph of the time shows one pupil, a young Winston Churchill, at an exotic Druidic gathering, dressed in long robes, a false beard providing the finishing touch to his outfit.

Carr-Gomm went on to take a degree in psychology and to train as a psychotherapist. Later, he returned to Druidry, seeing it as a means of integrating the ecological and spiritual concerns of our times. 'People tend to operate either on the level of cause – the spiritual dimension, or effect – the ecological dimension,' he explains. 'Druidry enables them to combine the two.'[7]

On taking over the reins of the OBOD in the mid-1980s, Carr-Gomm's first aim was to return Druidry to its roots. The Druids belonged to the priestly caste of the Celts, who can be traced back to the Bronze Age. But most modern-day knowledge of the Druids relies heavily on accounts given by the Greeks and Romans – and since the Romans suppressed the Druids in the first century AD, most of their reports are far from flattering. One Roman historian, however, concedes that the Druids searched into 'things most secret and sublime'.[8] Certainly, they appear to have been concerned with philosophical, theological and educational issues including astronomy, poetry, natural medicine, omens and sacrifices.

Some years ago, Carr-Gomm rediscovered a manuscript owned by Ross Nicholls, to whom, he says, many Druidic secrets had been passed down. Mysteriously lost for several years after his death, its recovery has, says Carr-Gomm, helped to reclaim the ancient wisdom for posterity. Now, he is concerned with finding an expression of Druidry which is 'appropriate and relevant to the twentieth century'. And that means bridging the gap between the New Age and the pagan scene. 'One of the reasons I like Druidry is that it has a much more grounded quality than a lot of New Age thinking. Druidry is connected to the earth, our heritage and our roots – it has a shamanistic component.'

Carr-Gomm holds workshops and retreats all over the world.

Using ceremony, meditation and visualization, he aims to show trainees that their individual journey is part of the natural process. 'By getting individuals to relate to the sun, to trees and stars and stones, Druidry takes the integrative experience a step further than straightforward psychotherapy,' he says.[9] Those interested in becoming Druids themselves can sign up for the Order's correspondence course. Druids also work on a more practical level: Carr-Gomm has initiated environmental campaigns and has run a programme of planting sacred groves.

The Graigian Order, a New Age monastic community based in London also actively campaigns on green issues – and indeed calls itself the 'First Green Party'. Founded in 1971, members eat communal breakfast in the nude, consult the runes, read tarot cards and fight to protect the countryside, as well as London's heritage. Believing that spiritual development should go hand in hand with environmental issues, they practise 'natural psychology', based on Carl Jung's ideas, and aim to create a 'natural and sensitive world'.[10]

While the Graigian Order seeks a political voice, an organization known as the Movement or the Community seeks overt political power. The Movement's roots were laid two years before the foundation of the Graigian Order by Mario Rodriguez Cobo, an Argentinian businessman called Silo by his followers. Since its inception, it has grown to challenge many of the world's mainstream green political parties.

In 1969, Silo delivered his rallying speech from a rocky plain high in the Andes mountains. The 'harangue', or 'Sermon on the Mount', as it came to be called, was later published as *The Healing of Suffering*. 'This world is on the verge of exploding,' he announced. 'My brother, fulfil simple commandments, simple like these stones, this snow, and this sun that blesses us. Carry peace within yourself and carry it to others . . .'[11] Silo's aim was to bring about transformation within the individual which would eventually give rise to world transformation by means, he predicted, of 'total revolution', a 'historical rupture'.[12]

Aware that transformation held little appeal to the average man on the street, Silo set about acquiring political clout. 'Our tactic is to have access to power by setting up a parallel organization to the system and emptying it,' he said. 'When everything is chaotic, the people will choose us.'[13] Known at first as the Community for the Equilibrium and Development of the Human Being, in 1990 Movement membership stood at between ten and twenty thousand, and followers had spread Silo's message to more than forty countries worldwide, including Europe, the United States and South America.

In the 1980s, Silo's organization entered candidates for numerous political elections in America and Europe, sometimes polling more votes than the mainstream green parties. In various different countries, candidates called themselves representatives of the Greens, the Green Party, Green Ecologists, or Green Future. In Spain's 1989 European elections, the home-grown Greens suffered what one activist describes as a 'serious electoral setback',[14] when the Movement's green offshoot split the vote. Mainstream green parties were outraged. While many mainstream green voters were confused by Silo's Greens, others were won over by their prophecy of apocalyptic doom.

For those interested in personal transformation, Silo provided lengthy encounter sessions, group confessions and candle-lit meditations, sometimes aimed at coming to terms with death and often accompanied by New Age music. In the early days, birth and marriage rituals were conducted. Hermann Hesse's novel *The Glass Bead Game* was turned to for inspiration and advanced Siloists were known as Game Masters – after the intellectual élite who directed the evolution of mankind in Hesse's book. Silo himself was often referred to as Prime Magister, and was ranked by his followers with Mahatma Gandhi and Martin Luther King. He is, says a former Siloist, seen as 'a major prophet who is going to transform the world with his radical new ideas'.[15]

According to a Siloist from Manchester, England, the Movement provides an environment where people are able to understand more about themselves and other people. Then, he says, they will be able to 'transform the world'. In its transformed state, the planet will be ruled by something akin to a global brain.

Many members of mainstream green parties believe there is a conspiracy behind Silo's organization. Certainly, the 'mystery' to be found in nature has, over the centuries, given rise to numerous esoteric groups. One form of Druidry, revived in Britain in the eighteenth century, was inspired by the then-current upsurge in freemasonry until, according to some critics, it became 'dominated by masonic rituals'. In the mid-twentieth century, Gerald Gardner's revived form of witchcraft also relied heavily on freemasonry. Many of today's pagans, like Philip Carr-Gomm, are seeking to find their own way back to their roots in nature. Others continue to pursue esoteric paths.

Gerald Gardner was introduced to witchcraft by the Fellowship of Crotona, part of a masonic order introduced to Britain by Theosophist Annie Besant. Gardner was admitted to a secret order of witches within the Fellowship who claimed to be inheritors of a craft passed down to them through the centuries. The Fellowship of Crotona founded 'The First Rosicrucian Theatre in England', carrying on the intense interest in Rosicrucianism which had been revived at around the time the Theosophical Society was founded (see Chapter 1).

Rosicrucianism first arose during the Renaissance, the result, it now seems, of two 'Rosicrucian manifestoes' published in 1614 and 1615, and an alchemical romance, *The Chemical Wedding of Christian Rosencreutz*, which appeared in 1616. The movement draws from various esoteric mystery schools including the Hermetic tradition in which one form of alchemy has its roots.

The manifestoes announced the imminent arrival of a New Age of enlightenment: 'God hath certainly and most assuredly concluded to send and grant to the world before her end, which presently thereupon shall ensue, such a truth, light, life and glory, as the first man Adam had, which he lost in Paradise . . .' one of the manifestoes proclaims. While few as yet can read and understand 'that great book of nature', it continues, a time approaches when '. . . the World shall awake out of her heavy and drowsy sleep, and with an open heart, bare-head, and bare-foot, shall merrily and joyfully meet the new arising Sun'.[16]

Readers of the manifestoes were also invited to join a secret order which held the key to the forthcoming transformation. Long since declared a hoax, they aroused – and continue to arouse – intense excitement. The central theme of the manifestoes typified and encouraged a trend of thought that sees heaven on earth as being achievable through universal knowledge – a knowledge whose secrets could be found in nature.

The Hermetic tradition in which Rosicrucianism is founded stems from the esoteric wisdom found in a collection of ancient mystical books known as the *Hermetica*, dating from around the first century AD. The guiding principle of these works is that through enquiry into nature, and the relationship between the earthly world of mankind and the heavenly kingdom of God, the secrets of the universe can be uncovered, thereby bringing about heaven on earth: 'That which is above is like that which is below and that which is below is like that which is above, to achieve the wonders of the one thing,' according to the Hermetic *Emerald Tablet*.[17]

Such ideas had a tremendous hold in some seventeenth century circles, and have been passed on through the ages, surfacing today in the Hermetically-inspired magic rituals and ceremonies conducted by many pagans. The two-way harmony between inner and outer is akin to the New Age belief that personal transformation leads to world transformation.

One of the Rosicrucian manifestoes, the *Fama*, refers to a secret book called 'M' – the inspiration, perhaps, for John Score's name. What's more, Score remembered having lived in Atlantis in a past life – and in his fictional utopia *New Atlantis*, written around 1624, Sir Francis Bacon hints that his community was home to the Rosicrucian brothers. Called Bensalem, the most important organization in Bacon's utopia is Salomon's House, which is shrouded in secrecy and dedicated 'to the study of the works and creatures of God'. The highest office in Salomon's House is that of the 'interpreters of Nature', because in nature the divine will be found.[18] Like the Rosicrucian Brotherhood, the Brethren of Salomon's House go out disguised into the world at large, seeking the light of knowledge.

The Renaissance also saw a revival of interest in Arcadia as the earthly paradise. Sir Philip Sidney (1554–86), who was taught by one of the perpetrators of the Rosicrucian hoax, wrote the best-selling poem *The Arcadia* which was published posthumously in 1590; and in the seventeenth century artists Nicolas Poussin (1594–1665) and Claude Lorraine (1600–82) turned out their famous idealized Arcadian landscapes.

In the eighteenth century, the German man of letters Goethe (1749–1832) was inspired by the Rosicrucian manifestoes, and set part of his *Faust*, his story of man's quest to acquire superhuman powers of wisdom, in Arcadia. Goethe, a keen botanist and alchemist as well as a poet, believed he lived on the verge of a new era. He inspired Sigmund Freud (1865–1939), and is a favourite amongst many of today's New Agers.

In Greek mythology, Arcadia – which in reality is situated in the central Peloponnese area of Greece – was home to the pastoral deity Pan, who looked after flocks and herds. Pan appears in the children's classic *The Wind in the Willows* by Kenneth Grahame, as an aspect of the horned god who, together with the goddess, rules over the cycle of nature. Jonathan Porrit, former director of environmental campaign group Friends of the Earth (UK), has, no doubt tongue in cheek, expressed his surprise at 'how few people realize that *The Wind in the Willows* is a deeply subversive green tract, and should be kept away from children at all costs'.[19] Pan was also worshipped by the satanist Aleister Crowley.

Victor Anderson, the founder of the Faery Tradition of Witchcraft in the early twentieth century, had a vision of the horned god at the age of nine when he was initiated into the craft. Other pagans worship the Green Man, a deity associated with Arthurian legend who symbolizes regeneration: the power of nature to die and rise again. Pagans claim the Green Man is now resurfacing in order to rescue humanity from difficult times and to provide them with the chance to become one with the universe. Many pagans believe that it is only through the Green Man that we can unite with nature and our unconscious powers.

One of today's most influential witches, Miriam Simos or Starhawk, was initiated into Anderson's Faery Tradition at the age of seventeen. Born in 1954, Starhawk is a writer, feminist and political activist, believing in non-violent direct action through power from within. In Britain she has performed rituals at Greenham Common; in America she has protested against nuclear power plants and military bases. According to Starhawk, change will come about through collectively challenging the power structures. In her time she has worked as a psychotherapist but now lectures worldwide, conducts workshops and teaches rituals, training people to create states of consciousness divorced from the traditional power structures.

One of Starhawk's lecture venues has been the Institute in Culture and Creation Spirituality at Holy Names College in Oakland, California. Founded in 1977 by Matthew Fox, a Dominican monk, Starhawk's presence there, and Fox's admiration of her work, has fuelled controversy, while Fox's own teachings have sent the Vatican Congregation for the Doctrine of Faith scuttling to find evidence of heresy in his work. So far, Fox has simply had to undergo a year's silence, from December 1988 to 1989, under pressure from the Vatican. Since then, he has returned to the lecture circuit.

Matthew Fox preaches 'creation centred spirituality'. Rather than spreading the doctrine of original sin, he celebrates original blessing, and his lectures and bestselling books have won him a following from all denominations as well as the ecologically minded. According to Fox, religion, currently part of the ecological problem, must be transformed into the solution. Mother Earth, he says, is crying out for help and while she continues to bestow blessing upon blessing on mankind, humanity continues to destroy her. For Fox, Mother Earth today is Jesus Christ crucified, and Chernobyl is the twentieth-century cloud of unknowing. Christianity has for too long preached man's domination over nature, he claims. Spirit and earth need to be reunited so that, through man's reintegration with nature, a redemptive transformation can occur.

Fox argues that by suppressing the child within, we suppress the mystical. But although the child within must be reawakened, we must also take an adult, responsible approach to our spirituality. To neglect responsibility is to stifle creativity and so kill God. According to Fox, humanity's right brain, the area of mysticism, sensuality and synthesis, has shrivelled up over the past 300 years, bringing a divide between body and spirit and preventing us from seeing the whole. We should, he says, look to the old religions – whether of Africa, Asia, America or Europe – for inspiration. These religions, he says, embrace the entire cosmos, and hold within them the seeds which could renew both Mother Earth and Christianity.

By resurrecting human consciousness, we will resurrect Mother Earth and Christ. Then, humanity will be able to recognize the interdependency of all life, to reconnect to the universe and build a world of 'erotic justice'. Creation centred spirituality 'liberates because it moves us from head to body where heart and passion (the source of compassion) will be found'.[20] We have to wake up to the fact that the kingdom – and queendom – of Jesus Christ is with us.

To some extent, Fox can be seen to have taken on the mantle of the Jesuit priest Pierre Teilhard de Chardin (1881–1955) who, like Fox, came under strictures from religious superiors. Teilhard describes the coming of the kingdom of God as 'the "implosive" encounter in human consciousness of the "ultra-human" and the "Christic" impulses': 'I am,' he says, 'more and more convinced – judging from my own infinitesimal experience – that this process is indeed possible, and is actually in operation, and that it will psychologically transfigure the world of tomorrow.'[21]

A distinguished botanist and great nature lover, Teilhard de Chardin's religious convictions, like those of Fox, verged on pantheism. But, while 'pantheism seduces us by its vistas of perfect universal union', it would, he said, 'give us only fusion and unconsciousness;

for at the end of the evolution it claims to reveal, the elements of the world vanish in the God they create or by which they are absorbed . . .'[22] Christianity, for Teilhard, enabled one to 'be united . . . while remaining oneself'.[23]

Fox avoids the pantheist heresy of seeing the divine as contained within creation by preaching the doctrine of panentheism; the belief that everything exists in God. The grossest of all dualisms, says Fox, is that between the divine and us. One of the themes in his book *Original Blessing* is 'From Cosmos to Cosmogenesis: Our Last Divinization as Images of God Who Are Also Co-creators'. For Fox, dualism creates sin. Evil, he says, should be embraced: 'We . . . need to let sin be sin for a while. To allow sin its rightful and even instructive place in our own and others' lives.'[24] Moreover, he suggests, 'Perhaps the time has come to play with God more than to pray to God, and in our play true prayer will emerge.'[25]

Reiterating the creed filtered down through Rabelais, Crowley and wiccans, Fox preaches, 'Love life – and do whatever you want.'[26] But then Augustine of Hippo had said 'love and do what you will'. Once experience is embraced in totality, says Fox, even the crucifixion can be described as 'the perverse pleasure, the masochism and the sadism . . . and experience of natural ecstasy'.[27] For Fox, God is 'the lover', an 'erotic God'.[28]

Fox's cosmic, ecstatic embrace entails a shift from an either/or philosophy to the position of both/and – from the dualistic to the dialectic. Some argue, however, that the history of religion has always been dialectic and that Fox, far from seeking to oust dualism and take on dialectic, is instead seeking to uproot orthodox Christianity and instate a totalitarian religious system – the New Age.[29]

'The creation centred spiritual tradition represents the appropriate spiritual paradigm for our time,' Fox insists.[30] 'Every priest and every minister ought to get re-cycled in creation centred spirituality and fast.'[31] While looking forward to 'an ecological age' he preaches 'realized eschatology': 'Now is the time; Now is the place; Now is the occasion . . . Now is the moment of divine breakthrough . . . We have already died . . . Therefore heaven has already burst forth . . . it has burst forth – believe it or not – in the person of ourselves.'[32] Among those Fox cites as belonging to the 'family tree' of creation centred spirituality are Jung, Maslow, Norman O. Brown and 'New Age mystics such as . . . Marilyn Ferguson'.

Fox has found support among many ecology groups. The World

Wide Fund for Nature, on the other hand, has taken on its own team of religious advisors – the International Consultancy on Religion, Education and Culture (ICOREC), staffed by an international team of consultants drawn from all the major faiths. ICOREC's director, Martin Palmer, describes Fox as 'on the edge of the utopian'. Nevertheless, he believes that the relationship between spirituality and ecology will be a major topic of the 1990s. Only by rethinking our relationship with the earth, say ICOREC's leaders, will a New Age emerge. 'It will require a "death" to the way we have hitherto understood ourselves and our relationship with Nature . . . a journey from "mastery" to "mystery".'[33]

Many mainstream Christians ignore their responsibility to nature, says Palmer, pointing out that harvest festivals have traditionally been a celebration of overproduction. ICOREC, however, has devised harvest festival material which stresses the seriousness of our relation to nature and has already been used by innumerable churches worldwide. The organization has also held inter-faith services in a number of cathedrals and conducted an inter-faith service in the Basilica of St Francis of Assisi.

'In Christianity there is the tension between two stories – the utopian Garden of Eden story and the apocalyptic story of destruction,' says Palmer. 'Most of the time Christians are involved in the utopian model but they forget that God made a cosmic covenant and that God's concern is for the fulfilment of all of creation. The crucifixion wasn't just a human event, it was a cosmic event. We have interpreted everything in the Bible as solely to do with humanity. Now, there will be a big shift.'[34]

The path to the new, enlightened age will, however, be fraught with obstacles – not least those thrown down by Christian fundamentalists, who have described Palmer as the Anti-Christ on more than one occasion. 'Fundamentalists have a great fear of pantheism and believe that by taking nature seriously we are downgrading humanity and God,' Palmer explains. 'They fear we will end up worshipping nature.' The fundamentalists are also worried by pluralism. But according to Palmer, 'We don't believe any one faith has the answer. We believe we have to look for as many ways forward as possible.'[35]

Some say New Agers have seized upon environmental issues as a way to penetrate the Church and take it over in a time of division and uncertainty. Others believe it would do the Church no harm to be shaken up a little. According to Palmer, 'There are some for whom the terror of what we are doing to the world is too much. They ignore their responsibilities and say it's all in the hands of God because we are coming to the apocalypse.'[36]

In 1967, Arthur Koestler wrote, 'Nature has let us down, God seems to have left the receiver off the hook, and time is running out.'[37] In the 1990s, New Agers are saying, 'We have let nature down, we have left the receiver off the hook, and time is running out even faster.'

To save itself, then, New Agers believe that humanity must get back in touch with nature – both that of the world and the self. 'If the ecological community is ever achieved in practice, social life will yield a sensitive development of human and natural diversity, falling together into a well-balanced and harmonious whole,' writes anarchist Murray Bookchin – a favourite with many New Agers. 'The cast of mind that today organizes differences among humans and other life forms along hierarchical lines, defining the external in terms of its "superiority" or "inferiority", will give way to an outlook that deals with diversity in an ecological manner.'[38]

Attempts to do away with hierarchies, whether those of man over nature or man over man, have found expression in numerous schemes, whether those of anarchists, socialists or communists.

ELEVEN | COMMUNES AND COMMUNISTS

During the summer of 1980, a small group of people could be seen rolling a giant, twelve-foot cartwheel through the byways of Britain. Their route covered 1000 miles and took three months to complete. What united them was their vision of a new society, a viable, large-scale alternative culture where their theories could be practically applied. The Cartwheel manifesto was based on the principles of common ownership of land and houses, income sharing, non-discrimination and decision making by consensus.

The Wheelroll was a huge success, attracting widespread publicity. The group's message was welcomed by thousands: the new society would be politically just, economically fair and ecologically sound; their village-scale community would provide a solution for both unemployment and homelessness.

The longer term project, however, was a failure. 'In the months after the Wheelroll different interpretations of how the final aim of a large scale community was to be established emerged,' explains one Cartwheel member. 'This debate was never effectively resolved.'[1] Some members of the movement formed small communities – as distant from each other as the west coast of Scotland and the Irish island of Innisfree – and then broke away from Cartwheel. By the end of 1983, the Innisfree group had only two members, who have since moved on.

While Cartwheel's ideas went down well, their realization held problems. 'There is no doubt that Cartwheel knew where it wanted to go, the difficulty was how to get there . . . Interminable discussions took place . . . In this way the commitment to consensus effectively paralysed the group.'[2] It is the same old story – one that has dogged the fortunes of countless visionaries, including the nineteenth-century mill owner Robert Owen, often referred to as the pioneer or father of British socialism.

Owen's communities did, however, flourish – if briefly. Their relative success owed much, it seems, to the blatant Christian millennialism of his movement: 'Socialism by Robert Owen' appears in the 1853 *Cyclopedia of Religious Denominations* between chapters on the Shakers and Mormons.

Welsh-born Owen (1771–1858) aimed to build nothing less than a 'New Moral World'. After working as a draper's assistant in London, he became manager of a spinning mill in Manchester and eventually, on a business visit to Glasgow, met his future wife whose father owned the nearby New Lanark Twist Company. In 1800, he became its manager and part owner.

The industrial revolution had caused both a rise in unemployment and a break-up of society. Dismayed by what he saw about him, Owen drew up plans for self-supporting communities of about 1200 people. A philanthropist – phrenologists were forever pointing out the 'benevolence bump' on his forehead – his proposed Villages of Unity and Mutual Cooperation were framed within a vision of anti-capitalism, social reform and millennialism.

Owen first put his ideas into practice at New Lanark, transforming his 1500-odd mill workers into an experimental community, and the factory, a financial success, became known as 'Happy Valley'. The employees weren't always impressed by Owen's ideas, however. One of his methods was to give them marks for their everyday social behaviour – and to discipline them accordingly. But Owen had great faith in education. In a speech to his employees, delivered in 1816 at the opening of his Institution for the Formation of Character – a type of glorified school – he said, 'From this day a change must take place; a new era must commence.'[3] The Institution would look after children from the time they could walk in order to prevent them 'acquiring any bad habits' and would hold classes for older children, as well as their parents. The principles put into practice at New Lanark would, said Owen, 'enable mankind to *prevent*, in the rising generation, almost all, if not all of the evils and miseries which we and our forefathers have experienced'.[4]

Robert Owen was very much a man of his times. The growth of scientific knowledge in the seventeenth century had given rise to the eighteenth century Enlightenment, the philosophical movement which vested faith in reason and preached that mankind could reach perfection, not through the grace of Jesus but through progress. Dogma was viewed with scepticism, and liberty and equality usurped Christianity as the basis for individual and social life. Knowledge, for some, became synonymous with happiness.

Whereas many Christians lived in fear of failing to be one of the chosen elect, Robert Owen taught his followers that they might perfect themselves through their own efforts thereby freeing them from the bondage of uncertainty.

As one of his followers, George Holyoake, explained, Owen enabled him to be 'delivered by reason alone from the prison house in which I had dwelt with its many terrors'. Rather than perpetually worrying whether he was one of the elect, he was able to inhabit a 'land of self-effort and improvement', to enter 'the fruitful kingdom of material endeavour, where help and hope dwelt'.[5]

While denouncing the clergy and all existing religions, Owen preached a good deal of practical Christianity, his belief being that the millennium was the establishment of the social system, the New Moral World. Some of his followers saw him as none other than Christ returned: 'The fulness of time is come. Mankind are now able to bear the Truth,' said one. 'The Messiah has appeared.'[6]

The Book of the New Moral World took the place of the Bible at Owenist meetings, teaching that, 'The progress of knowledge now renders this revolution, in the general condition and character of mankind, so irresistible, that no earthly power can prevent, or much retard its course.'[7] Owenist lecturers were called social missionaries. But, though numerous of Owen's followers encouraged him to change his movement into a church, he would go no further than performing baptisms and funeral ceremonies.

The millennial drive of Owenism was immense: every time he founded a new community, or announced a new venture, he claimed it signalled the onset of Christ's reign on earth. The editorial in the first copy of his magazine *The New Moral World* (November 1, 1834) ran: 'This . . . is the great Advent of the world, the second coming of Christ – for Truth and Christ are one and the same. The first coming of Christ was a partial development of Truth to the few . . . The second coming of Christ will make Truth known to the many . . . the time is therefore arrived when the foretold millennium is about to commence . . .'.[8]

In 1824, Owen had visited a Shaker community at Niskeyuna, New York. The Shakers, or, to give them their full name, the United Society of Believers in Christ's Second Coming, were founded in northern England in the mid-eighteenth century, an offshoot of the Quakers. Their leader, Mother Ann Lee, was seen by followers as the Head Eldress, with Jesus the Chief Elder, and in 1774 she led them to America.

The Shakers' successful practice of communal living impressed Owen and even the German socialist Friedrich Engels (1820–95) corresponded with them. Today, only a handful of Shakers survive, and their continued recognition rests largely in the popularity of their simple furniture designs. Each year, more and more of their belongings are auctioned off; in 1990, millionaire chatshow personality Oprah Winfrey paid more than £100,000 for a Shaker chest.

A year after visiting the Shakers, Owen bought a settlement in Indiana from the Rappites, named after their leader Father George Rapp who, like the Shakers, believed in the imminent arrival of Christ. The village, called Harmony, was rechristened New Harmony, and in May 1825 some 900 Owenites – and hangers-on – moved in. Soon, however, they split into separate communities and by June 1827 New Harmony could no longer be called Owenite.

More than twenty Owenite communities were founded in Britain and America during the first half of the nineteenth century. Few of them lasted more than two or three years and in none of them was complete communism attained. For most communitarians, there was simply too much mud, work and talking – and there were also leadership struggles. The aim was universal perfection – but who was perfect enough to educate people for the future heaven on earth? It was the same problem that had beset the Enlighteners. Claude Helvetius (1715–71), one of the prime Enlighteners, believed that the reins of power should be handed over to 'enlightened despots'. Leading figures in today's New Age movement seem to view themselves as mystically enlightened despots, or 'spiritual warriors', who will 'creep in under cover of darkness', and effect an internal revolution within the masses.

In 1789, when Owen was eighteen, the French Revolution had sparked off anxiety on both sides of the Atlantic, heralding innumerable last days prophets, their voices mingling with those of self-styled saviours. According to one historian, the French Revolution was 'a sort of atomic bomb of which the fallout is still at work'.[9] The dreams of perfectibility were about to be fulfilled, so it seemed. Mankind was about to realize his earthly paradise. The Russian Mikhail Bakunin (1814–76), 'the father of modern anarchism', who believed in a violent seizure of power, looked on the French Revolution as a 'Revelation', bringing 'not the mystic but the rational . . . not the divine but the human Gospel, the Gospel of the Rights of Man'.[10]

The poet William Wordsworth (1770–1850), caught up in the mood, claimed, 'Bliss was it in that dawn to be alive, but to be young was very heaven.' Bliss was ushered in to France with the Cult of Reason which, for a time, became the country's official religion. Time began again, France's calendar was turned to year one – and the length of hours, weeks and months was changed. On 20 brumaire (November 10, 1793), two months after the announcement 'terror is the order of the day', a Festival of Reason was held in Paris. The opera singer Mme Maillard, dressed to symbolize the goddess of Reason, led a procession to Nôtre Dame which was declared a Temple of Reason, and a hymn to Liberty was sung:

Descend, O Liberty, daughter of Nature:
The People have recaptured their immortal power:
Over the pompous remains of age-old imposture
Their hands raise thine altar.[11]

The Revolutionaries' bible was Jean Jacques Rousseau's *Social Contract* (1762). 'Man is born free; and everywhere he is in chains', the book begins, putting forward the idea that if citizens gave up their rights and possessions to the 'general will', something which exists inside each individual as well as within society as a whole, they would achieve freedom and goodness for all. Rousseau's 'general will' seems to be much the same as today's New Agers' cosmic consciousness. And like many of today's leading New Agers, Rousseau has repeatedly been accused of totalitarianism. Rousseau believed that once humanity tuned in to the general will, each individual would be 'forced to be free'. Likewise, today's New Agers believe that the universal 'shift in consciousness' will suck in everyone, willy nilly.

An odd man out among the Enlighteners, Rousseau distrusted their faith in scientific knowledge, believing instead in the benefits of a simple life and an inward knowledge. Again, the parallel with today's New Agers is apparent. Moreover, Rousseau was confident that humans could perfect themselves through realizing their inner potential, although institutions persistently stifled their natural bent. Given freedom from authoritarian discipline, the goodness of human nature would flower spontaneously, along with moral sentiments. But of course, within an imperfect society, man might choose to be a perfect murderer as readily as a saint.

The problem with Christianity, according to Rousseau, is that it is 'a wholly spiritual religion concerned solely with the things of heaven . . . Provided that [man] has nothing to reproach himself for, it does not matter to him whether all goes well or badly here on earth'.[12] The argument is repeated today by many New Agers.

Taking much of his inspiration from Rousseau's idea that man belonged to a natural community from which he had become estranged by civilization, Samuel Taylor Coleridge (1772–1834) in 1794 aimed to set up a community beside the Susquehanna river in Pennsylvania based on what he called pantisocracy – the 'System of No Property'. According to Coleridge, 'Property . . . is beyond doubt the Origin of all Evil.'[13] The project was set to be a model for social regeneration but failed when Coleridge became disillusioned on hearing fellow-poet Robert Southey's (1774–1843) plans to bring a servant with him.

Of course there were plenty of people who disagreed strongly with Rousseau. Joseph de Maistre (1753–1821) believed that the noble savage was nothing more than a fanciful illusion and that nature, far from being uncorrupted, was cruel and violent. A 'remarkable and terrifying prophet', de Maistre was horrified by the French Revolution. Interestingly, he was a mason; in the nineteenth century masons repeatedly claimed that they were responsible for the Revolution.

The Comte de Saint-Simon (1760–1825), the founder of French socialism, disagreed with Rousseau in that he believed the future society would be governed by industrialists and scientists and that spiritual matters would also be handed over to industrialists. Many of Saint-Simon's followers turned to mysticism; others went on to join one of the several Fourierist communities which sprang up in the later nineteenth century.

Like Rousseau, Charles Fourier (1772–1837) believed that mankind could achieve universal harmony by being given the chance to develop free from the evil influences of society. It was society therefore, that had to be reformed, and the way to do it, Fourier believed, was to split it up into separate units or *'phalanges'* of about 1500 inhabitants each. Everyone would live in the same building, workers would continually change their jobs, everyone would receive a minimum wage and the excess would be distributed according to the amount of capital invested, the labour carried out and the talent contributed. Attempts were made to found several Fourierist communities in both France and America but, like Owen's, they faltered.

In William Morris's *News From Nowhere* (1890), the visitor is surprised to learn that the citizens of the future live in ordinary households. 'Remember again,' he is told, 'that poverty is extinct, and that the Fourierist phalangsteries and all their kind, as was but natural at the time, implied nothing but a refuge from mere destitution. Such a way of life as that, could only have been conceived of by people surrounded by the worst form of poverty.'[14] The society portrayed in *News From Nowhere* has no government – the Houses of Parliament are used to store manure – and comes near, at any rate, to being the ideal anarchist utopia. When the new world first came into being, a citizen explains, the 'way of life was the spirit of the Middle Ages, to whom beauty and the life of the next world was such a reality, that it became to them a part of the life upon the earth'.[15] Now, however, Christianity has disappeared and the citizens of utopia live out the religion of humanity.

Fourier's blueprint for heaven on earth included something akin to a computer dating agency – a 'system of licence' – so that mutual love, publicly acknowledged, should constitute the sole requirement for living together – a system which was sometimes put into practice in Fourierist communities in America. He also foresaw the need for air conditioning, predicted that the seas would run with lemonade and suggested that children, organized into Little Hordes, should do the communities' dirty work.

Some of Fourier's ideas inspired the New England Transcendentalists who came together in 1836 and numbered among them poet and essayist Ralph Waldo Emerson (1803–82), Amos Bronson Alcott, father of *Little Women* author Louisa M. Alcott, and writer and critic Margaret Fuller, the 'sibyl' of the group. One of the exchanges for which Margaret Fuller is best remembered is her unmistakably New Age announcement, 'I accept the universe' – and Thomas Carlyle's reply, 'Gad! she's better!' The Transcendentalists 'claimed for all men what Protestant Christianity claimed for its own elect'.[16] They believed that through intuition – what they termed 'transcendental reason' – they could find a form of government beyond democracy in which the individual conscience would act as the supreme authority, forming a link with cosmic purpose. Again, there is a close similarity with New Age political thinking.

Henry David Thoreau (1817–62) – the 'hermit of Walden' who built himself a shack by Walden Pond where he proceeded to live and write the classic *Walden, or Life in the Woods* (1854) – also occasionally referred to himself as a Transcendentalist. But both he and Emerson refused to live at Brook Farm, the supposedly idyllic, semi-socialist community founded by Transcendentalist George Ripley in 1841. 'I had rather keep bachelor's hall in hell than go to board in heaven,'[17] said Thoreau, while Emerson considered it unnecessary that 'the writer should dig'. According to the novelist Nathaniel Hawthorne (1804–64), who joined the community for a year, 'It is my opinion that a man's soul may be buried and perish under a dung heap or in a furrow of the field, just as well as under a pile of money.' He thought that some members of the community neglected their share of the work, and in his novel *The Blithedale Romance* (1852) he portrayed Brook Farm in a highly unflattering light. While Hawthorne thought community life stifled the individual, others thought Brook Farm lacked community spirit. After two years, Brook Farm was changed into a Fourierist community, which seemed to herald its ruin. Fruitlands, founded by Bronson Alcott, was even less successful. There, the members' diet – vegetarian because animal products were thought to corrupt the soul – did not allow carrots or potatoes on the menu because their roots grew downwards rather than reaching towards heaven. 'He had tried but he was a failure,' wrote Louisa M. Alcott of her father years later. 'The world was not ready for Utopia, and those who attempted to found it only got laughed at for their pains.'[18]

The Transcendentalists received little attention at the time but later Thoreau's essay 'Civil Disobedience' (1849) was picked up by the British Labour Party and the Fabians, and New Agers admire him as a champion of the individual conscience.

Numerous 'free thinkers' floated from community to community. Owenites became Fourierists, and dropped in on Transcendentalists. Few communities lasted long, but the work went on.

Owen and Fourier were also an inspiration to Britain's first town planners who, in the late nineteenth century, began to create garden suburbs and cities – places of work and residence built on cheap land and intended to avoid the evils of the city. Two of the earliest examples are Port Sunlight, built for the workers at Unilever, and Bournville, begun in 1895 for chocolate maker George Cadbury's employees. The first independent garden city was Letchworth, near London, designed in 1904 and intended to be an arcadian idyll with trees and winding roads.

Karl Marx (1818–83), the founder of modern international Communism, was quick to condemn the likes of Owen and Fourier, describing their experimental utopias as mere 'castles in the air'[20] or 'recipes for the cook-shops of the future'.[21] Meanwhile, he locked himself up in the British Library, sometimes fainting with exhaustion at his desk as he wrestled with ideas. Marx's sidekick Engels had more time for the Owenites. Condemning the 'religious bigotry and stupidity of the English respectable middle class', he held that 'in order to find people who dared to use their own intellectual facilities with regard to religious matters, you had to go amongst the uneducated, the "great unwashed", as they were then called, the working people, especially the Owenite Socialists'.[22]

While generally condemning religion as a form of oppression, several Marxists have sought to find in medieval religious sects the spirit of revolutionary socialism. Engels wrote admiringly of Thomas Munzer and the Anabaptists and Otto Bauer saw the Anabaptists as the forerunners of modern socialism. In the 1520s, Munzer formed a League of the Elect and led some 8000 peasants in battle against the Princes, believing that then and there the second coming would occur. The peasants were immediately overcome, and thousands slaughtered, while Munzer was captured, tortured and beheaded.

But whether the medieval sects found the core of their inspiration in the vision of an egalitarian society or the kingdom of heaven on earth is one of the chicken and egg conundrums which has yet to be cracked. Today, people are still arguing as to whether the British Labour Party was an outgrowth of Marxism or radical Christianity.

As we push towards the year 2000, it is interesting that, in October 1990, for the first time since its inception, Britain's Labour Party ended its annual conference with a rousing rendition of William Blake's most famous prophetic poem: 'And we shall buiiiild Jerusalem, in England's green and pleasant land.' Many experts have pointed out how closely the Marxist vision tallies with Biblical eschatology – and Marx himself referred to the Communist state as the kingdom of heaven on earth. The lost paradise is seen as the prehistoric Communist society where humankind lives 'in edenic harmony with nature'; the expulsion from paradise tallies with the industrial, capitalist society; the coming of the messiah corresponds to the 'proletarian-revolutionary interruption of history' and the millennium is the earthly heaven in which the proletariat will rule before the final perfection – Communism or the kingdom of heaven itself.

But whether, and to what extent, socialists simply commandeer the rhetoric of religion to inspire their followers is uncertain. There is, however, no doubt that the idea of being on a divine mission to reinstate God's kingdom is heady stuff – and an effective weapon, as the Crusades have shown. Moreover, as David McLellan points out in *Marxism and Religion*, other Marxists have suggested that 'new religions . . . direct energies towards a form of life which is not yet in existence'[23] and that religion 'provides the first and earliest rebellions of the proletariat with their ideology'.[24] Maybe Marx wasn't being entirely dismissive when he referred to religion as the opium of the people. Maybe he was suggesting that it gave the masses a taste of heaven on earth, or the high to remain constant to their vision.

Just as the 'giant utopia' of religion is often seen as a threat to socialism, the reverse applies, too. In Britain during the 1840s, the Christian Socialist movement sprang up, apparently out of a worry that socialism 'must be Christianized or it would shake Christianity to its foundation, precisely because it appealed to the higher and not to the lower instincts of the men'.[25] Marx had no time for Christian Socialists, describing them as Feudal Socialists. For, while writer Charles Kingsley (1819–75), the most prominent Christian Socialist, believed it was out of keeping with the kingdom of God that capital should reside in the hands of a privileged few, he looked back fondly to a time when the masses were governed by a squire and parson.

In America, the Social Gospel movement took off in the late nineteenth century under the auspices of Walter Rauschenbusch (1861–1918) who claimed that 'the business before us is concerned with refashioning this present world, making this earth clean and sweet and habitable'.[26] The 'fellowship of righteousness' must happen here, he said, as Jesus had announced in the New Testament. Whereas the fundamentalists were awaiting the imminent second coming of Christ, members of the Social Gospel movement embarked on a heaven on earth construction project. Perfection, they believed, should not be an individual goal to be realized eventually in an other-worldly heaven, it should be achieved in the here and now. Once social, economic and religious improvement was underway on earth, the 'great day of the Lord for which the ages waited' would be attained.[27]

While the Marxists favoured revolution, others favoured non-violent resistance – among them *War and Peace* author Count Leo Tolstoy (1823–1910). Around 1879 Tolstoy underwent a spiritual crisis from which he emerged with a faith in an extreme form of Christian anarchism. 'Mankind has outgrown the era of external religious precepts, and no one believes in them any more,' he later wrote.[28] Determined to realize and establish the kingdom of God on earth, he eventually worked and dressed as a peasant, became a vegetarian, espoused total pacifism, repudiated his former literary works, and divided his property among the members of his family. His work ethic has sometimes been declared a forerunner of the Russian mystic Gurdjieff's, although according to Gurdjieff's one-time partner Ouspensky, who tried to interest Tolstoy in his mystical investigations, the Count loved work for work's sake rather than as a means to enlightenment.

Mahatma Gandhi began to read Tolstoy after moving to South Africa in 1893, and was particularly affected by *The Kingdom of God is Within You*, published that year, a book which claims the world would be a better place without governments, armies, police forces and prisons. It was, apparently, from Tolstoy that Gandhi came to espouse what he called satyagraha, or non-violent resistance, and the two corresponded briefly. In *The Aquarian Conspiracy* (1980), Marilyn Ferguson describes satyagraha as an attitude that 'transforms conflict at its source, the hearts of the participants', and cites both Gandhi and Thoreau as carrying forward the 'concept of the powerful committed minority',[29] helping to bring about a political paradigm shift. Gandhi also used Thoreau's *Civil Disobedience* to inspire Indians and Africans to non-violent resistance.

In April 1889, Tolstoy received a parcel from the United States containing tracts and brochures written by members of a Shaker community. Like Robert Owen, he was impressed by their lifestyle although, unlike Owen, it was their ideal of chastity that most struck him. While the idea filled him with horror, he was convinced that the practice of chastity would bring about a 'joyful transformation'.[30] Tolstoy's numerous moral tracts and stories gained him an international discipleship, and numerous Tolstoyan sects sprang up, including some in Britain. He died at eighty-two of pneumonia a few days after secretly leaving his home in order to live in solitude.

Communism was practised in Imperial Russia by several radical Christian sects, including the pacifist Dukhobors or Spirit Wrestlers who believe in reincarnation and the guidance of the spirit within the individual rather than the teachings of the Bible. Persecuted by the government and Orthodox Church, they were stoutly defended by Tolstoy who, along with the Quakers, helped thousands of them to emigrate to Canada, where they still remain.

Imperial Russia was not taken with Tolstoy's anti-Church writings, and he was excommunicated in 1901. Following the 1917 Marxist Revolution, however, the same works were exploited by Soviet cultural authorities – although Lenin (1870–1924) nonetheless condemned Tolstoy for 'preaching one of the most odious things on earth, namely, religion'. For Lenin, religion was 'a sort of spiritual booze'[31] – a remark more clearly condemnatory than Marx's reference to it as 'the opium of the people'.

As far as religion was concerned, Lenin had more in common with the anarchist Mikhail Bakunin than with Marx. For Bakunin, there was 'no need to discuss the problem of eternal salvation, since we do not believe in the immortality of the soul. We are convinced that the most harmful of all things, for humanity and for truth and progress, is the Church . . . who by her dogmas, her lies, her stupidity and her ignominy, seeks to destroy logical thinking and science . . . If the progress of our century is not to be a lying dream, it must make an end to the Church'.[32] Lenin and Bakunin have both been described as 'apocalyptic zealots' by one historian, and certainly Bolshevism has often been described as a secular religion.

Hundreds of Westerners flocked to the Soviet promised land – or 'sugar candy mountain'. Some set up communes and stayed to be persecuted in later years by Stalin; others simply visited and returned with prophetic messages. 'I have been over into the future and it works,' announced American investigative journalist Leonard Steffens after visiting the Soviet Union in 1919. Stalin trained as a priest in a theological seminary in Tiflis, living for several months with the family of Gurdjieff. It was particularly under Stalin's rule of terror in the 1930s that admission to the Communist Party became enveloped in ritual religious symbolism.

H.G. Wells could, in the years Stalin was carrying out his mass murders, proclaim that, though 'crazy with suspicion and persecution, ruled by a permanent Terror, Russia nevertheless upholds the tattered banner of world collectivity and remains something splendid and hopeful in the spectacle of mankind'.[33]

One of the most bizarre – and gruesome – stories associated with a quasi-socialist utopian community is that of the demise, in 1978, of the People's Temple, based deep in the heart of Guyana and led by American messiah-cum-revolutionary figure Jim Jones. A tape recording of the last moments of the Communist experiment carries the voice of an American woman: 'Is it too late for Russia?' she asks. 'At this point,' Jones replies, 'it's too late for Russia.' Minutes later, more than 900 members of the community swallowed cyanide-laced Fla-Vor-Aid, and died. 'Those who cannot remember the past are condemned to repeat it' was daubed on the wall of the community's central building. The communards – over a thousand of them – studied Russian and read Lenin's *What is to be done?* and *On Marx and Engels*. Jones himself professed to be a staunch Stalinist.

Jones had founded the People's Temple in the United States in 1956. Based in San Francisco, he preached a personalized Christianity, dismissing much biblical teaching and performing healings – and even, so it is claimed, resurrections – and involving himself and his organization in numerous welfare programmes, for which he won several humanitarian awards. Actress Jane Fonda, governor of California Jerry Brown and former US vice-president Walter Mondale had all, at one time, given Jones their support.

In 1977 he and many of his followers moved out to paradise, as Jones described it. Guyana – a 'cooperative socialist republic' – became the home of his agricultural community on some 4000 acres of cleared jungle. Based on racial brotherhood and socialism, it attracted socialist utopians and utopian socialists, along with the vaguely idealistic and those in search of a leader. As the months wore on the religious input decreased, but the messianic urgency – and paranoia – was upgraded.

Paranoia was what dominated much of the Cold War, with fundamentalists painting the drab reality of the Communist bloc in livid colours and picturing its leaders as a succession of Anti-Christs. Out of this supposed hell, however, rose Gorbachev – the 'avatar of the New Age' as New Age leaders described him in his early years in office. Both supporters and critics of the Soviet leader point to his frequent use of terms such as 'global village', 'new era', 'world transformation' and 'New Age' as evidence of his spiritual leaning.

'The collapse of the Leninist project marks the end of the era of socialism in one bloc,' according to Martin Jacques, editor of *Marxism Today*. 'Heaven on earth is an impossibility. A utopian dream lies in ashes.'[34] But as the grip of Communism relaxes, Western New Age and New Religious Movements have been rushing into the Eastern bloc, offering their own variety of heaven on earth to fill the vacuum. In 1989, the guru Bhagwan Shree Rajneesh, latterly known as Osho, announced, 'And this is the state of the whole Soviet Union: the people have become like children. No church, no programming, no God, no prayer – they have become so innocent that meditation will go deep down in them faster than in any other country.'

The prophets of paradise needed no further prompting. Before long, the Scientologists had opened a centre in Leningrad, aided by a Mission Starter Pack – a type of Scientology first aid kit costing $40,000 at the last count – and established footholds in Hungary and Czechoslovakia. The drug rehabilitation programme Narconon, a Scientology offshoot, opened a clinic in Moscow with, claim Narconon officials, 400 beds, and the Hare Krishnas, many of whom were imprisoned during the 1980s by the Soviet authorities, were released and presented by the authorities with a property to use as their Moscow temple. Everywhere, say onlookers, citizens of the Eastern bloc are turning to meditation, visualization, spirit channelling and other such New Age practices.

The Soviets are not simply pulling themselves out of a spiritual vacuum; they are marching towards capitalism, and many new religions, together with the New Age movements, are offering them the twin-pronged paradise of material and spiritual wealth. On one level there is the help offered by the violently anti-Communist Rev Sun Myung Moon, leader of the Moonies. In April 1990, following his world media conference held in Moscow, Moon held a private meeting with Gorbachev in the Kremlin, and promised to encourage Japanese businessmen to look into investment opportunities in the Soviet Union. On another level, there is the 'prosperity counselling' and 'prosperity consciousness' offered to the ordinary Soviet citizen by many New Age outfits.

As early as 1986, New Age guru Werner Erhard was importing the religion of 'self' to the Soviets. That year, he led a five-day seminar in Moscow for sixty-five Soviet managers and scholars. The Forum, the standard five-day seminar offered by Erhard's organization, offers participants 'a breakthrough . . . into a new dimension of possibility' and promises to 'produce . . . a decisive edge in your ability to achieve'.[35] Other courses in Erhard's battery include 'Excellence', 'Accomplishment' and 'High Performance'.

In 1989, Erhard's in-house magazine reported a speech given by representatives of the USSR's Znaniye Society or All-Union Knowledge Society, an organization concerned with the education of Soviet citizens: 'At this important point in our growth, we need good captains, good managers, good trainers,' they announced. 'In this respect we are interested in the programs and work that Werner Erhard has to offer. The intrinsic nature of our Perestroika requires that we invoke the creative thinking of the masses of people.'[36]

Following the 1988 Armenian earthquake the Maharishi Mahesh Yogi's Transcendental Meditation blossomed in the Soviet Union. Soviet meditators claimed their techniques would help restore 'coherence and stability' throughout Armenia. In December 1987, the organization announced: 'Already 3500 Armenians have learned TM in recent weeks, and hundreds more are learning each day.'[37] Osho, however, warned Gorbachev not to put his trust in the Maharishi's 'hocus pocus', pointing to a report that former President Marcos of the Philippines had hired TM consultants in 1984 and, sixteen months later, had been kicked into exile.

Dr Geoffrey Clements, vice-chancellor of Britain's Maharishi University of Natural Law, has suggested that the introduction of a 'coherence creating programme' by meditators in West Germany helped bring down the Berlin Wall. Osho, on the other hand, wary of the Wall's collapse, warned, 'Don't be in such a hurry to tear down the Berlin Wall because when my sannyasins transform East Germany it will be needed to keep people out.' What Osho wanted was to see 'Buddha and Marx dancing hand in hand' along the Wall's parapet. Instead, he saw the rise of capitalism and all its evils – Eastern Europe might be spiritually poor but the West was spiritually bankrupt. By allowing in the capitalists and religionists, he warned, the Eastern bloc would spoil what 'all utopians, all the people who have any vision for the future have been dreaming for, for centuries'.[38]

The day the Brandenburg Gate was opened, a branch of the Unification Church dumped a truck-load of its promotional leaflets in the Pariser Platz. 'They hear the word "unification" and think it must be good,' said one observer. On New Year's Day 1990 the

Moonie-sponsored *Washington Times* reported a conference staged by the Moonie-related International Security Council between US and Russian military experts. And the Kirov Ballet of Leningrad has entered into an official partnership with the budding Moonie-owned Universal Ballet Company, based in Washington DC. A brochure for the company's dance academy features a large picture of UBC founder Moon. In the early 1990s Moonie rock group The Original Mind Band toured Bulgaria, Romania, Hungary and Czechoslovakia.

Osho's parting shot to a Soviet television crew who visited his Indian ashram was, 'Please tell Gorbachev from me, allow everything, but don't allow Christianity again! Beware! Don't allow any of the priests of any religion into the Soviet Union if you want to save Communism!'[39]

In March 1990, Raisa Gorbachev welcomed several young representatives of Youth Ending Hunger, the children's branch of Erhard's Hunger Project, at the Kremlin. The Hunger Project aims to eliminate world hunger through the New Age method of 'commitment'. The delegation comprised students from twelve countries including the UK, what was then East and West Germany, Canada and Ghana. The 'world runners', who grew out of the Project have held marathons in Moscow for the past four years, and recently created a Siberian marathon, too. One British supporter told how the runners battled against the winds blowing across Gorky Park, cheered on by crowds of Muscovites calling: '*Za mir bez goloda. Za mir, za mir.*' (For a world without hunger. For peace, for peace – *mir* means both peace and world.) 'Even the soldiers, stoic, stern and trained to remain aloof, laughed and smiled along with us,' he reported.[40] Soviet press and television coverage has introduced millions of Soviets to the Project.

Musician John Denver, acolyte of Werner Erhard, has also done much to spread his guru's 'self-religion' Eastwards. In 1988 ten Soviets on a UN Peace Exchange programme attended a conference at Denver's Windstar Foundation, an educational organization deep in Colorado's Rocky Mountains which 'seeks to communicate a vision of the Earth as a living organism whose growth depends on its continuing existence as a unified whole'.[41] Denver was also approached by Glavkosmos, the commercial arm of the Soviet space programme, when it was considering asking a US citizen to be the first US civilian to go up in a manned Soviet spacecraft.

In December 1989, Moscow hosted a Global Forum of Religious and

Political World Leaders. The brainchild of a Japanese businessman, its aim was to provide a discussion ground for the development of global unity. British MP David Alton was one of the delegates. 'Innumerable religions were represented, and a lot of good came out of the event,' he said. 'But it made me feel vaguely uneasy. The language used was often New Age – they talked of self-deification and creating reality in your mind.'[42] Gorbachev left the Baltic crisis to attend the final day of the conference – despite having turned down a meeting with Britain's Labour Party leader Neil Kinnock on account of the political situation. One participant recalls that there was a 'wonderful moment' when hundreds of people, including Gorbachev, gathered in the Kremlin and intoned the mystical sound OM.

According to David Alton, 'Religion can help shore up a troubled society, and a religion without the hierarchy of the Church – like the New Age – could suit Gorbachev very well.'

Critics of the New Age, who claim its followers are encouraged to become 'self'-centred to the point of apathy, suspect the Soviet authorities are importing the New Age as quickly as possible in the hope that it will turn people inwards and reduce their political activities. The mainstream religions, on the other hand, are seen as a political threat, they say. Others believe the New Age has an intensely political message – none other than a world takeover. Certainly, in its early days, the New Age movement was outspoken about, and had absolute confidence in, its revolutionary capabilities. As long ago as 1970 Charles Reich claimed that beside the new consciousness 'a mere revolution, such as the French or the Russian, seems inconsequential'.

However, just as the kingdom of heaven on earth is generally seen in rather vague terms as being 'blissful' so, according to the historian Eric Hobsbawm, writing in 1990: 'Socialists gave practically no thought to what a socialist economy and society should be like, until forced to improvise suitable measures after they became governments.'[43] As Osho put it: 'You may have sometimes seen a dog who runs after a car, barking, and with great speed. And if the man in the car stops, the dog looks all around, embarrassed – "What to do now?" – miles of unnecessary running and barking. And that happens to all revolutionaries. Miles of trouble! Fighting, murder, being killed, jailed and when they get into power they look just like the dog, embarrassed. "What to do now?"'[44]

The answer, for some, was to set about changing humanity. Lenin

had attempted to create Soviet Man, turning for help to the physi-
ologist and behaviourist Ivan Petrovich Pavlov (1849–1936), whose
work on reflex reactions with dogs and bells seemed to open wide the
doors to perfectibility. But to usher in the New Age, it is not enough
simply to change man's behaviour; man's consciousness must be
changed. Once the transformation has been effected, government can
be thrown out and some other form of social order installed – an order
which has a close affinity with Murray Bookchin's version of anarchism. 'Anarchism is not only a stateless society but also a harmonized
society,' he writes, and stresses the importance of 'unrepressed sensuality and self-directed spirituality', 'communal solidarity and individual development', 'regional uniqueness and worldwide brotherhood',
'spontaneity and self-discipline'.[45] It is almost a blueprint for how
New Agers promote themselves, although they put forward words
such as autarchy (self-government) and heterarchy (government by
an ever-changing leadership, depending on the qualities called for)
to describe themselves. At the end of the day, however, the New
Age vision of society seems most akin to the mystical anarchism
foretold by Joachim of Fiore – or Joachim de Flore as he is sometimes
known.

Just how pervasive Joachim's prophecy has been can be seen from
an interview with the French political philosopher Roger Garaudy.
A former Christian and former member of the Political Bureau of the
French Communist Party, Garaudy converted to Islam at the end of
the 1970s. 'I came to Islam,' he says in an interview with the French
magazine *Krisis*, 'with the Bible in one hand and *Das Kapital* by Marx
in the other. I have decided not to abandon either of them.' When
asked what hope there is in the world today, he says: 'Utopia is
the necessary horizon of all politics, even though we know that this
horizon is always pushed back farther and can never be reached.'
And when asked who lives at the horizon, he agrees that it is none
other than 'Joachim de Flore and the Age of Spirit'.[46]

New Agers are, however, doing their best to see that the horizon is
reached. Just as the medieval spirituals imagined they were ushering
in Joachim of Fiore's Age of the Spirit, so many of today's New
Agers seem to see themselves as an inner core of spiritually advanced
individuals bringing about the transformation of the individual and so
society. Perhaps one of the more pressing questions for the anarchic,
transformed New Age of radical self-responsibility and spirituality is
how will its luminaries cope with being a chosen people.

TWELVE | THE CHOSEN ONES

O ne of the most successful myths of all time is that the world is split into heroes and villains. The heroes – the chosen people – will inherit the world and become citizens of heaven on earth. The villains will be exterminated. It is there in the Bible's Book of Revelation, and it is there in the ideology of countless fascist political leaders. Often, the boundaries of religion and politics become blurred.

This chapter looks at groups whose members believe they have a right to heaven on earth, and who slam the gates in the face of all those who fail to meet their criteria.

Tickets to the earthly paradise have often been valid only for a chosen few, whether of a particular colour, race, nation or IQ rating. In uncertain times the tickets become all the more precious – and many of their owners become charged with a protectionist zeal: it appears that we need villains in order to confirm we are heroes, that we must see bodies rotting in hell to ensure we are truly in heaven.

During the Cold War, the hero/villain divide was quite clear cut. Now, with the boundaries blurred, onlookers are predicting a rise in groups intent on building their own barriers and proclaiming they are the heroes – and a consequent rise in the persecution of 'villains'.

'What we have now are utopias without universal hope, sectional utopias, at a time when a world increasingly organized globally, and whose problems require global treatment, actually calls for a new universalism,' wrote Eric Hobsbawm in 1990. The groups he sees emerging are informed by 'worse visions and more dangerous dreams, such as religious fundamentalism, nationalist zealotry, or more generally, that racially tinged xenophobia which looks like becoming the major mass ideology of the *fin de siècle*.[1]

The chosen people – of whatever creed, colour, or nationality – are, so they are usually led to believe, marked out by destiny for a role in something greater than their individual identities. Their leaders have mastered the inspired language of religious rhetoric, laden with symbolism and prophetic utterances, and their meetings are rich in ritual and ceremony so that, while the disciples wait for heaven on earth to transpire, they can undergo the ultimate mystical experience – loss of self.

Those without the necessary qualifications for entrance to the ranks of the élite quickly set about making their own ideologies, their own religions and their own happy valleys. The very fact of their exclusion from a particularly earthly paradise simply fires their attempts to create their own heaven on earth.

'White Man's Heaven is Black Man's Hell,' went the words to the Black Muslims' popular anthem, back in the 1960s. Currently undergoing a resurgence, the Black Muslims or Nation of Islam grew up in response to the white man's grip on heaven on earth. For too long, whites had taken freedom and riches for themselves, leaving the blacks in poverty and slavery. Christianity, it seemed, had simply fuelled the situation: 'This white man's Christian religion,' said Black Muslim leader Malcolm X, 'further deceived and brainwashed this "Negro" to always turn the other cheek, and grin, and scrape, and bow, and be humble, and to sing, and to pray and to take whatever was dished out by the devilish white man; and to look for his pie in the sky, and for his heaven in the hereafter, while right here on earth the slavemaster white man enjoyed *his* heaven.'[2] Heaven on earth would, however, be returned to blacks – by the Nation of Islam.

The movement was founded in 1930 in Detroit by Wallace D. Farad, also known as Wali Fard. According to Black Muslim teaching, Fard – a 'brother from the East' – was a member of the tribe of Muhammad ibn Abdullah, Islam's great prophet. Fard's mission was to return negroes to Islam, God's one true religion. He began by preaching the Quran and Bible in negroes' homes, and taught his growing flock that the American negroes were directly descended from Muslims who had become separated from the Nation of Islam. Elijah Muhammad, born Elijah Poole in Georgia in 1897, met Fard and was soon converted and appointed to the position of Supreme Minister.

According to Black Muslim teaching, black people were the original inhabitants of the earth, and founded the Holy City of Mecca thousands upon thousands of years ago. In time, a scientist called Mr Yacub rebelled against Allah and, with a small breakaway group, set up a genetics laboratory on the island of Patmos in Greece – where the author of the Bible's Book of Revelation experienced his vision, according to Christian tradition.

That was about 6600 years ago. On Patmos, Mr Yacub allegedly bred from his black followers a bleached race of devils – the white man. Hundreds of years passed before the white devils were perfected, at which point they swarmed to the mainland and turned what had been an earthly paradise into a living hell.

These white devils would rule the world for 6000 years until, in the twentieth century, with the onset of the last days, a black messiah would be born who would save the negroes and return them to their own people. The saviour was, said Elijah Muhammad, none other than Fard – 'God in Person' – whose arrival signalled the onset of the end-times. Now was the time for the negroes to save the Lost-Found Nation of Islam, and found a Black Islamic state.

In 1934, Fard disappeared and the movement's leadership passed to Elijah Muhammad. But it wasn't until Malcolm X appeared on the scene in the late 1950s that the Black Muslims gained notoriety. Outspoken and charismatic, Malcolm X, born Malcolm Little in 1925, gave vent to black bitterness, built up by years of white supremacy. 'I *believe* in anger,' he said. 'The Bible says there is a *time* for anger.'[3]

By acquiring their own unique mythology, Black Muslims were able to retrieve at least some sense of self-determination. While the Patmos story provided a spiritual vision, genetics gave them scientific evidence that they were not merely equal with the white man but superior to him. After reading the Austrian abbot and geneticist Gregor Mendel's *Findings in Genetics*, Malcolm X was convinced that 'if you started with a black man, a white man could be produced; but starting with a white man you never could produce a black man. And since no one disputes that there was but one Original Man, the conclusion is clear'.[4]

Today, T-shirts printed with 'Original Man' are worn by numerous supporters of the Black Power movement – and the Nation of Islam, which in 1990 had an estimated 10,000 members in the USA, is growing more and more vociferous – not least due to the highly controversial leadership of Louis Farrakhan. Viewed as a demi-god by many of his followers, he is notorious for his anti-semitic remarks and rarely moves without the protection of an armed bodyguard.

In 1984, Farrakhan reportedly referred to Judaism as a 'dirty religion' and to Hitler as a 'great man'. Certainly, he has been quoted as saying to Jews: 'You're the scriptwriters. You're the Hollywood producers who gave us Little Black Sambo and Bug-Eyes and Stepin Fetchit. What've we done to you? We didn't burn you in no oven! We didn't paint no swastikas on your synagogues! Who wrote the textbooks who wrote us out of history?'[5]

In 1990, however, Farrakhan claimed he had described Hitler as 'wickedly great' and that he wanted to end the bitter enmity with the Jews – although he added that Jews are part of 'a small clique who use their power and knowledge to manipulate the masses against the best interests of the people'.[6] A great conspiracy theorist, Farrakhan described how in 1985 he had a vision in which he was taken up into what appeared to be a giant wheel – a type of spaceship is how he described it – where Elijah Muhammad, who had died ten years earlier, told him of various schemes by high level government officials.

One Black Muslim theory is that whites deliberately aim to turn blacks into drug addicts. As a result, the movement has set up numerous clinics to help followers kick the addiction, as well as masterminding anti-crime patrols. Black Muslims are now attempting to enter the political mainstream, putting forward candidates for Congress and local office.

Malcolm X was prepared to use violence to help Black Muslims achieve their heaven: 'The goal has always been the same,' he said, 'with the approaches to it as different as mine and Dr Martin Luther King's non-violent marching, that dramatizes the brutality and the evil of the white man against defenceless blacks. And in the racial climate of this country today, it is anybody's guess which of the "extremes" in approach to the black man's problems might personally meet a fatal catastrophe first – "non-violent" Dr King, or so-called "violent" me.'[7]

As it turned out, Malcolm X was the first to be assassinated. Martin Luther King, the prime leader of the civil rights movement, was killed in 1968 and Malcolm X was killed in 1965. Two years earlier he had been expelled from the Black Muslims, on account of having said, on hearing of President Kennedy's assassination: 'The chickens are coming home to roost.'[8] Malcolm X's murderers were followers of Elijah Muhammad.

Dr King's vision of the promised land – the American dream of equal opportunity when all people would live as one nation, and when blacks would have equal rights in voting, housing and education – has not materialized. Many, of whatever colour, no longer want it. Separation is the only answer, they say.

Malcolm X's father was a staunch supporter of Marcus Garvey (1887–1940), the Jamaican prophet of both the Rastafarians and the Back to Africa movement. Garvey believed the black people of the world should return to Africa, the land from which their forefathers had been taken as slaves. 'Look to Africa when a black king shall be crowned, for deliverance is near,' he allegedly told his followers. In 1930, when Ras Tafari (1892–1977) was crowned Emperor Haile Selassie I of Ethiopia, many considered him to be the king of whom Garvey had spoken. Innumerable preachers hailed him as the messiah and he was worshipped as a living God.

In the late 1950s, Rastafarianism took off in Britain and North America while in Jamaica, Prince Edward C. Edwards summoned an all-island convention of Rastafarians to a twenty-one-day celebration. About 3000 followers turned up, some having sold their worldly goods beforehand, convinced that the convention would be followed by a mass exodus to Ethiopia, or paradise. No such exodus occurred.

According to Garvey, 'We were the first fascists. We had disciplined men, women and children in training for the liberation of Africa. The black masses saw that in this extreme nationalism lay their only hope and readily supported it. Mussolini copied fascism from me but the Negro reactionaries sabotaged it.'[9]

In 1922 Garvey caused uproar among the black integrationist leaders when he met with Edward Young Clarke, the acting imperial wizard of the Ku Klux Klan. Like white supremacists, Garvey disapproved of integration and supported emigration. 'Between the Ku Klux Klan and the Moorfield Storey National Association for the Advancement of "Colored" People group, give me the Klan for their honesty of purpose towards the Negro,' he said. 'They are better friends to my race, for telling us what they are, and what they mean . . .'[10]

Founded in Tennessee after the American Civil War (1861–5), the Klan was originally intended to take the form of a secret vigilante group aimed at deterring blacks from taking up their newly gained rights. Klansmen wore white cloaks and hoods, burned large fiery crosses, castrated and killed blacks, and destroyed their property. Within a few years, when the whites had regained political control in the South, the movement died down. Then, in 1915, the American film director D.W. Griffith portrayed Klansmen as heroes in his film *Birth of a Nation*. That same year saw the revival of the KKK.

This time it supported white Protestants against Catholics, Jews and blacks. Fuelled by anxiety over mass immigration, membership of the Klan peaked at between four and five million in the 1920s – even President Warren G. Harding was a member – but declined again at the end of the decade, a decline prompted by the arrest of a charismatic Klan leader for the rape and murder of a young woman.

During the 1950s the Klan gained a new lease of life, spurred on by the US South's bitterness against the civil rights movement – in particular the supreme court's desegregation decision in 1954. Today, the Klan, or the 'Invisible Empire' as one of its three main divisions is known, continues to dress in its white regalia and protest against Martin Luther King Day, although these days many members choose to wear army fatigues.

Blacks continue to receive threats from the Ku Klux Klan. In 1981 a black teenager was allegedly beaten to death and hung from a tree by the organization. Testifying at the trial, a Klan member said that the murder was a show of Klan strength in Alabama.[11] The Klan vision of heaven on earth is a world filled with white Anglo Saxon Protestants. In 1988, a KKK Grand Giant (the group constantly awards colourful titles to its leaders) reportedly announced that the black race was founded before Adam, that the white race was founded by Adam and that Jews were founded after Adam – the offspring of Satan and Eve.[12]

At the time the Ku Klux Klan was founded in America, Britain's unquestioning belief in its own supremacy was in its heyday. In the eyes of the British, not only were they superior as a nation, but Anglo Saxons were superior as a race. Some were convinced the world was waiting to hear of their scientific advances, others that the savages were waiting to hear of Protestant Christianity; they were God's chosen people and, once they had evangelized the world, an earthly paradise would ensue.

The Bible was regularly used to license hatred – not least by the respected Christian Socialist Charles Kingsley. Discussing the slaughter of the tribal Dyaks of Sarawak, Malaysia, by Englishman James Brooke – later known as Rajah Brooke – Kingsley wrote: 'Sacrifice of human life? Prove that it is *human* life. It is beast-life.'

He concluded that, in keeping with the Old Testament, he would, 'Like David, "Hate you with perfect hatred, even as though you were my enemies." I will blast you out with grape and rockets. "I will beat you as small as the dust before the wind." '13

In 1849, Thomas Carlyle – 'a prophet disguised as a man of letters' – wrote 'The Nigger Question'. In his view, those born lords had the right to dominate those born to serve, using the 'beneficent whip' if necessary. Charles Darwin's theory of evolution helped give scientific credence to the right of might, and his name was attached to a movement known as Social Darwinism. By applying the 'survival of the fittest' theory to human society, Social Darwinism justified power politics, imperialism and war.

Many nineteenth century thinkers believed that, in the fullness of time, when evolution had run its course, an earthly paradise would transpire. Some believed the gates of Eden would be opened to all humanity – provided that everyone had developed their 'higher nature'. More often, those who weren't 'naturally selected' would fall by the wayside, and be barred admission to the heaven on earth.

In 1869 Darwin's cousin, the eugenicist Sir Francis Galton, wrote in his *Hereditary Genius*: 'There is nothing either in the history of domestic animals or in that of evolution to make us doubt that a race of sane men may be formed, who shall be as much superior mentally and morally to the modern European, as the modern European is to the lowest of the Negro races.'14 In his later years, Galton wrote a novel about a utopia called Kantsaywhere – a land in which only those who received marks above a certain level in exams were allowed to marry. More than 2000 years earlier, in the plans for his Republic, Plato had put forward the idea of positive eugenics – plans which seem to have impressed the School of Economic Science (see Chapter Two). 'We must,' he had said, '. . . mate the best of the men with the best of our women as often as possible . . . and bring up only the offspring of the best.'15 By selecting only those with a 'natural aptitude' for a rarified education, Plato hoped to produce an aristocracy of talent – the Philosopher Rulers – whose minds would be converted 'from a kind of twilight to the true day'.16 First, however, the Philosopher Rulers must display 'natural qualities' – including bravery and beauty.

Like Plato, Adolf Hitler aimed to breed an élite of physically perfect beings. Many Germans, offered hope and bread by their Führer, believed paradise was in the offing. Many Jews, used as guinea pigs in the 'racial hygiene' sterilization experiments carried out in concentration camps, were mentally and physically scarred for life, or died.

Plato has been described as a ruthless authoritarian, as a racist – and as the first totalitarian. Certainly, his *Republic* rests on the belief that nature has created some men to rule and others to be ruled and that there is a 'natural relation of control and subordination'.[17] Moreover, in his ideal state, authority will be invested in the chosen rulers by the use of a 'noble lie' or 'some magnificent myth that would in itself carry conviction to our whole community'.[18]

But Plato was writing about a fictional community. Hitler attempted to put his myth – a myth based on race – into practice. 'We want to make a selection from the new dominating caste,' he said to an aide in 1930, 'which is not moved, as you are, by any ethic of pity, but is quite clear in its own mind that it has the right to dominate others because it represents a better race.'[19] What he was looking for was 'a conception which enables the order that hitherto existed on an historic basis to be abolished, and an entirely new and anti-historic order enforced and given an intellectual basis . . . And for this purpose the conception of race serves me well'.[20]

The race he came up with was that of the Aryans: 'It was the Aryan who laid the groundwork and erected the walls of every great structure in human culture,' he claimed.[21] By choosing to murder and torture millions of Jews, Hitler was simply actualizing the prejudice and persecution of hundreds of years.

Sometime in the thirteenth century BC, it is generally believed, the Israelites were forced into service under an Egyptian pharaoh until eventually Moses led them out of bondage, across the Red Sea to the Promised Land. Several hundred years later, in 586BC, Jerusalem fell to the Babylonians and the Jews were exiled for about fifty years. In Christian times, the fall of Jerusalem to the Romans in 70AD ended the Jewish nation. Afterwards, the Jews lived scattered throughout Christian Europe with no nationality and no territory of their own. They still, however, remained Jews – the chosen people: 'For thou art an holy people unto the Lord thy God', says the Bible, 'The Lord thy God hath chosen thee to be a special people unto himself, above all people that are upon the face of the earth'.[22] Other Jewish religious teachings describe how all the nations which have ever ruled over Israel will be put to the sword and an age of bliss, peace and righteousness will be instated. The chosen people will rule over the world, the earthly paradise, the centre of which will be the gloriously restored Israel.

So, secure that one day they would live in God's kingdom on earth, the Jews withstood their hardships, and the laws of their religion helped give them an identity, to bind them together however far they might be from their homeland and those of their faith. Christians were taught that the Jews were the murderers of Christ – and, to add to their outrage, the Jews persisted in refusing to acknowledge his divinity. By the second century, preachers were spreading the word that the Anti-Christ would be a Jew – a belief which became so widespread that it was adhered to even by the medieval theological scholar St Thomas Aquinas.

By the Middle Ages, Jews were viewed as devils with horns and hooves. Attempts were even made to make them wear horns on their hats in everyday life. Jews ate babies, they practised black magic and revelled in filth, but thankfully they would be exterminated along with the Anti-Christ before Christ's second coming.

Gradually, some Jews had been returning to Jerusalem, which in the seventh century had fallen into the hands of Muslims. At the end of the eleventh century, the Christians, who had taken over the Jews' belief that they were the chosen people, rose up, determined to win back and Christianize what they saw as their holy city. The First Crusade took off, culminating in 1099 when the Crusaders converged on Jerusalem, exterminating Jews and Muslims alike. 'A Christian glories in the death of a Muslim because Christ is glorified,' said St Bernard.[23] Some Jews took shelter in their synagogue and were burned alive. Thousands of Jews were murdered during the Second Crusade, too. If, however, Jews agreed to be baptised into the Christian religion, they were spared. In 1543, Martin Luther suggested that Jews' synagogues and homes should be destroyed 'for the honour of God and of Christianity'.[24]

Hitler's justification and methods for putting anti-semitism into practice drew on much nineteenth century and current thinking. In *The Foundations of the Nineteenth Century*, published in 1911, Houston Stewart Chamberlain wrote: 'The Indo-European, moved by ideal motives, opened the gates of friendship: the Jews rushed in like an enemy, stormed all positions and planted the flag of his, to us, alien nature . . .'[25]

Social Darwinism allowed Hitler to justify might is right: 'The whole work of nature,' he said in a speech at Munich, 'is a mighty struggle between strength and weakness – an eternal victory of the strong over the weak. There would be nothing but decay in the whole of nature if this were not so. States which offend against this elementary law fall into decay.'[26] One interpretation of Hitler's rule states: 'Monism [the belief that there is only one substantial thing in the universe] tinged with popular Darwinism figured prominently in the outlook of the National Socialist leadership. It was one of the few ideological elements that dominated Hitler's thinking throughout his career and that he did not manipulate in accordance with tactical needs.'[27]

Friedrich Nietzsche was not anti-semitic himself – in fact, he said that 'the mere presence of a German hinders my digestion'[28] – but his belief that the suffering of slaves was insignificant since 'almost anything we call higher culture is based upon the spiritualizing and intensifying of cruelty'[29] must have rung true with Hitler. Moreover, his passion for the triumph of the will and 'the air of the heights', together with his belief that 'religions are affairs of the rabble',[30] proved irresistible to the Nazi propaganda machine. 'One day,' said Nietzsche, prophetically, 'there will be associated with my name the recollection of something frightful – of a crisis like no other before on earth.'[31]

Carlyle also gave backing to Hitler's belief in power and the concept of the hero – apparently Hitler wept when one of Carlyle's works was read to him. And Richard Wagner's vast, overwhelming operas, provided him with mindless mythic emotionalism – as did the films of Leni Riefenstahl. The first film Riefenstahl directed focused on the mysterious, magnetic and terrifying pull of bleak mountain ranges – Nietzsche's 'air of the heights'.

In 1936 Riefenstahl directed *Triumph of the Will*, the film of one of Hitler's impeccably orchestrated Nuremberg rallies. By actualizing an impulse towards some larger, mythic sphere of being, Hitler liberated the unconscious of the masses – in a manner Jung might have been proud of. By losing themselves to the Führer, they experienced a heavenly loss of self.

Hitler constructed a world of archetypes – one of which was the SS, the Nazi Party's élite military force. Its members, their uniforms emblazoned with runic symbols and the death's head, were to strip themselves of all remnants of humanity until they embodied pure violence – and pure superiority. The SS, selected in accordance with Nazi principles of eugenics, provided Hitler with his racial elite and, as his Order of Knights, were intended to, and did, take on mythic proportions.

Hitler has been described sometimes as a brilliant, sometimes as a ham-fisted psychologist. As Michael Billig points out in *Fascists*, he wouldn't have had to look far among the psychologists of the day to find a basis for his racism and élitism. In 1896 G. Le Bon had written of a 'race soul' and claimed there was a vast difference between the feelings of Jews and Aryans. Two years later he wrote that 'above all the destiny of peoples is woven with the qualities of souls'.[32] A highly-regarded expert on crowd behaviour, Le Bon's theories on the subject were taken up by Freud. Both saw that the individual could experience a loss of self by losing themselves in a mass situation, leading to a feeling of 'invincible strength'.[33]

Some experts believe Hitler must have read Le Bon. Certainly, in *Mein Kampf* (1925–6) Hitler describes how at a mass meeting the individual succumbs to 'the magic influence of what we designate as "mass suggestion"'[34], responding to the call of 'mysterious powers'.[35] He celebrated the 'sacred collective egoism',[36] believing 'the individual is transitory, the *Volk* is permanent', adding: 'It is essential that the individual should slowly come to realize that his own ego is unimportant when compared with the existence of the whole people . . . above all he must realize that the freedom of the mind and will of a nation are to be valued more highly than the individual's freedom of mind and will.'[37]

In 1934, Carl Jung announced: 'The Jews have this peculiarity in common with women: being physically the weaker they have to aim at the chinks in their opponent's armour . . . The Jew, as relatively a nomad, never has and presumably never will produce a culture of his own, since all his instincts and gifts require a more or less civilized host-people for their development . . . The Aryan unconscious has a higher potential than the Jewish.' For Jung, the 'precious secret of the Germanic peoples' was 'the creatively prophetic depths of soul'.[38] Two years later, he suggested that Germans should be regarded as victims of the 'Semitic experience of Allah',[39] and that National Socialism was the result of the German's desire to cleanse themselves of Judaeo-Christianity and return to their mystical pagan roots, expressed by the Wotan archetype – 'a fundamental attribute of the German psyche . . . the truest expression and unsurpassed personification of a fundamental quality that is particularly characteristic of the German'.[40]

In Wagner's *Ring* Wotan breaks Judaeo-Christian morality and creates the liberated German, a pagan redeemer who restores unity with nature. Many looked on Wagner as having created a new religion from the mythical, Aryan past. It is interesting that many naturist groups sprang up in Germany during Hitler's reign. He himself encouraged the masses to take part in open air physical exercises – perhaps attempting to nurture a desire for control together with a return to mythical, primal, instinctual man. A modern naturist magazine describes how 'nudity seems fused with the expanse of nature'.[41]

According to Wilhelm Reich, 'mystical feelings are a source of nationalistic ideology'; he adds, ''Patriarchal family attitudes *and* a mystical frame of mind are the basic psychological elements of fascism and imperialistic nationalism in the masses.'[42] Thousands of clients streamed into his Sex-Pol clinic in Berlin in the 1930s. According to Reich, the German Communist Party, by ignoring the connection between individual – including sexual – needs and politics, had opened up the doors for the masses to surge towards Nazism. Both Reich and Norman O. Brown emphasized a need for total Being, for a full-blooded experience of life rather than a rational, disconnected approach. It was a need which fascism satisfied. The rational mind was to be dispensed with and instead a 'mindless' state, relying on experience rather than 'history', instated. In 1933, as pile upon pile of books were consigned to bonfires, Goebbels hailed the end of Jewish intellectualism and the arrival of an era when once again the German spirit could reign supreme.

Much of this ideology is precisely that of the New Age – in which Jung is extremely influential. Feeling and intuition dominate intellect, the heart dominates the head, and the community dominates the individual. The aim is to become self-actualized within the group experience. History and 'stories' from the past are simply a limiting belief; the individual must break through and forge their own all-powerful destiny.

Members of the British fascist organization the National Front admire Jung – particularly for his work on racial memories and archetypes. The masses, they say, are not moved by reason but by the 'hidden forces of the human soul'. Moreover, like New Agers, they say that '*instinct* and *feeling* . . . are the primary forces in people'.[43]

Hitler advocated a type of mystical progress – much as did the Jesuit priest Pierre Teilhard de Chardin, who was in the Far East during World War II, studying science and writing philosophical and religious essays. Beloved by today's New Agers, Teilhard believed that all discoveries – including the atom bomb – would help bring about a single nation. Like Hitler, it seems that for Teilhard de Chardin, the ends – the one world – justified the means. According to Teilhard, individuals should subsume themselves to the single nation, humanity should 'fix their eyes, as one man, on one same thing ahead of them'. Fascism, he said, allows 'the preservation of the élite', it 'opens its arms to the future' and might 'possibly represent a fairly successful small scale model of tomorrow's world'.[44]

New Agers would prefer not to be an élite; they would prefer everyone to be as spiritually enlightened as they are. But until that time, their task is to bring enlightenment to the uninitiated, so that everyone might live together in the earthly paradise. Those who fail to listen, who insist on remaining separate, will either be swept in to the New Age against their wishes – or will be consigned to the hell of the outside world.

America, according to Hitler, was 'half-Judaized, half negrified'[45] – and there were plenty who sympathized with the sentiment. The story of Nazism in America winds in and out of religious, racist and even mainstream political circles, each feeding off the other's belief that they are the chosen people. In the 1930s and 40s, the American Father Charles Coughlin was giving outright support to Hitler, and spreading anti-semitism across America's airwaves, attracting millions of listeners.

By the end of the 1980s, membership of the Ku Klux Klan, which had revived alongside the Civil Rights movement, was estimated at anything between 5000 and 15,000. The disparity was caused by the numerous white supremacy and neo-Nazi quasi-Klan groups which had erupted. In 1989, former California Klan Grand Dragon Tom Metzger was hosting a cable television chat show, *Race and Reason*, which was shown on more than twenty cable systems in more than fifty-five US cities, promoting his, and his guests', white supremacist views. Metzger campaigns for a white separatist state – just as many blacks seek a black separatist state. A leader of both the White American Political Association and White Aryan Resistance, a host of neo-Nazi skinhead gangs swell his ranks.[46]

Also in 1989, a cable system in Cincinnati carried an advertisement placed by a group calling themselves the White American Skin Heads. 'Join the American Nazis and smash Red, Jew and Black Power' it proclaimed.[47] That same year, David Duke, formerly an Imperial Wizard of the Knights of the KKK, won a seat as an independent

Republican in the Louisiana state legislature. In 1990 he received forty-four per cent of the Louisiana vote, almost becoming one of the state's representatives in the senate. A neo-Nazi activist in his teens, Duke spoke in his campaign of feeling the 'hand of destiny' moving among his supporters. He is also the founder of the National Association for the Advancement of White People which sends out tapes of the late American Nazi leader George Lincoln Rockwell who styled himself on Nazi leaders – and admired Malcolm X.[48]

Duke had previously stood for the Populist Party which, until 1986, was the electoral front of Willis Carto's right-wing Liberty Lobby. The Liberty Lobby's weekly tabloid *The Spotlight* has advertised teaching materials from Identity Christianity preachers. Identity Christianity has its roots in British Israelism – an attempt to prove that Anglo Saxons are the chosen people. In 1649 Englishman John Saddler wrote the *Rights of the Kingdom*, wherein he tried to demonstrate that the British were the true Israelites. Nearly 150 years later, in 1793, Richard Brothers, a former naval officer, announced that he was 'nephew of the Almighty' and began to spread the word of a new religion, Anglo-Israelism. Two years later, Brothers was sent to prison for prophesying the destruction of the monarchy, and from there to an asylum. The gospel of British Israelism was, however, carried on in the nineteenth century and both Queen Victoria and King Edward VII were patrons of the movement. Today the British Israel World Federation has some two million adherents both in Britain and America, where some British Israelites have settled. British Israelite beliefs have received little support from scholars.

According to some accounts, British Israelism took off in earnest across the Atlantic with car manufacturer Henry Ford. In 1920, a newspaper owned by Ford published a series of anti-semitic articles culminating in a book called *The International Jew: The World's Foremost Problem*. The articles were written by William Cameron, a British Israelite who referred to the Anglo Saxon Celtic race as the chosen people.

Cameron went on to found the Anglo Saxon Federation of America whose secretary, Howard Rand, published *Destiny*, a magazine which propounded similar views; he has also promoted Identity Christianity literature.[49]

Identity Christianity, like British Israelism, teaches that the lost tribes of Israel left the Middle East and founded the New Israel in Britain, from where many of their number crossed to the New

World. Those who call themselves Jews, teach Identity Christians, are in fact imposters, the 'seed of Satan'. Blacks, and indeed all non-white people, are sub-human 'mud people'.[50] Pastor Pete Peters spreads his Identity Gospel through a syndicated extremist radio programme *Scriptures of America*.

Also in the late 1980s, a group known as the Church of Jesus Christ Christian, founded in north America in 1946, attempted to gain a stronghold in Britain. The church has close lines with Identity Christianity.

Many of these groups are at the extremist end of what has been termed America's New Christian Right (NCR) – those Christians who are committed to bringing God back into American politics. Religion – and in particular Protestantism – has been an important factor in American politics ever since the Pilgrim Fathers landed at Cape Cod, and scripture is more often invoked in American politics than anywhere else in the western world. According to Steve Bruce, an academic expert on the NCR, the movement 'has limited appeal to anyone outside the WASP world because its arcadia – the one nation under God which was blessed – is white and Protestant. There are no parts for Catholics, Jews, or blacks in the sacred history of the new Christian right'.[51]

A – if not the – leading figure within the NCR is Jerry Falwell, a Southern Baptist minister. Falwell was the front man of the Moral Majority from its foundation in 1979 until its demise in 1989. Despite describing it as 'God's Guerilla Army' Falwell has denied it was a religious organization.[52] In August 1985 Jerry Falwell took part in the Unification Church's God and Freedom Banquet and made a speech celebrating the notoriously right-wing Moon's early release from jail for tax evasion and obstruction of justice.[53]

One of the Moral Majority's causes was to boost Reagan's popularity. Ideally, Falwell wanted God as president, but God's chosen man would do. Reagan came to his presidency trailing clouds of doom, claiming: 'If we don't get our house in order we're not going to be able to stop the apocalypse because we're going to deserve all we get . . .'[54] Reagan promised America would be reinstated as 'that God-given place between two oceans . . . a shining house on the hill'. Again, on Jim Bakker's PTL (Praise The Lord) network in 1980, he announced: 'We may be the generation that sees Armageddon.'[55] The Old Testament Book of Ezekiel tells how the the northern land of Gog will lead a mighty army against the people of Israel 'as a cloud to cover the land', whereupon 'there shall be a great shaking in the land of Israel'.[56] For Reagan, Gog was none other than Russia – the 'Evil Empire'.

Many supporters of the NCR now view the 1948 birth of Israel and the 1967 Israeli capture of Jerusalem as signalling the approach of Christ's second coming, and as a result are keen supporters of the state of Israel. For these 'Christian Zionists', however, the Jews themselves, as Bible expert Hal Lindsey's bestselling book *The Late Great Planet Earth* makes clear, are useful simply for the role they play in the drama of the apocalypse. In this vision of the end times, Israel will be invaded by an Arab-African army as well as the Russians. The Russians will kill millions of Jews, turn on and slaughter the Arab-African troops, and God will kill five-sixths of the Russians. Finally the Anti-Christ will lead Western civilization against the Communist Chinese, and the world will end. Before this all kicks off, however, Born Again Christians will be taken up from the world in a rapture and their role will be taken over by 144,000 Jews who will become evangelical Protestants. Finally, Christ will return to earth with the Born Again Christians and the millennium will begin.

Falwell's forecast was more succinct: 'From Genesis to Revelation the message is clear . . . there will be a nuclear holy war over Jerusalem and the Russians will come out second best . . . if we are ready for it.'[57]

On his election to President, Reagan appointed several NCR leaders positions within the administration. It wasn't an altogether fortuitous decision. Interior Secretary James Watt of the Assemblies of God argued there was little point in protecting the environment when the second coming was about to occur, and on one occasion announced to a White House committee: 'I do not know how many future generations we can count on before the Lord returns.'[58] Eventually he attempted to defend his egalitarian principles, saying, 'We have every kind of mixture you can have. I have a black. I have a woman, two Jews and a cripple.'[59] The statement cost him his post.

By turning abortion into an issue, the NCR became a mass movement. Abortion, thundered numerous preachers, was murder, and abortion clinics were bombed by Jesus activists. Abortion was referred to as a holocaust – the Nazi holocaust. Willis Carto of the Liberty Lobby was meanwhile publishing white supremacist tracts and material demonstrating that the Nazi holocaust was a myth. The National Front, too, have claimed that the holocaust never really happened – as have The Way and various fascist theoreticians in France.

It all smacks of George Orwell's 'two plus two equals five' in *1984*. Or of New Age teaching that 'you create your own reality'. But what in God's name could replace the crumbling myth of the Evil Empire? As it turned out, for many, the New Age fitted in neatly.

THIRTEEN | YOU HAVE THE POWER

For thousands of years communities, secret brotherhoods and loosely-affiliated networks have heralded the New Age, the arrival of heaven on earth. From the ascetic Essenes guarding their specialized knowledge on the shores of the Dead Sea, to the pockets of wild-eyed libertines touring Europe during the Middle Ages, to the intrigues of the Rosicrucians and the other-worldly intellectualism of the Theosophists, innumerable groups have believed that they have the power to bring about a new era.

Today's New Age has garnered from its heritage a spiritual hotchpotch of abstruse theories and esoteric snippets, sprinkled with a liberal dose of Eastern exoticisms. The result: a vast umbrella movement embracing countless groups, gurus and individuals, bound together by a belief that the world is undergoing a transformation or shift in consciousness which will usher in a new mode of being, an earthly paradise.

Rather than filing itself away under philosophical or theological labels, the New Age provides seekers with a spiritual core around which they can orbit, picking up whichever rays of enlightenment they feel hit the mark, or resonate with their own inner truth. By dismissing logical argument, by putting intuition above intellect and feeling above theory, the New Age happily embraces wildly differing creeds. For the New Age is not 'either/or' but 'both/and', as its proponents so often insist. Therein lies much of its appeal: the New Age has something for everyone. While it attracts its fair share of confirmed 1960s children, it also draws in businesspeople, so-called 'New Age yuppies', health professionals, lawyers – anyone who wants to take control over their life and at the same time escape, just for a while, from the monotony of everyday existence. It does help, however, if you are reasonably well off: the New Age brand of enlightenment doesn't come cheap.

What distinguishes a New Age convert? At one extreme, the New Age is a fashion item: at the beginning of the 1990s, several magazines and newspapers ran New Age fashion spreads, the clothes ranging from a return to 1960s psychedelic gear to white, loose-fitting outfits intended to symbolize the spiritual purity and holistic values of the wearer. Casual New Agers wear the clothes, sport crystal jewellery, read the odd book and attend a course now and again. At the other extreme are the committed New Agers. And while some might still be wearing their original 1960s clothes, many wear business suits, sport Filofaxes and only betray their spiritual allegiances when they open their mouths: key New Age words such as 'commitment', 'empower-ment', 'transformation', 'integrity' and 'unity' come tumbling out in a tone of high seriousness.

While today's New Age revival can in part be attributed to the approach of the millennium and the threat of the environmental crisis, it is the desire for power and control which accounts above all for the current upsurge of interest in the movement. Despite its aversion to labels, the New Age can be summed up by one simple phrase: you have the power.

Power is, it appears, an increasingly valued commodity in the latter part of the twentieth century – one which mainstream religions often fail to provide. Instead, they tend to emphasize powerlessness – and besides, say New Agers, most mainstream religions treat women appallingly and are divorced from real life. Whereas at first the twentieth century saw a drifting away from religion, the New Age marks a return to an all-embracing, all-powerful spirituality.

Of course, the heady sense of being privy to supposedly secret information has lured people towards esoteric paths for centuries. But what is different about the twentieth century search for power and control is that rather than simply being sought after by fringe groups or oppressed sections of society – as, for instance, with the revolutionary millennial sects of the Middle Ages – it is all-pervasive.

Over the past few decades, the average man and woman has been bombarded with information revealing how traditional seats of authority – the Church, the government and the family – have failed and deceived them. In tandem with such revelations, social commentators have been claiming that humanity is feeling increasingly out of control over everything from the minutiae of everyday life to world events which threaten their very existence. Not only are we living in a rapidly changing world, but also the mass media is continually making us aware of the situation. Many people were already half way to the conclusion that the self was the only place where they could locate Truth. The New Age simply pushed them over the edge by handing them the tantalizing concept of the 'empowered self'.

In the late 1960s, American psychiatrist Robert Jay Lifton described the new type of being produced by modernity as 'Protean man' – named after the shape-shifting Greek God Proteus. 'Protean man,' he said, 'is incapable of maintaining an unquestioning allegiance to the large ideologies and Utopian thought of the nineteenth and early twentieth centuries.'[1] Modern man was, he claimed 'confused about limits'. The response to this crisis was, he said, twofold. Some people chose to 'hold fast to all existing categories', creating 'nostalgic visions of restoring a golden age of exact boundaries, an age in which men allegedly knew exactly where they stood'. The opposite response, he said, was 'to destroy, or seek to destroy, all boundaries, in the name of an all-encompassing oneness'.[2]

The New Age sets out to break down the boundaries of reality, the boundaries of religions, the boundaries of nations and the boundaries of mind-body-spirit. Boundaries imply alienation and separation – and for the New Age, separation is the greatest evil. True to its 'both/and' doctrine, the New Age also returns men and women to a golden age – one in which they are all-powerful, no less than gods. In practice, however, it is often the New Age leader or guru who has the power: the follower will be told to locate truth in his or her inner self – but the leader will interpret what the inner self says. And although the New Age teaches a profound sense of 'self'-responsibility, many converts seem eager to hand over all semblance of personal decision-making to a leader who provides direction on everything from their choice of partner to what to eat and how often to wash.

The New Age also allows no boundaries between God and man – hence the difficulty with the Judaeo-Christian God who is seen as separate from his creation, and hence the New Age teaching that *you* are God. There must also be no distinction – no 'separation' – between the individual's reality and the outside reality, a doctrine which gives rise to the New Age maxim: you create your own reality.

For some converts, the maxim can be immensely liberating; for the unconverted, it can be infuriating: logical argument becomes impossible. In practice, 'you create your own reality' lays itself open to abuse. The emphasis on self can easily lead to selfishness, and even callousness: one New Age convert, explaining his philosophy of life, remarked that of course he could treat women how he liked because it was up to them how they chose to experience his behaviour. On a larger scale, some New Age groups teach that since people are 'responsible for' and 'create' their own reality, there is no point in giving to charity. During the massive 1985 Live Aid campaign, at least one New Age group staunchly refused to contribute any money. Although some of today's New Agers are active campaigners on issues which concern them, many have decided that a meditation or a dance will work just as well.

The idea that you create your own reality can also create profound feelings of guilt: someone suffering from an illness might be told that it is simply their 'story' – and it is up to them to get rid of the victim mentality and change the punchline. The New Age tends to dismiss the existence of absolutes, among them pain and death, which are often seen as simply yet another dogma. The one absolute which the New Age does promote is the power of the self.

New Agers themselves are often quite open about the dangers of self-discovery. LSD turned breath-control therapist Stanislav Grof recently co-wrote *The Stormy Search for The Self*,[3] advising seekers on how to deal with crack-ups on the path towards enlightenment. Others are worried not so much about the psychological as about the spiritual dangers of the New Age. Some leaders of established religions are so horrified by the emphasis on power that they are convinced Satan is behind the movement – a demonic puppeteer pulling the strings with the ultimate aim of effecting a world takeover.

Many New Agers actively promote the movement as being both dangerous and covert – and even the charge of Satanism is transformed into an attribute by some prominent New Age figures who see Satan not as the Anti-Christ (against Christ) but as the ante-Christ (before Christ), preparing the way for heaven on earth. Virtually all the derogatory remarks made about the New Age can also be seen as the very essence of what makes the movement so attractive: the New Age is not 'either/or' but 'both/and'.

Some believe that, before long, the New Age will develop an orthodoxy. While this would, in a sense, strip the New Age of what it is, it might help to ensure that New Age leaders are prevented from taking advantage of their spiritual authority: followers would have some code of practice against which they could measure their leader's behaviour; something concrete to hang on to in times of uncertainty. While some New Agers are happy to flit from group to group, others become totally dependent on the movement and if their faith is shaken they can feel immensely let down. Sometimes, the disillusionment can be shattering, and the struggle to rebuild their lives well-nigh overwhelming.

While there are countless New Age leaders whose behaviour towards their followers is faultless, there are a number who have abused the power which their personal charisma, together with the persuasiveness of their teachings, has given them. These leaders are accountable only to themselves – and their followers have little, if any, means of redress. The story of the Movement of Spiritual Inner Awareness (MSIA) provides a good illustration of the problem. Teachings within the movement encourage followers to reject criticism of them or their leader as 'negative'. Specific charges of malpractice by MSIA leaders are dismissed as tales that cannot be substantiated short of 'personal experience'. Those who become unhappy within the movement have either to obliterate any negative thinking, or leave it.

The founder of MSIA is Roger Hinkins. Born in Rains, Utah, in 1934 to Mormon parents, Hinkins was an ordinary kind of child, distinguished from his schoolfellows only by his claimed ability to see the auras or colours surrounding people. After gaining a degree in psychology, Hinkins took a job as an English teacher at Rosemead County High School, California.

Then the transformation occurred: falling into a coma following a kidney stone operation in 1963, Hinkins claims to have undergone a profoundly enlightening near-death experience and, on returning to the living, became aware that a spiritual being – John the Beloved – had entered his body. In Christian belief, John the Beloved is St John the Evangelist, one of Christ's apostles. From then on, Hinkins adopted the name of John-Roger, or J-R. He also claimed he was the embodiment of the Mystical Traveller Consciousness – a being, so his followers came to believe, which appears only once every 25,000 years, and without whom it is virtually impossible to reach God or the 'soul realm'.

In his spare time, J-R began to lead evening classes, preaching his new-found spirituality and gradually gathering a group of firm devotees around him. Meanwhile, he continued his more mundane teaching at Rosemead until, one day, the headmaster walked into his classroom to find the lights extinguished and curtains drawn: J-R had been introducing his pupils to hypnosis. Deciding that his spiritual teachings took priority, J-R and the school went separate ways.

J-R continued to spread his message, asking for small financial offerings from his followers. By 1971, interest had grown to such an extent that he and his followers founded the Movement for Spiritual Inner Awareness. By the mid-1970s, the Movement had attracted thousands of devotees in America and was beginning to take off in Europe. Members subscribed to spiritual study courses known as Soul Awareness Discourses and, when unable to be with J-R in person, listened to cassette tapes or watched videos of their guru.

In the United States MSIA became a legally incorporated church with a hierarchy of ministers licensed to perform baptisms and marriages – as well as New Age therapies such as aura balancings and innerphasings. In time, the organization expanded to include the Purple Rose Ashram of the New Age and the University of Santa Monica – an educational institution devoted to New Age study. J-R also had plans for a New Atlantis project in the Bahamas. 'We bring forward the "close" of one age and unlock and fling open the doors to the New Age,' wrote J-R in 1973. '. . . Soul Consciousness is again being presented to those Souls who can recognize it. This is the work of the Movement of Spiritual Inner Awareness – this is the work that I have come to do.'[4]

During the 1980s J-R launched a yearly International Integrity Award. Its recipients have included Mother Teresa of Calcutta, Bishop Desmond Tutu, Stevie Wonder and Lech Walesa. Followers of MSIA have also included Beach Boy Carl Wilson, socialite and author Arianna Stassinopoulos Huffington, actress Sally Kirkland and Bruce Gyngell, the managing director of British television company TV-am.

J-R also features in a cable TV programme syndicated throughout America, and *Life 101*, a self-help book he co-authored, hit the New York Times bestseller list. One of his many previous books, *You Can't Afford the Luxury of a Negative Thought*, has also been immensely popular.

In 1978, J-R launched Insight, a 'personal growth' seminar, with the help of Russell Bishop, a key figure within John Hanley's Lifespring (see Chapter Six). 'I said I was coming down to do battle for the soul,' wrote J-R in a letter to his ministerial board. 'And so we brought Insight Transformational Seminars into being . . .'[5] Before the launch of Insight, J-R introduced the new programme to MSIA ministers. He announced he had just returned from a four-day mountain-top meeting in Hawaii, attended by 'the spiritual hierarchy of the planet', including Jesus and other 'ascended masters'.[6]

Insight literature says the programme is aimed at 'enhancing productivity, contentment and success in personal and professional life'. Through an elaborate series of seminars, it claims to provide 'a new way of living' by 'making it possible to move through our deepest – often unconscious – limiting beliefs, freeing us to accept and express ourselves as we really are'.[7]

The promise has enticed businesspeople, actresses, teachers, lawyers, medical professionals and media personalities. Most newcomers are introduced by word of mouth; some qualified therapists and medical professionals have recommended the seminar to their clients. An offshoot, the Insight Consulting Group has provided time management consultancies for several top-notch organizations.

While top Insight facilitators have repeatedly denied that the organization has any links with MSIA, most Insight seminars are run by MSIA ministers, and trainees on the courses are introduced to the teachings of J-R. Among themselves, ministers have also admitted and applauded the fact that many people have come to MSIA from Insight.

While J-R provided purpose and stability for numerous lost souls of the 1960s, others, who had willingly latched on to the power of the Mystical Traveller, slowly began to feel that it was not something they could shake off so easily. Some felt that to leave J-R's fold was to condemn themselves to an everlasting cycle of death and rebirth with no hope of ever reaching heaven. Although ministers say it is possible to belong to any religion and still belong to the religion of MSIA, J-R's spiritual system teaches a belief in reincarnation and karma.

In the 1980s, controversy broke out within the Movement, fuelled by allegations made against J-R. Apparently, he had told some of his closest followers that their only route to paradise was through having sex with him. Some followers left the movement – defections which J-R explained away by saying they had become infected with a powerful negative force known as the Red Monk. Their best friends deserted them to avoid contagion.

Most of J-R's followers choose to 'check things out against their own experience and test it against their own reality'. If they choose to see J-R as blameless, then he is blameless, they believe. When presented with the allegations made against J-R, a lawyer and leading figure within MSIA said, 'I have no personal knowledge. I wasn't there at the time,'[8] and added that to check out the facts would necessitate concentrating on the negative.

Insight seminars are also rooted in New Age thinking. They focus on words such as love and trust, but are run in a curiously authoritarian manner. Trainees are prevented from leaving the room – usually a hotel conference room – where the trainings take place and must commit themselves to a list of guidelines or rules. Exits are guarded by volunteer graduates of previous trainings known as the 'Sentry Team'. 'They don't want you to be in control of the situation,' said one Insight trainee. 'They want to make you conform so that you obey.'[9] The Sentry Team, believe they are helping the newcomers in their midst to achieve enlightenment. And, for some, they are.

Trainees are encouraged to participate in a therapeutic-cum-mystical exercise in which they are told to go down into their inner worlds, to forgive themselves for themselves and to throw out white light, a type of spiritual energy. Guided meditations are conducted and a tremendous amount of hugging and swaying to gentle music takes place. In Insight II, or 'The Opening Heart', trainees are referred to as 'dirty bottles' – Insight is the clean water which flushes them out.[10] On subsequent courses, trainees must complete a 'quest'. One woman lectured on her sexual problems to passers by, another flew to Paris and walked down the Champs Elysée, another went swimming with dolphins. Then there are the 'survival' days, when the 'Wilderness Team' takes trainees on an outward bound course, swinging from ropes and so forth. One man, who had been looking forward to 'getting down and actually doing something', was told he had to spend the day carrying a leader's bags – even feeding him his lunchtime sandwiches. The courses encourage childlike behaviour to emerge. On one occasion, trainees were told to walk down the street asking passers by why they were happy. 'My husband's just been diagnosed with cancer,' was the reply from one ashen-faced woman.[11]

A vast amount of networking takes place at Insight courses. It begins when trainees are encouraged to put other trainees up for the night and continues into providing them with money for further courses and even jobs. To pay for subsequent courses trainees are prepared to cook and clean for other course participants; one woman was encouraged to ask her parents for the money she would be left in their will.[12]

Many people feel empowered by the courses, others claim they have been deceived, or 'had'. One such person rebelled and attempted to found 'Outsight' – a group intended to show that people didn't need rules or the Insight philosophy to enjoy themselves. The group met once or twice, practised 'OM' meditations – and soon petered out: without a firm leader, they simply didn't know what to do.

Insight is now targeting schools in the USA via the Achievement and Commitment to Excellence (ACE) programme, a seminar for high school students. 'I know that as we go out to schools we don't "advertise" our inner relationship with you or the church . . . mainly because of the separate [sic] of church and state,' wrote Insight's chief executive officer in a 1990 memo. 'At the same time I want you to know that we are very proud to be your friends, to be ministers in MSIA and very blessed to be doing this work.'[13]

Education is a constant bug-bear to New Agers, seen as a 'training towards alienation'[14] and school as a 'brutal machine for destruction of the self'.[15] Many believe that they themselves will never be free of the programming instilled into them in their childhoods. But they are determined that their children will fare better, that the next generation will be brought up with holistic, spiritual values. Nonetheless, while children might be introduced to enlightened forms of education, there is no way of preventing the educators from passing on the programming they received in their childhoods. The problem of who will educate the educators is one which, down the ages, has constantly confronted movements intent on breaking through into a new era.

In search of a solution, today's New Agers are increasingly taking their children out of mainstream institutions and educating them at home, or sending them to Steiner or Montessori schools. Maria Montessori (1870–1952) worked with the Theosophists for nine years at a cultural centre in India, and Rudolf Steiner (1861–1925) was a Theosophist before breaking away to form his own movement, Anthroposophy. Followers of the late Rajneesh have also formed their own school.

The Ko Hsuan Rajneesh school, lying surrounded by woods and

fields deep in England's Devonshire countryside, gets round the eternal problem of who will educate the educators by letting the children take the lead. Inside the entrance hall a handful of small scruffy children lie on the floor surrounded by roller skates and wellingtons. One shows the way through to the breakfast room where the headmaster, Sharna – or John Groombridge as he was known before he became a devotee, or sannyasin, of Rajneesh – is swamped under a pile of pupils.

According to Sharna, 'The kids are helping me find my deeper inside. They keep on throwing me back against myself. They let me know when I am being horrible, and when I am vulnerable they are so accepting and loving. The longer the school goes on the more they teach us and the less we teach them.' Rajneesh, says Sharna, made it 'really clear that generally adults screw kids up. Kids have an innate wisdom which if you give them space and freedom to use, they will. The best thing you can do for kids is to get out of their way. We learn so much from kids. They help us to reconnect to the kid within ourselves'.

The school has some sixty pupils from Europe and America. Fees are more than £1000 a term, making it prohibitively expensive for most parents – but then the unorthodox manner in which the school is run would not make it an attractive prospect to people who weren't themselves sannyasins. The curriculum is based around Osho's Five Dimensions of learning – the fifth being the art of dying or meditation in which the children seek to find the eternal within themselves. One subject – supernature – is devoted to the exploration of unexplained phenomena such as ley lines and ghosts. 'For one of the classes, we dropped the kids off in the middle of nowhere to see if they could find their way back,' says Sharna. 'Several moved in the right direction and decided it might be something to do with magnetism – so we sent them out again with magnets strapped to their heads.' Meditation is the first lesson of the day. It is optional for the children and consists of six minutes' speaking gibberish, six minutes' laughing about nothing and six minutes' silence.

'I was at another school before I came here,' says a thirteen-year-old pupil. 'It made me scared. Here, I love it. I have met Osho lots of times. He makes me feel good inside – he understands. He makes me feel very centred, very loved.'

According to Sharna, Britain's educational legislation is a desperate measure to regain nationalistic powers by destroying individuals and turning human beings into cramming machines. 'Our whole educational background is based on fear of survival. You are taught that life is an arduous struggle and you have to beat it, that if you don't learn, someone else will get that good job and you will have no money. Everybody is desperately planning for retirement from the time they go to school. Our kids live their lives for one thing and that's for joy, for their own joy – not for survival or money. At least they won't be able to manipulate our children. We have created a totally different space where most values are turned around and inside out.'

A dozen or so children gather in a classroom for an English lesson – today they can choose to learn a list of spellings. 'There are too many words – I'm going to die,' shrieks one boy, rolling on the floor. Another boy is curled up on a cushion in the corner reading Tolkein. 'Hey man, I can give you a read. I would really like that!' yells another pupil, then starts jumping around crying, 'I'm so happy! I'm so happy!' The teacher and one or two other pupils join in. Outside the classroom, a girl in the courtyard is hugging one of her teachers. 'What's a historical fact?' asks another girl. 'Some stupid date when some king died,' replies the teacher. 'Yaa Hoo! I Love You' is scrawled on the blackboard.

'Osho has allowed us space to grow,' says another teacher. 'He has freed us from fear and taught us love. We pass that on to the kids, but they teach us, too.' According to Sharna, 'Most children are being educated not to be awake or alive. We give children space and continually encourage them to look at and question their truth. If they don't lose that they won't have to waste their lives trying to find it again. We don't force them down somebody else's road.'

'Morals with these kids are a joke. We will not teach them somebody else's ideas of good and bad – that can never be your own truth. Your own truth can only come from inside you. For the first time in my life I have actually seen that the natural way for human beings to grow is through sensitivity and care and appreciation of beauty.'

One former Ko Hsuan pupil is now learning to be an accountant, another is training in photography, some have started their own rock band and one or two of the girls have won bit-parts in Indian films. 'They are going for what they want,' says Sharna. 'They're just enjoying their lives.'[16]

While other groups such as Transcendental Meditation, the School of Economic Science and the Church of Scientology have their own schools, New Age thinking is, say some, entering the educational arena through more discreet doors – particularly through the emphasis on experiential learning. Some parents' groups in the United States are claiming that their children's schools have become laboratories for New Age experimentation with regular classes in guided visualization and meditation.[16]

The movement towards enlightened methods of education was influenced by Jean-Jacques Rousseau and later by Johann Pestalozzi (1746–1827). In the 1960s, the rise of Summerhill, Suffolk, the so-called 'free school' founded by A. S. Neill (1883–1973), was influential in spreading the idea that the child rather than achievement should be put first. Interestingly, in the early 1920s, when Neill was running a progressive school at the Dalcroze Institute near Dresden, he met Gurdjieff. Gurdjieff wanted to set up his Institute for the Harmonious Development of Mankind at the Dalcroze Institute and persuaded the owner of the property to cancel his lease to Neill. Eventually, the owner was persuaded his move had been wrong and, in court, said that Gurdjieff had hypnotized him into agreeing to his demands.

Of course adults have not entirely given up hope that they might be released from their 'programming' in readiness for the New Age. That is why so many New Age teachings and training courses are flourishing. One organization that many adults and even companies are turning to in order to re-examine themselves and learn how to live 'authentically' is the Findhorn Foundation, which attracts more than 4000 visitors each year.

An international spiritual community based on the north east coast of Scotland, the Findhorn Foundation aims to create a 'spiritually based, holistic planetary culture'. Home to some 200 people, its main emphasis is on running courses for like-minded New Agers. The foundation has 'no formal doctrine or creed' but aims to put the underlying principles behind all major world religions into practice through 'the way we relate to each other, how we work and how we express concern for the earth'. Findhornians believe that 'an evolutionary expansion of consciousness is taking place in the world, creating a human culture infused with spiritual values'. Members of the Foundation recently developed the Transformation Game – a board game which provides 'a remarkable new way to experience and express you or deepest self'.

One of the numerous courses run at Findhorn in 1990 was 'Creating

Your Own Reality': 'Everything in your life is there because you chose it, because you created it – the beauty, the pain, the joy, the fear, the sheer magnificence,' ran the description. 'Life is an ongoing exploration of how we co-create with God.' While most courses are rooted in self-transformation, others promise that, for instance, 'your memory ability will improve by 300–500%'.

The Findhorn community was founded in 1962 by Peter and Eileen Caddy, together with their friend, Dorothy Maclean. Dismissed from their jobs as managers of a Scottish hotel, Peter and Eileen moved into a caravan near Findhorn with their three children, deciding to devote their lives to following the messages Eileen received from some higher force. Sometimes the demands appeared ludicrous such as when Eileen's inner voice instructed her to grow vegetables on a seemingly barren, sandy plot. But with the help of Dorothy, who was also able to tune in to the spirit of plants, the vegetables flourished, producing prodigious results – including 42lb broccoli and 60lb cabbages, and the attention flooded in. In 1975, the hotel which Eileen and Peter had been turfed out of was bought by the Findhorn Foundation.

'What seemed eccentric in the sixties is mainstream today,' says the Foundation. 'We know that everything is alive and interdependent. We are all essential crew on Spaceship Earth.' In the early years, Peter and Eileen Caddy were said to have exerted a charismatic control over the community but the Foundation has evolved into a movement constantly striving to run itself on principles of sharing, keeping in front of itself the ideals of healing separateness and 'dis-ease' both within the individual and, more importantly, the planet. Indeed, full membership is reserved for those who have already got to grips with their own growth and are seeking to move into planetary healing and growth.

Findhornians tend to believe that a divine force is working behind everything. Take, for instance, the example of a planned trip to Botswana, part of the International Youth Wilderness Expedition – an exchange between young people of southern Africa, the Soviet Union, Sweden and the United Kingdom run by Findhorn and sympathetic organizations in the other countries. At the last minute it was discovered that the seats booked on the flight to Botswana were a 'figment of someone's imagination'. However, everyone was able to rearrange their lives to leave three weeks later: 'a miracle of divine coordination' – or perhaps simply that everyone had flexible schedules. The new seats would be more expensive, but it was decided that rather than putting off the expedition, it would be 'easier and more graceful (and a safer bet) to manifest the cash'.

The exchanges were designed to teach the participants about the environmental problems facing the respective countries, and to provide 'a greenhouse for young people from four very different cultures to cultivate their relationships to one another and to prune their outdated, unfounded beliefs and prejudices against one another'.

Alongside the Foundation a number of independent businesses have sprung up and the Foundation itself has an annual turnover of more than £2 million. There have been complaints that it is becoming too worldly, that the sense of enlightenment has disappeared and that the accent is now on physical and entrepreneurial expansion rather than spiritual growth. The Foundation, however, aims to 'work with finances through trust and attunement' – and work is described as 'love in action'.[17]

Recently, the Foundation has begun to run an increasing number of courses for businesspeople such as working retreats for consultants and managers and seminars in 'Intuitive Leadership'. While Findhornians are keen that their outlook should influence the mainstream business world, the more mundane need for cash has also influenced the development. The need to face up to the harsh realities of life is a constant source of soul-searching – and growth – for the movement.

Education is certainly one means by which the New Age is entering the mainstream: education of children, education of adults and education of businesspeople. How firm a foothold the New Age now has in everyday life cannot be exactly determined but, if language forms a reliable barometer, it has achieved a fair degree of success: key New Age terms such as 'empowerment' and 'transformation' are now part of everyday parlance.

While New Age ideas are seeping through into the mainstream, some New Age groups are making a concerted effort to gain access to power through political channels. A leading member of Programmes, the business set up by Robert d'Aubigny, founder of 'self religion' Exegesis, was invited to a 'highfliers' conference organized by the British Conservative Party in 1988[18] and Conservative MP Ken Warren is on the company's board of directors. Silo's Movement (see Chapter Ten) has been causing confusion within green political parties worldwide and American New Age leader Barbara Marx Hubbard received more than 200 delegate signatures on petitions to put her name in nomination for the Vice Presidency at the 1984 Democratic Convention. Moreover, several high-profile figures have been associated with New Age guru Werner Erhard's Hunger Project and British MP Jim Lester has sat on its advisory council.

Another British MP swears by Transcendental Meditation as a stress reliever and former British Prime Minister Margaret Thatcher has used the ancient Indian system of mind-body-spirit health treatment Ayur-Veda, which reportedly includes Transcendental Meditation twice daily.[19]

The New Age is not simply gaining access to business and politics; it is even affecting royalty. Britain's heir apparent has gleaned inspiration from his spiritual mentor, explorer and Jungian philosopher Laurens van der Post. In 1986 Prince Charles stunned a group of Canadians with his musings on the meaning of the human soul. 'I rather feel deep in the soul of mankind there is a reflection as on the surface of a mirror, of a mirror-calm lake, of the beauty and harmony of the universe,' he said. 'But so often that reflection is obscured and ruffled by unaccountable storms. So much depends, I think, on how each one of us is introduced to and is made aware of that reflection within us. I believe we have a duty to our children to try to develop this awareness, for it seems to me that only through the development of an inner peace in the individual and through the outer manifestation of that reflection, that we can ever hope to attain the kind of peace in this world for which we yearn.'[20]

Whether or not Prince Charles considers himself 'New Age', the New Agers have used his words to give backing to their beliefs. On television in 1990, Charles declared himself concerned with humanity's 'crisis of the spirit' and advocated the need for man to find a kinship or oneness with nature.[21] In October that same year, the Prince visited Glastonbury, the haven of innumerable New Agers, where he drank from the Chalice Well – allegedly brimful with miracles, like everything else in Glastonbury. After trailing his hand in the water, he climbed Glastonbury Tor, where, according to one legend, King Arthur and his knights are in a deep sleep, awaiting the time when they will wake up to usher in a New Age.[22]

The New Age emphasizes magic and miracles – and such beliefs have found their echo in the 1980s' upsurge of miraculous sightings in Ireland where suddenly, it seemed, statues of the Virgin Mary were moving at every turn. Charismatic evangelicals too, with their belief in speaking in tongues and in healing miracles also demonstrate a liking for spiritual powers.

New Age leader Frank Natale has apparently worked with Charles Dederich, founder of Synanon, the drug rehabilitation programme which flowered into a full-blown religion, humanistic psychologist Carl Rogers, Gestalt psychologist Fritz Perls, Indian guru Muktananda, the Theosophists' chosen messiah J. Krishnamurti, altered states researcher John Lilly and Zen expert Alan Watts. He was also part of Abraham Maslow's research on 'self-actualized personalities'. Today, he runs seminars in 'Skills for the New Age' which apparently, through his 'wizardry', have brought 'clarity, power and magic back into the lives of all those who have been willing to participate in his seminars'.[23]

While some Christians describe the New Age emphasis on power as satanic, many are themselves increasingly emphasizing power – some to an extent which vies with the bizarreness of many New Age practices. The Christians' power, however, comes from the God without, not from the deified self. The Power Team, an American-based group, tours the world pumping iron for Jesus. Its members blow up hot water bottles, crack blocks of stone with their heads and punctuate their shows with cries such as 'I declare war on the Anti-Christ'. Even the name of televangelist Robert Schuller's programme – *The Hour of Power* – can be seen as indicating the general trend within both Christianity and the New Age.

According to Natale, 'The Old Age was filled with obligation, struggle, sacrifice, suffering, punishment, blame, self-pity, victimhood and martyrdom. These were the foundations of the old time religion. The Age of Consciousness is replacing these with clarity, responsibility, mastery, creativity, power, enthusiasm and love . . . The Old Age was a time of creating unconsciously. The New Age creates reality consciously and therefore the future can be changed at will. The more you become conscious, the more the New Age becomes more real than the old.'[24]

Like New Agers, many evangelicals, seek 'one world' – the Christians a world peopled by those of their faith, the New Age a world peopled by those of their consciousness. 'In every age, even in the Old Age, many had discovered their new age,' says Frank Natale. 'The New Age, the Age of Consciousness is a personal experience. It happens for each person individually, so stop waiting for some monkey to lead the way, do it for yourself now.'[25]

For many evangelicals, the apocalypse is about to happen now, too.

Many mainstream religions have come under immense criticism for their attitude towards women. 'Wives, submit to your husbands as to the Lord' is a favoured Bible quotation of many fundamentalist Christians. The New Age, supposedly peopled by 'enlightened' individuals, has also been criticized for its attitude towards women: Rajneesh might have chosen women as leaders within his community but it was because he valued their vulnerability and passivity rather than their dynamic qualities. And goddess spirituality, which celebrates the divine within women, cuts little ice with women who are struggling for equal rights and equal pay. Instead, say some women, it diverts attention from the real issues. But the New Age seems to have lost all sense of what is real.

And just as New Agers are profoundly anti-thought and analysis, religious fundamentalists, rather than questioning and challenging their scriptures, accept their every word as absolute truth.

Many fundamentalists see the New Age as the New Evil Empire – and New Agers return the compliment. Nonetheless, fundamentalist religion clearly has much in common with the New Age. And both are on the rise as we approach the millennium. In 1988, for the first time since the 1960s, the Church of England showed increases in attendance and membership – a rise attributed to the evangelicals.

'The modern age opened with the destruction of God and religion,' wrote a group of post-modernists in 1986. 'It is ending with the threatened destruction of all coherent thought.' The document was titled *After Truth*.

The last word goes to a Rajneesh sannyasin: 'The only thing the New Age is absolutely missing is a simple intelligence or understanding to sift between the seed and the chaff in its abundant harvest of esoteric nonsense. The danger of the New Age is that amidst all the spiritual slogans that sound like truth there *are* actually a few pearls of wisdom. But for that one real mystic rose there are ninety-nine plastic look-alikes that cost less, last longer and promise instant enlightenment.

'The real pilgrimage to Truth takes guts, integrity and putting your whole life at stake – the New Age variety takes Visa, Mastercard and putting aside three minutes a day chanting under a pyramid teepee for lower interest rates. All in all, it seems the attraction of the New Age is that people aren't actually interested in the "real" . . .'[26]

REFERENCES

CHAPTER ONE: MYSTERY AND MASTERY

1. Quoted in Alec R. Vidler, *The Church in an Age of Revolution* (London, 1987), p. 118.
2. Ianthe Hoskins, 'Of Dogma and Doctrine' *The Theosophical Journal* January/February 1990, Vol. 31, No.1.
3. Bruce Campbell, *Ancient Wisdom Revived* (Berkeley, California, 1980), p. 33.
4. ibid. p. 93.
5. Radha Burnier, 'On the Watch-Tower' *The Theosophist*, Feburary 1990, Vol. III, No.5 (Adyar, Madras).
6. *A Theosophical View of Human Races* (Illinois).
7. ibid.
8. Dr Yves Marcel, *Theosophy, A Perennial Wisdom for a New Age*, The Blavatsky Lecture delivered at the Annual Convention of the Theosophical Society in England, 30 July 1989 (England).
9. *A Theosophical View of Human Races*, op cit.
10. Plato, *Timaeus and Critias* (Harmondsworth, 1977), p. 137.
11. ibid, p. 145.
12. K. Lankheit (ed), *The Blaue Reiter Almanac* (London, 1974), p. 250.
13. Unpublished letter, quoted in Richard Ellman, *The Man and the Masks* (Oxford, 1979), p. 121.
14. Quoted ibid, p. 97.
15. Norman Cohn, *The Pursuit of the Millennium* (London, 1970), p. 109.
16. Unpublished Golden Dawn notebook, quoted in *The Man and the Masks*, op cit, p. 96.
16a. 'Manifesto From the Three Chiefs' in G. M. Harper, *Yeats's Golden Dawn* (Wellingborough, 1987), p. 287.
17. Leaflet, Theosophical Society.
18. *The International Order of the Round Table Jubilee Book 1908–1983*, (Coventry).
19. ibid.

20. Friedrich Nietzsche, *Thus Spoke Zarathustra* (London, 1969), p. 41.
21. Marilyn Ferguson, *The Aquarian Conspiracy* (London, 1988), p. 30.
22. Cited in Nicholas Goodrick-Clarke, *The Occult Roots of Nazism* (Wellingborough, 1985), p. 101.
23. ibid, p. 104.
24. Alice A. Bailey, *Problems of Humanity* (London, 1947), pp. 147–58.
25. *A Theosophical view of Human Races*, op cit.
26. ibid.

CHAPTER TWO: AWAKENINGS

1. Bernard Shaw, *Plays Pleasant and Unpleasant*, Vol. I (London, 1898), p. vii.
2. H. G. Wells, *A Modern Utopia* (London, 1925), p. 328.
3. Philip Mairet, *A. R. Orage A Memoir* (London, 1936), p. 59.
4. *The New Age*, 17 March 1910.
5. Letter, 23 May 1921 in *Katherine Mansfield's Letters to John Middleton Murry* (London, 1951).
6. G. I. Gurdjieff, *Meetings With Remarkable Men* (London, 1985), p. 79.
7. ibid, p. 90.
8. P. Ouspensky, *In Search of the Miraculous* (London, 1950), p. 19.
9. J. G. Bennett, *Gurdjieff Today* (Sherborne, 1974), p. 47.
10. ibid, p. 16.
11. Katherine Mansfield, letter to Koteliansky, 19 October 1922. Cited in Gillian Boddy, *Katherine Mansfield, The Woman and the Writer* (London, 1988), p. 149.
12. G. I. Gurdjieff, op cit, pp. 284–5.
13. James Webb, *The Harmonious Circle* (London, 1980), p. 261.
14. Louis Pauwels, *Gurdjieff* (Douglas, 1964), p. 5.
15. Letter, November 1922 in *Katherine Mansfield's Letters to John Middleton Murry*, op cit.
16. ibid, October, 1922.
17. P. Ouspensky, op cit, p. 55.
18. William Seabrook, *Witchcraft, its Power in the World Today* (New York, 1940), pp. 207–8.
19. *Resurgence*, November/December 1990.
20. Quoted in Peter Hounam and Andrew Hogg, *Secret Cult* (Tring, 1985), p. 36.
21. G. I. Gurdjieff, *Beelzebub's Tales to his Grandson* (London, 1985), p. 51.
22. J. G. Bennett, *Gurdjieff Today*, op cit, p. 34.
23. Internal document.
24. Internal document.
25. Hermann Hesse, *Journey to the East* (London, 1956), p. 21.
26. Plato, *The Republic* (London, 1987), p. 289, p. 240.
27. Interview with author, 1990.

28. Plato, *The Republic*, op cit, p. 240.
29. Interview with author, 1990.

CHAPTER THREE: DO WHAT YOU WILL

1. Rabelais, *Gargantua and Pantagruel* (London, 1981), p. 151.
2. I Corinthians 7:1–9.
3. Alan Watts, *This Is It* (London, 1978), p. 113.
4. Chung Hwan Kwak, *Outline of the Principle: Level 4* (New York, 1980), p. 214.
5. Tim Brown, *Daily Telegraph*, 31 December 1990.
6. Marquis de Sade, *The Complete Justine, Philosophy in the Bedroom and other Writings*, trans. R. Seaver and A. Wainhouse (New York, 1966), p. 204.
7. ibid, p. 345.
8. ibid, p. 344–5.
9. ibid, p. 246.
10. Aleister Crowley, *The Book of the Law* (London, 1938).
11. *The Confessions of Aleister Crowley* (London, 1989), p. 850.
12. ibid, p. 853.
13. ibid, p. 852.
14. ibid, p. 851.
15. ibid, p. 854.
16. Edward Carpenter, *The Drama of Love and Death* (London, 1912), p. 247.
17. *Chains ov thee Mind*, Thee Temple Ov Psychick Youth booklet, (1988).
18. Henry Chadwick, *The Early Church* (Harmondsworth, 1978), p. 35.
19. Norman Cohn, *The Pursuit of the Millennium* (London, 1970), p. 156.
20. ibid.
21. ibid, p. 175.
22. ibid, p. 176.
23. ibid, p. 176.
24. ibid, p. 149.
25. Henri, Comte de Saint-Simon, *Selected Writings*, ed and trans F. Markham (Oxford, 1952), p. xxxviii.
26. *Bible Communism* (Brooklyn, New York, 1853), pp. 26–31.
27. Letter from J. M. Shepherd to James Barr, 8 August 1885, cited in Herbert Schneider and George Lawton *A Prophet and A Pilgrim* (Columbia, 1942), p. 464.
28. Interview 1989.
29. Janet and Stewart Farrar, *The Life and Times of a Modern Witch* (London, 1987), p. 81.
30. Interview 1990.
31. *The Times*, 17 February 1967.
32. Quoted in Deborah Davis, *The Children of God* (Michigan, 1984), p. 189.
33. Quoted in Eileen Barker *New Religious Movements* (London, 1989), p. 171.
34. ibid.
35. Quoted in *The Children of God*, op cit, p. 183.
36. ibid, p. 123.

36a. *Heaven's Children* (Zurich, 1987), p. 391.
37. Rajneesh, *Tantra: the Supreme Understanding* (London, 1978).
38. Rajneesh, *From Sex to Superconsciousness* (Poona, 1979).
39. *Space Aliens took me to their Planet*, pamphlet published by the British Raelian Movement.
40. Jason Bennetto, *Western Daily Press*, 7 January, 1989.
41. Janet and Stewart Farrar, op cit, p. 87.
42. Friedrich Nietzsche, *The Birth of Tragedy*, trans W. A. Haussmann (Edinburgh & London, 1909), p. 27.
43. *Healing Sex* leaflet.
44. *Soul Centering* leaflet.
45. Timothy Leary, *The Politics of Ecstasy* (London, 1970), p. 189.

CHAPTER FOUR: CHEMICAL ENLIGHTENMENT

1. R. Gordon Wasson, *Soma: Divine Mushroom of Immortality* (New York, 1969).
2. Aldous Huxley, *Brave New World* (Harmondsworth, 1975), p. 53.
3. ibid, p. 71.
4. ibid, p. 53.
5. ibid, p. 18.
6. ibid, p. 173.
7. Rosemary Ellen Guiley, *The Encyclopedia of Witches and Witchcraft* (New York, 1989), p. 255.
8. Timothy Leary, *The Politics of Ecstasy* (London, 1970), p. 69.
9. Alan Ginsberg, introduction to Timothy Leary *Jail Notes* (New York, 1970), p. 9.
10. Timothy Leary, op cit, p. 193.
11. Quoted in Jeff Nuttall, *Bomb Culture* (London, 1968), p. 199.
12. Barbara L. Goldsmith, 'La Dolce Viva' in *The New Journalism* (London, 1980), p. 249.
13. Timothy Leary, op cit, p. 184.
14. ibid, p. 54.
15. Quoted by Alan Ginsberg, *Jail Notes*, op cit, p. 12.
16. Timothy Leary, *Jail Notes*, op cit, p. 61.
17. Quoted by Alan Ginsberg, introduction to *Jail Notes*, op cit, p. 9.
18. *The Independent*, 11 February 1989.
19. Timothy Leary, *Info Psychology, A Revision of Exo Psychology* (Falcon Press, 1987).
20. Alan Ginsberg, op cit, p. 8.
21. Weston La Barre, 'Twenty years of Peyote studies' *Current Anthropology I*, 1 January 1960, pp. 45–60. Cited in Bryan Wilson, *Magic and the Millennium* (London, 1975), p. 414.
22. Barbara L. Goldsmith, op cit, p. 249.
23. *Gnosis, A Journal of Western Inner Traditions*, No. 16, Summer 1990.
24. Tom Wolfe, *The Electric Kool-Aid Acid Test* (London, 1989), p. 51.

25. ibid, p. 117.
26. Susan Sontag, *Against Interpretation* (London, 1987), p. 274.
27. Alan Watts, *This Is It* (London, 1978), p. 141.
28. Tom Wolfe, op cit, p. 243.
29. Alan Watts, op cit, p. 135.
30. William James, *The Varieties of Religious Experience* (London, 1985), p. 387.
31. Church of the SubGenius pamphlet.
32. *Rolling Stone*, Issue 585, 23 August 1990.
33. ibid.
34. Gerrard Winstanley, 'The New Law of Righteousness', 1649, 'The Law of Freedom in a Platform', 1652, in *Journey through Utopia*, Marie Louise Berneri (London, 1987), pp. 147, 152, 172.
35. Quoted in *The Independent Magazine* 12 August 1989.
36. *The Confessions of Aleister Crowley* (London, 1989), p. 490.
37. Thomas De Quincey, *Confessions of an English Opium Eater* (London, 1982), p. 75.
38. ibid, p. 72.
39. ibid, p. 75.
40. ibid, p. 73.
41. William James, op cit, p. 387.
42. Virginia Berridge, 'Fenland Opium Eating in the 19th Century', *British Journal of Addiction*, no. 72, 1977, pp. 275–84, quoted in *The Oxford Companion to the Mind*.
43. Charles-Pierre Baudelaire *Les Fleurs du mal, Petits poemes en prose, Les paradis artificiels*, trans Arthur Symons, (London, 1925), p. 246.
44. Aldous Huxley, *The Doors of Perception* (London, 1990), p. 54.
45. Bernard Lewis, *The Assassins*, (London, 1967), pp. 6–8
46. ibid.
47. *The Age*, 8, 10 and 11 September 1990; *Times on Sunday*, 18 October 1987.
48. Arthur Koestler, *The Ghost in the Machine* (London, 1989), pp. 336–9.
49. Quoted by Marc Galanter in 'Cults and Zealous Self-Help Movements: A Psychiatric perspective', *The American Journal of Psychiatry*, 147:5, May 1990, p. 547.
50. William S. Burroughs, Brian Gysin and Throbbing Gristle, *Research*, 1982, p. 64.
51. *Rapid Eye*, 1986.

CHAPTER FIVE: BE ALL YOU CAN BE

1. Alan Watts, *This Is It* (London, 1978), p. 134.
2. Eternal Flame leaflet.
3. Timothy Leary, *The Politics of Ecstasy* (London, 1970), pp. 223, 182.
4. Leonard Orr, *Rebirthing in the New Age* (California, 1980).
5. Sir Edward Dyer 'My Mind to Me a Kingdom Is', *Oxford Book of English Verse* (Oxford, 1979), p. 49.

6. B. F. Skinner, *Walden Two* (New York, 1960), p. 163.
7. ibid, p. 240.
8. B. F. Skinner, *About Behaviourism* (New York, 1974), p. 225.
9. Abraham Maslow, *Toward a Psychology of Being* (New York, 1982), p. 105.
10. ibid, p. 197.
11. ibid, p. 214.
12. ibid, p. 212.
13. Pauline Kael, quoted in *Halliwell's Film Guide* (London, 1986), p. 26.
14. Sri Aurobindo, ashram leaflet.
15 T. M. P. Mahadevan, *Outlines of Hinduism* (Bombay, 1954), p. 239.
16. William Blake, 'A Memorable Fancy', in *Complete Writings*, ed. Geoffrey Keynes (Oxford, 1972), p. 154.
17. William Blake, 'Proverbs of Hell', *Complete Writings*, op cit, p. 150.
18. Quoted in Rasa Gustasis, *Turning On* (London, 1969), p. 42.
19. R. D. Laing, *The Politics of Experience* (London, 1990), p. 119.
20. Gestalt leaflet.
21. William Blake, *Complete Writings*, op cit, p. 179.
22. Robert Heinlein, *Stranger in a Strange Land* (London, 1990), p. 92.
23. ibid, p. 392.
24. Charles Manson, letter from prison, quoted in Donald A. Nielsen, 'Charles Manson's Family of Love: A Case of Anomism, Puerilism and Transmoral Consciousness in Civilizational Perspective', *Sociological Analysis* Vol. 45, No. 4, Winter 1984, p. 328.
24a. Ed Sanders, *The Family* (London, 1972), p. 224.
24b. Benjamin Lee Whorf, *Language Thought and Reality* (Cambridge, Massachusetts, 1973), p. 263. Reprinted from *Theosophist* (Madras, India), January and April issues, 1942.
25. Fritz Kunz, *The Men Beyond Mankind* (London, 1934)
26. L. Ron Hubbard, *Dianetics* (New Era Publications, Redhill, Surrey, 1988), p. viii.
27. ibid, p. 94.
28. *New York Times*, 2 July 1950. Quoted in Russell Miller, *Bare-Faced Messiah* (London, 1988), p. 208.
29. *The Times*, 29 January 1986.
30. *What Is Scientology*, 1978. Quoted in *Bare-Faced Messiah*, op cit, p. 264.
31. Interview, 1990.
32. Life Training course hand-out.
33. ibid.
34. Cosmic Vortex leaflet.
35. ibid.
36. James Channon, *The First Earth Battalion*, (USA, 1979).
37. Delta Force report, *Army Leadership Development, Power Down to Power Up*, (Carlisle, Pennsylvania, 1982).
38. John A. Swets and Robert A. Bjork 'Enhancing Human Performance: An Evaluation of New Age Techniques Considered by the US Army', *Psychological Science*, Vol. 1, No. 2, March 1990, and interview, 1990.
39. Kevin Garvey, report of private conversation, 1977.

40. Luke Rhinehart, *The Book of est* (New York, 1976), p. 211.
41. Aldous Huxley, *Brave New World* (Harmondsworth, 1975), p. 24.
42. Fyodor Dostoevsky, *The Devils* (Harmondsworth, 1971), pp. 243–4.
43. Adelaide Bry, *est: 60 hours that transform your life* (London, 1977), p. 153.
44. *Fontana Dictionary of Modern Thought*, ed Alan Bullock and Oliver Stallybrass (London, 1977) p. 517.
45. Luke Rhinehart, *The Dice Man*, (London, 1989), p. 69.
46. ibid, p. 415.
47. Luke Rhinehart, *The Book of est*, op cit, p. 185.
48. William Bartley, *Werner Erhard: The Transformation of a Man*, (New York, 1978).
49. Luke Rhinehart, *The Book of est*, op cit, pp. 11, 13.
50. Robert Heinlein, op cit, p. 134.
51. Luke Rhinehart, op cit, p. 189.
52. Robert Heinlein, op cit, p. 130.
53. Horizon television programme, 1990.

CHAPTER SIX: THE PROSPEROUS SELF

1. Hunter S. Thompson, *San Francisco Examiner*, 22 February 1988.
2. Press reports, 1989.
3. Interview.
4. Luther, *Colloquial* (collected 1566 by J. Aurifaber), Ch. 20.
5. Robert Jay Lifton, *Boundaries: Psychological Man in Revolution* (New York, 1970), p. 6.
6. Arthur Koestler, *The Ghost in the Machine* (London, 1989), pp. 322–3.
7. Robert Jay Lifton, op cit, p. 29.
8. Norman Vincent Peale, *The Power of Positive Thinking*, (Kingswood, 1963), pp. viii–ix.
9. Catherine Ponder, *Open Your Mind to Receive* (California, 1983), cover copy.
10. ibid.
11. The Way leaflet.
12. ibid.
13. Letter from Victor Paul Wierwille to the Way Corps, 24 May 1979.
14. *The Sunday Post*, 30 November 1986.
15. Way leader Craig Martindale, quoted in Carol Coulter *Are Religious Cults Dangerous* (Dublin, 1984), p. 56.
16. Quoted in Russell Miller *Bare-Faced Messiah* (London, 1988), p. 285.
17. Randy Bright, *Disneyland's Inside Story* (New York, 1987), Introduction.
18. Umberto Eco, *Faith in Fakes* (London, 1986), p. 19.
19. Quoted in Leonard Mosley, *Disney's World* (New York, 1985), p. 287.
20. ibid, p. 232.
21. Catherine Mayer, 'The American Dream and the great escape', *The Economist*, 11 January 1986.
22. Charles Reich, *The Greening of America* (London, 1972), p. 152.

23. ibid, p. 15.
24. ibid, p. 204.
25. ibid, p. 326.
26. Judson Jerome, *Families of Eden* (London, 1975), p. 110.
27. Trainee's course notes.
28. ibid.
29. Interview, 1990.
30. Rajneesh, quoted in *Rajneesh Times*.
31. Peter Morgan, director Institute of Directors, quoted in *The Times*, 12 March 1990.
32. Seminar brochure.
33. Andrew Kopkind, *The Real Paper*, quoted in Nora Sayre, *Sixties Going on Seventies* (London, 1974).
34. William Bartley, *Werner Erhard The Transformation of a Man*, (New York, 1978), pp. 166–8.
35. Forum brochure.
36. David Kirp and Douglas Rice, 'Fast Forward – Styles of California Management', *Harvard Business Review*, January–February 1988.
37. Robert D'Aubigny in 'Transformation Express' *Everyman*, BBC 2, 25 November 1979.
38. ibid.
39. Interview with author, 1989.
40. Kim Coe in 'Transformation Express'.
41. Interview with author, 1990.
42. Programmes leaflet.
43. Interview with author, 1990.
44. 'Transformation Express'.
45. Interview with author, 1989.
46. Interview with author, 1991.
47. *The Financial Initiative Context Document*, December 1983, p. 16.
48. ibid.
49. Interview with author, 1990.
50. Quoted by Sarah Binning in unpublished article.
51. Lecture given by management trainer, mid-1980s.

CHAPTER SEVEN: LIVING GODS

1. Interview with author, 1991.
2. Interviews with author, 1989.
3. Quoted in K. M. Sen, *Hinduism* (Harmondsworth, 1972), p. 110.
4. Tal Brooke, *Riders of the Cosmic Circuit* (Tring, 1986), p. 52.
5. Lecture, 1973, quoted in Muz Murray, *Seeking the Master*, (Sudbury, Suffolk, 1980).
6. Rajneesh, 'The Sound of Running Water', in *Rajneesh Times International*, 16 February 1989.

7. Rajneesh, 'Zen: The Mystery and Mastery of the Beyond', Discourse 1, 8 January 1989, in *Rajneesh Times International*, Vol. 2, No. 3, 16 February 1989.
8. Osho, 'The Invitation', 21 August 1987, in *Osho Times International*, Vol. 3, No. 6, 16 March 1990.
9. Interview with author, 1989.
10. ibid.
11. Quoted in Tal Brooke, op cit, p. 145.
12. Interview with author, 1989.
13. Rajneesh, 'The Light on The Path', in *Rajneesh Times International* Vol. 2, No.3, 16 February 1989.
14. Rajneesh, 'Om Shantih Shantih Shanti', Discourse 13, 6 March 1988, in *Rajneesh Times International*, Vol. 1, No. 7, 16 April 1988.
15. Interview 1989.
16. ibid.
17. *Here & Now* magazine, March 1988.
18. Osho, 'The Invitation', in *Osho Times International*, Vol. 3, No. 6, 16 March 1990.
19. Saniel Bonder, *The Divine Emergence of the World-Teacher*, (California, 1990), p. 132.
20. ibid.
21. Interview with author, 1991.
22. Frans Bakker, 'Radical Healing', *Human Potential* magazine, Vol. 15, No. 3, Autumn 1990.
23. Interviews with author, 1991.
24. Thomas Carlyle, *Heroes & Hero Worship* (London, 1898), p. 13.
25. ibid, p. 11.
26. Frederic Harrison, *A New Era* (London, 1889), p. 12.
27. Frederic Harrison, *Science and Humanity*, (London, 1879), p. 7.
28. Frederic Harrison, *A New Era*, op cit, p. 10.
29. ibid, p. 5.
30. Frederic Harrison, *Autobiographic Memoirs*, Vol. 2, (London, 1911), p. 288.
31. Rajneesh, from *Rajneesh Bible*, in *Rajneesh Times International*, 16 October, 1988.

CHAPTER EIGHT: EASTERN PROMISE

1. *Maharishi News Release*, December 1989.
2. *Maharishi News Release*, January 1990.
3. Maharishi University of Natural Law Press Statement, December 1989.
4. Cooper Whiteside Norman and Margaret Calvert Norman 'Building For Heaven on Earth', *The Fairfield Source*, September 1990, p. 27.
5. ibid.
6. *Maharishi News Release*, January 1990.
7. Cooper Whiteside Norman and Margaret Calvert Norman, op cit, p. 26.

8. *Maharishi News Release*, December 1989.
9. Duncan Campbell, 'Heaven on Earth', *New Statesman and Society*, October 1990, p. 11.
9a. A. C. Bhaktivedanta Swami Prabhupada, *Chant and Be Happy* (Los Angeles, 1985), p. 77.
10. Stasvarupa Dasa Goswami, *Prabhupada*, (Los Angeles, 1984), p. x.
11. Interview with author, 1990.
12. Satsvarupa Dasa Goswami, op cit, p. 65, p. 171.
13. Interview with author, 1990.
14. A. C. Bhaktivedanta Swami Prabhupada, *Sri Iospanisad*, (Los Angeles, 1974), p. xi.
15. Interview with author, 1990.
16. *The Bhagavad Gita*, trans. Juan Mascaro, (London, 1988), p. 83.
17. A. C. Bhaktivedanta Swami Prabhupada, *Bhagavad-Gita As It Is*, (Philippines), p. 489.
18. Satsvarupa Dasa Goswami, op cit, p. 259.
19. Interview with author, 1989.
20. Satsvarupa Dasa Goswami, op cit, p. 245.
21. *Sunday Times*, 24 August 1986.
22. *The Times*, 21 July 1988.
23. Interview with author, 1990.
24. Alan Watts, *This Is It* (London, 1978), p. 91.
25. *The Upanishads*, trans. Juan Mascaro, (Harmondsworth, 1965), p. 52.
26. Henry Miller, *Tropic of Capricorn* (London, 1980), p. 11.
27. Akira Kasamatsu and Tomio Hirai, 'An Electroencephalographic Study on the Zen Meditation (Zazen)', in C. T. Tart, *Altered States of Consciousness* (New York, 1969), pp. 489–501.
28. Interview with author, 1990.
29. Rabindranath Tagore, quoted in Juan Mascaro's introduction to *The Upanishads* (London, 1965), p. 17.
30. Fritjof Capra, *Tao of Physics*, (London, 1983), p. 16.
31. Sivananda, *Sivananda's Lectures: All India Tour (1950)*, (Rishikesh, 1951), p. 424.
32. Cited in Muz Murray, *Seeking the Master* (Sudbury, Suffolk, 1980), p. 262.
33. ibid, p. 261.
34. Fritjof Capra, op cit, pp. 15–16.
35. Bede Griffiths, *A New Vision of Reality* (Tiruchy), p. 12.
36. ibid, p. 2.

CHAPTER NINE: WESTERN REVELATIONS

1. Adriaane Pielou, 'Mother Knows Best – And It's the Worst', *You* magazine, 1 October 1989.
2. *Wall Street Journal*, 5 December 1989.
3. The Book of Daniel, 7:13–14, 27.

4. Revelation, 20:4.
5. ibid, 22: 6–7.
6. The Gospel According to St Matthew, 16:28.
7. Sir George Trevelyan, *Operation Redemption* (Wellingborough, 1981), p. 93.
8. Geza Vermes, *The Dead Sea Scrolls in English* (London, 1987), p. 118.
9. ibid, p. 286.
10. ibid, p. 105.
11. ibid, p. 117.
12. ibid, p. 72.
13. ibid, p. 73.
14. Peter Lemesurier, *The Armageddon Script*, (Salisbury, 1981), p. 248.
15. Elizabeth Prophet, *Forbidden Mysteries of Enoch, The Untold Story of Men and Angels*, (Livingston, Montana, 1983).
16. ibid.
17. ibid.
18. ibid.
19. Omraam Mikhael Aivanhov, *A Philosophy of Universality*, (Frejus, 1988), p. 156.
20. ibid, p. 35.
21. ibid, p. 19.
22. Interview with author, 1990.
23. ibid, p. 62.
24. ibid, p. 80.
25. ibid, p. 75.
26. ibid, p. 176.
27. Interview with author, 1990.
28. ibid, p. 76.
29. *Diggers and Dreamers, Guide to Communal Living*, (Dunford Bridge, 1989).
30. Revelation, 3:10–12.
31. *The Plain Truth*, (Worldwide Church of God, Pasadena, California), March 1989.
32. *The Plain Truth*, November/December 1989.
33. *The Government that Will Bring Paradise*, (Watch Tower Bible and Tract Society of Pennsylvania), 1985.
34. *The Watchtower* (Watch Tower Bible and Tract Society of Pennsylvania) 1 June 1990.
35. *The Government that Will Bring Paradise*, op cit.
36. *Mankind's Search for God*, op cit, p. 371–2.
37. 1 Thessalonians, 5:3.

CHAPTER TEN: GREEN SPIRITUALITY

1. Interview with author, 1990 (and following quotations).
2. Richard Falk, *This Endangered Planet*, (New York, 1972), pp. 428–34.
3. Interview with author, 1990.

4. Thomas Traherne, 'Centuries of Meditations' in F. C. Happold, *Mysticism*, (London, 1988), pp. 368–70.
5. Findhorn Foundation brochure, 1990.
6. Interview with author, 1990.
7. ibid.
8. Ammianus, cited in Rosemary Ellen Guiley, *The Encyclopedia of Witches and Witchcraft* (New York, 1989), p. 107.
9. Interview with author, 1990.
10. Graigian Order leaflet.
11. Interviews with author, 1990 and Joe Conason, Jill Weiner, 'The Fake Greens', *Village Voice*, 26 December 1989.
12. ibid.
13. ibid.
14. Interview with author, 1990.
15. ibid.
16. Frances Yates, *The Rosicrucian Enlightenment* (London, 1986), pp. 256–7.
17. Rosemary Ellen Guiley, op cit, p. 160.
18. Francis Bacon, *New Atlantis* (Oxford, 1915), p. 46.
19. *The Sunday Telegraph*, 2 December 1990.
20. Matthew Fox, leaflet, On Creation-Centred Spirituality.
21. Teilhard de Chardin, 'Letters from a Traveller' in F. C. Happold, *Mysticism*, op cit, p. 39.
22. Teilhard de Chardin, *The Divine Milieu* (London, 1960), p. 103.
23. ibid, p. 106.
24. Matthew Fox, *Original Blessing* (London, 1983), p. 161.
25. ibid, p. 283.
26. Matthew Fox, *On Becoming a Musical Mystical Bear* (New Jersey, 1976), p. 76.
27. Matthew Fox, *Whee! We, Wee All the Way Home: A Guide to Sensual, Prophetic Spirituality*, (Santa Fe, 1981), p. 93.
28. Matthew Fox, *Original Blessing*, p. 283.
29. Margaret Brearley, 'Matthew Fox: Creation Spirituality for the Aquarian Age', *Christian Jewish Relations*, Vol. 22, No. 2, 1989.
30. Matthew Fox, *Original Blessing*, op cit, p. 26.
31. ibid, p. 23.
32. ibid, p. 105.
33. *New Road*, bulletin of the WWF Network on Conservation and Religion, No. 5, p. 7.
34. Interview with author, 1990.
35. ibid.
36. ibid.
37. Arthur Koestler, *The Ghost in the Machine* (London, 1989), p. 339.
38. Murray Bookchin, 'Post Scarcity Anarchism' (1974), in *The Anarchist Reader*, ed George Woodcock (London, 1980), p. 370.

CHAPTER ELEVEN: COMMUNES AND COMMUNISTS

1. Jan Bang, 'Cartwheel', in *Digger's and Dreamers, Guide to Communal Living* (Dunford Bridge, 1989), p. 23.
2. ibid, p. 26.
3. Robert Owen, *A New View of Society* (London, 1923), p. 97.
4. ibid, p. 113.
5. George Holyoake, *Gygones Worth Remembering*, Vol. 2 (New York, 1905), p. 238. Cited by Walter E. Houghton in *The Victorian Frame of Mind, 1830–1870* (Yale, 1957), p. 51.
6. John Finch, *The Millennium* (1837), p. 24, cited in J. F. C. Harrison, *Robert Owen and the Owenites in Britain and America* (London, 1969), p. 126.
7. Robert Owen, *The Book of The New Moral World* (London, 1836), p. xi.
8. *New Moral World*, 1 November 1834, cited in J. F. C. Harrison, op cit, p. 133.
9. Alec R. Vidler *The Church in an Age of Revolution* (London, 1987), p. 11.
10. G. P. Maximoff (ed), *The Political Philosophy of Bakunin* (Glencoe, 1964), p. 192.
11. Quoted in Emmet Kennedy, *A Cultural History of the French Revolution* (Yale, 1989), p. 343.
12. Jean-Jacques Rousseau, *The Social Contract*, (Harmondsworth, 1968), p. 183.
13. E. L. Griggs (ed), *Collected Letters of Samuel Taylor Coleridge*, Vol. 1, (Oxford, 1956), p. 214.
14. William Morris, *News from Nowhere* (London, 1986), p. 238.
15. ibid, p. 298.
16. Catherine Albanese, *Corresponding Motion: Transcendental Religion and the New America* (Philadelphia, 1977), p. 64.
17. Henry Thoreau, *Journal*, ed Bradford Torrey and Francis H. Allen, Vol. 1 (Boston, 1906), p. 227.
18. Lousia M. Alcott, *Silver Pitchers*(1876), cited in Donald Koster, *Transcendentalism in America* (Boston, 1975), p. 14.
19. Rosabeth Moss Kanter, *Commitment and Community: Communes and Utopias in Sociological Perspective*, (Harvard, 1972), p. 166, cited in Judson Jerome, *Families of Eden* (London, 1975), p. 66.
20. Karl Marx and Friedrich Engels, *The Comunist Manifesto*, (London, 1980), p. 117.
21. Karl Marx, *Capital: A Critique of Political Economy* (Harmondsworth, 1976), p. 99.
22. Friedrich Engels, 'Socialism: utopian and scientific', in Marx and Engels, *On Religion* (New York, 1964), p. 291.
23. Franz Borkenau, *Der Ubergang vom Feudalen zum Burgerlichen Weltbild* (Paris, 1934), p. 158, quoted in David McLellan, *Marxism and Religion* (London, 1987), pp. 126–7.
24. Otto Bauer, *Sozialdemokratie, Religion und Kirche* (Vienna, 1927), p. 21, quoted in *Marxism and Religion*, op cit, p. 81.

25. John Malcolm Ludlow, letter to F. D. Maurice, in F. Maurice *Life of F. D. Maurice* (1884), Vol. 1, p. 458, quoted in Alec R. Vidler, *The Church in an Age of Revolution*, op cit, p. 96.
26. Walter Rauschenbusch, *Christianity and the Social Crisis* (New York, 1907), p. 422.
27. Walter Rauschenbusch, *Christianizing the Social Order* (New York, 1912), p. 42.
28. Leo Tolstoy, *The Kreutzer Sonata* (London, 1985), p. 281.
29. Marilyn Ferguson, *The Aquarian Conspiracy*, op cit, pp. 217–8.
30. Leo Tolstoy, letter, 10 February 1890, quoted in 'Translator's Introduction', *The Kruetzer Sonata*, op cit, p. 7.
31. Lenin, 'Socialism and Religion', *Collected Works* Vol. 10 (Moscow, 1982), p. 83.
32. Bakunin, *Oeuvres*, Vol. IV (1910), in *The Anarchist Reader*, ed George Woodcock (London, 1980), p. 88.
33. H. G. Wells, *The Work, Wealth and Happiness of Mankind* (London, 1932), p. 507.
34. *The Alternative. Politics for a Change*, ed Ben Pilott, Anthony Wright, Tony Flower (London, 1990) p. 248.
35. Forum brochure.
36. *The Review*, January 1989, p. 9.
37. Maharishi News Release, December 1989.
38. Osho Commune International Press Release, Poona, 1989.
39. *Rajneesh Times International*, 16 March, 1989, Vol. 2, No. 5.
40. *Network News* Issue 1, Vol. II, 1988.
41. Windstar conference report, *Link Up* magazine, Winter 1988.
42. Interview with author, 1990.
43. Eric Hobsbawm, 'Lost Horizons', *New Statesman and Society*, 14 September 1990.
44. 'Zen Fire, Zen Wind', Discourse 3, 1 February 1989, in *Rajneesh Times International*, Vol. 2, No. 5, 16 March 1989.
45. Murray Bookchin, *Post Scarcity Anarchism* (1974), in *The Anarchist Reader*, op cit, p. 370.
46. *Krisis*, No. 3, September 1989, trans in *Gnosis, A Journal of Western Inner Traditions*, No. 16, summer 1990.

CHAPTER TWELVE: THE CHOSEN ONES

1. Eric Hobsbawm 'Lost Horizons', *New Statesman and Society*, 14 September 1990.
2. Malcolm X, *The Autobiography of Malcolm X*, (London, 1987), p. 257.
3. ibid, p. 483.
4. ibid, p. 270.
5. *Observer Magazine*, 9 September 1990.
6. *Washington Post*, 1 March 1990.
7. Malcolm X, op cit, p. 496.

8. ibid, p. 411.

9. J. A. Rogers, *World's Great Men of Colour* (New York, 1947), p. 602, quoted in Tony Martin *Race First* (London, 1976), p. 60.

10. Amy Jacques Garvey (ed), *The Philosophy and Opinions of Marcus Garvey* Vol. II (London, 1967), p. 71, quoted in *Race First*, op cit, p. 344.

11. *The Independent*, 21 May 1987.

12. *Financial Times*, 18 August 1988.

13. Charles Kingsley, *His Letters and Memories of His Life*, Vol. I (London, 1877), pp. 374–5.

14. Francis Galton, *Hereditary Genius* (London, 1892), p. x.

15. Plato, *The Republic* (London, 1987), p. 240.

16. ibid, pp. 347, 326.

17. ibid, p. 222.

18. ibid, p. 181.

19. Otto Strasser, *Ministersessel oder Revolution?* pp. 12–14, quoted in Alan Bullock, *Hitler, A Study in Tyranny* (London, 1988), pp. 399–400.

20. Hermann Rauschning, *Hitler Speaks* (London, 1939), p. 229.

21. Adolf Hitler, *Mein Kampf* (London, 1974), p. 343.

22. Deuteronomy, 7:6.

23. Quoted in Julian Pettifor and Richard Bradley, *Missionaries* (London, 1990).

24. M. Gilbert, *Exile and Return* (London, 1978), p. 20.

25. H. S. Chamberlain, *The Foundations of the Nineteenth Century* (London, 1911), pp. 330–1.

26. Speech at Munich, 13 April 1923, from *Adolf Hitler's Reden*, ed Ernst Boepple (Munich, 1934), p. 44, quoted in *Hitler, A Study in Tyranny*, op cit, p. 399.

27. H. G. Zmarzlik, 'Social Darwinism in Germany, seen as a historical problem', in *Republic to Reich*, ed H. Holborn, (New York, 1973), quoted in *Fascists* Michael Billig, (London, 1978), p. 14.

28. Friedrich Nietzsche, *Ecce Homo* (London, 1988), p. 60.

29. Friedrich Nietzsche, *Beyond Good and Evil* trans. Helen Zimmern (Edinburgh & London, 1914), pp. 176–7.

30. Friedrich Nietzsche, *Ecce Homo*, op cit, p. 126.

31. ibid.

32. G. Le Bon, *Psychologie des Temps Nouveaux* (Paris, 1920), p. 17, quoted in *Fascists*, p. 21.

33. G. Le Bon, *Psychologie des Foules*, (Paris, 1897), p. 17.

34. Hitler, op cit, p. 435.

35. ibid, p. 428.

36. Norman H. Baynes, *The Speeches of Adolf Hitler, 1922–39*, Vol. I (Oxford, 1942), p. 866.

37. ibid, pp. 871–2.

38. Carl Jung, *Zur gegenwartigen Lage der Psychotherapie*, VII (1934), quoted in Leon Poliakov, *The Aryan Myth* (London, 1974), pp. 373–4.

39. Carl Jung, 'Wotan' in *Essays on Contemporary Events* (London, 1988), p. 23.

40. ibid, p. 17.

41. *Health and Efficiency* magazine, Vol. 92, No. 3.
42. Wilhelm Reich, *The Mass Psychology of Fascism* (Harmondsworth, 1975), p. 163.
43. *Spearhead* 67, quoted in *Fascists*, op cit, p. 29.
44. Teilhard de Chardin, *Science and Christ* (London, 1968), pp. 140–1.
45. *Hitler's Table Talk, 1941–4* (London, 1953), p. 624.
46. Adrian Monck, 'The Klan Marches into the parlour' *The Guardian*, 27 February 1989.
47. Adrian Monck, op cit.
48. Ian Ball, 'New-look Klan stirs up the old embers' *Daily Telegraph*, 21 February 1989. John Cassidy, 'Ex-Klan wizard claims victory in state election' *The Sunday Times*, 19 February 1989. *Sunday Telegraph*, 14 October 1990.
49. Leonard Zeskind, *The 'Christian Identity' Movement*, (USA, 1986).
50. ibid.
51. Steve Bruce, *The Rise and Fall of the New Christian Right* (Oxford 1988), p. 89.
52. ibid, p. 86.
53. Thomas W. Case, 'The Mooning of America's Conservatives' *Fidelity*, March 1989, p. 38.
54. John Pilger, *Heroes* (London, 1989), p. 150.
55. *The Guardian*, 21 April 1984.
56. Ezekiel, 38:19.
57. John Pilger, op cit, p. 149.
58. *Sunday Times*, 5 December 1982.
59. *Time*, 26 December, 1983.

CHAPTER THIRTEEN: YOU HAVE THE POWER

1. Robert Jay Lifton, *Boundaries* (New York, 1969), p. 59.
2. ibid, p. xi.
3. Christina and Stanislav Grof, *The Stormy Search for Self* (Los Angeles, 1990).
4. J-R, *Baraka*, (1973), quoted in *Los Angeles Times*, 15 August, 1988.
5. Movement literature.
6. ibid.
7. ibid.
8. Interview with author, 1990.
9. Interview with author, 1990.
10. ibid.
11. ibid.
12. ibid.
13. *Washington City Paper*, 7–13 December 1990.
14. Charles Reich, *The Greening of America* (London, 1972), p. 220.
15. ibid, p. 119.
16. Fergus M. Bordewich, *New York Times Magazine*, 1 May 1988.

17. Findhorn quotes from Findhorn Foundation brochures and memos.
18. *Daily Telegraph*, 27 October 1980.
19. *Daily Express*, 19 May 1989.
20. *Daily Telegraph*, 6 May 1986.
21. *The Earth in Balance*, May 1990.
22. *Daily Mail*, 30 October 1990.
23. Seminar brochure.
24. Frank Natale, 'The Age of Consciousness', *Kindred Spirit*, Autumn 1990, Vol. 1, No. 12, p. 22.
25. ibid, p. 20.
26. *Rajneesh Times International*, 16 May 1988.

INDEX